Shimmers
of
Pearl

by

Arianne Richmonde

Arianne Richmonde's full-length novels in *The Pearl Trilogy*, *Shades of Pearl, Shadows of Pearl and Shimmers of Pearl*, follow the tumultuous and heart-rending love story between Pearl Robinson and Alexandre Chevalier. All three books are Amazon best sellers in erotic romance.

Praise for *The Pearl Trilogy:*

'*The Pearl Trilogy* is a must read!! OMG! I loved the Fifty Shades and Bared to You series…but this one is a topper!! I laughed and cried - it's so well written. So many twists and turns and just when you think you know where this story is going….you don't! It's frustrating, and oh, about every emotion you have - you'll feel it. I love the fact that it's written about a 40 year-old female…that's my age…Now, if only I could meet a hot Frenchman like Alexandre Chevalier…'

-A.J Cox.

'All three books flowed wonderfully and had the perfect ending for the wonderful trilogy. If you haven't read this trilogy yet, put it on your Must Read list!! I look forward to more from Arianne Richmonde!!'

—Sassy and Sultry Books

'The wait for this final book in the series was well worth it. There were twists I never would have imagined….the best erotica series I have read to date. Arianne Richmonde I look forward to the next book, you truly are a delight to read.'

—Megan Cain Loera

Praise for *Shades of Pearl:*

'This was a great book, Pearl was such a great character that she won me over from the start. The sex scenes were just how I like them, hot heavy and very sensual when the time was right, I loved the fairytale aspect to this book, the great hero, the female lead who had traits she did not like about herself, the evil family member, I would highly recommend this to all who love a great love story with sex, that would be most of us then, 5/5'

—*Confessions of a Bookaholic*

'I recommend this book for those who enjoy a wonderfully written first person narrative, romantic erotica, with lots of dialogue and plenty of well-done descriptive scenes.'

—*Swept Away By Romance*

'*Shades of Pearl* has been written to an exceptional standard, it captivates its audience from the first page and keeps you entertained until the very end. The characters are so well described, allowing images to run wild in your head. The story makes you laugh, scream and cry and leaves you wanting more.'

—*Nade Ferrabee*

'As a fan of the erotica genre and, most recently, the 50 Shades phenomenon, I was thrilled to find this book so incredibly steamy but without the hard side of hard kink to it.'

—*Jenny Baldwin*

Praise for *Shadows of Pearl:*

'I'm mad, I'm sad, I've been crying, I want to hit some characters in the book…well more than one person actually!

This book was an **AMAZING** read for me. It started off where *Shades of Pearl* left off. The book grabbed me right from the start and I did not want to put it down. I personally love Arianne Richmonde's writing style. I think she did an excellent job with these characters and the story line was VERY original.

I WANT BOOK 3 NOW!! I need to know what will happen next. Arianne left this reader wanting and needing **MORE**. I know without a doubt, that book 3 is a **MUST READ** for me!'

—*Swept Away By Romance*

'Let me say that *Shadows of Pearl* made for a FREAKING awesome story filled with so much drama…oh, how I loved the drama. It was a big page turner for me and when things got crazy oh how I got sucked in!'

—*Momma's Books Blog*

'I am a fan of the 50 Shades of Grey series and the Bared to You series. As I liked both this one was a surprise and I loved it. I thought this was better than both of them put together. I found a new author who can't write fast enough. Arianne Richmonde is a new fave for me.'

—*Amazon reviewer*

'This book has twists and turns that I never expected. I thought this might be another knock off of Fifty but Oh, no! This book holds it's own and I loved every word of it!'

—*Samantha Addison*

Praise for *Shimmers of Pearl:*

'Awesome; full of heart, tears and much laughter. This book flows together and feels so real and true I forgot I was actually reading a story. I love these characters. If you want to read something great, get these books.'

—*Dawn M. Earley*

'Wow, this had me on the edge of my seat, or rather bed. I have loved the whole trilogy of Pearl & I am sad that this is the end, I love how this author writes, she made me believe I was watching the whole thing like a film in my head which is just how I like to read my books, watching them play out and imagining the characters.'

—*Confessions of a Bookaholic*

'**Shimmers of Pearl** is what a true erotic book should be; great story line, wonderful characters, and some of the **HOTTEST** sex/love scenes I've read in a while. This is where the author's writing shines. I could really feel the attraction and desire that Pearl and Alexandre had for each other. Their chemistry was amazing and their need for each other leapt off the pages.
Arianne Richmonde did a wonderful job, not with just the story and characters but also with her skillfully crafted descriptive writing. The whole Pearl Trilogy has simply captivated me.'

—*Swept Away by Romance*

'Holy hotness for sure! Arianne Richmonde more than delivered with book 3!!!'

—*Sassy and Sultry Books*

This book is a work of fiction. Names, places, characters and incidents are either a product of the author's imagination or are used fictitiously. Any resemblance to actual events, locales or persons, living or dead, is entirely coincidental.

Cover design © by: Arianne Richmonde

About the Author

Arianne Richmonde is an American writer and artist who was raised in both the US and Europe. She lives in France with her husband.

As well as *The Pearl Trilogy* novels she has written a short story, *Glass*. She is currently writing her next novel, *Pearl*, from Alexandre's point of view.

For more information on the author visit her website:

www.ariannerichmonde.com

Dedication

To all my amazing readers who are rooting for Pearl and Alexandre and who have thrown *Shadows of Pearl* across the floor in frustration. Thanks for all your love, support, feedback and patience. This book is for you.

Acknowledgements

Kiki, my lady in shining armor who came along just when I needed her most. Cheryl and Lisa, again, thank you. All my fabulous readers, and bloggers who have recommended my books to their friends and followers, and last but not least, E L James for sharing so many of her fans with me, thank you.

1

I'm still staring in disbelief at Laura's sinister, black, front door. I have not moved from this park bench. The only thing that has changed in the last ten minutes is the music I'm listening to on my iPod. The Blues have been replaced with Patsy Cline's *Sweet Dreams.* That is all I have left – dreams of Alexandre and memories of how it used to be between us. Could I really have just imagined the intensity of our bond, our passion? 'He was in lust with you,' Laura told me, just twenty minutes ago, and I now see that what she said was true. Alexandre walked through her door. What more proof do I need that it is over between us?

He is still in love with her, his ex fiancée. This horrific fact is seeping through my veins like green poison, sapping me of energy, rendering me drained, making me feel as if my life has been nothing but a lie for the last five months.

Laura's words, 'rebound' and 'detour' to describe who and

what I am to Alexandre are ringing in my ears. Twice, I have tried to get up from where I'm sitting. I want to rap at that foreboding, black door and confront him, but my muscles are weak – I can hardly move. Laura has been plotting and scheming to get him back all along and he was waiting, as she said, for her to click her fingers.

Click.

And he rushed back to her like an eager dog.

I fumble about in my beautiful, red Birkin bag for my cell phone. I need to speak to Alessandra Demarr. Maybe she can clear a few things up for me.

My memory slides back to that moment when I fled Alessandra's house, when I found that photo of her and Sophie together in an intimate embrace. I had the notion that they had set me up and that Sophie was trying to destroy my life by wheedling herself in on my film projects; infiltrating her way into HookedUp Enterprises. Alexandre testified to her innocence, swore that her motivation came from nothing more than her desire to help out her girlfriend and get us out of a sticky situation when Samuel Myers wasn't good for the money. I didn't believe him. But now I see that Alexandre could have been telling the truth. I have been so 'hooked up' on Sophie that I was blind to what was really going on… Laura, my real enemy from word, Go.

Laura told me that Sophie actually liked me, confirming what Alexandre had also said. Either I am living some sort of Hitchcockian nightmare, where everyone is conspiring to drive me to a loony bin, or they're right – I have misjudged Sophie – wrongly accused her. There I was, obsessing about my future sister-in-law, when it was Laura I should have been looking out for, all along.

Alessandra picks up her phone after several rings. She sounds groggy and I realize that it's only eight a.m. Los Angeles time; she isn't an early riser. Too bad, I can't wait. Rise. And. Shine.

"It's Pearl," I say with urgency. "Sorry to wake you."

I hear a growling yawn. "Can you call back, I was sleeping - I thought it was a family emergency." Her sleepiness is evident - her Italian accent is more pronounced than usual.

"Well, considering that you and I could have been family, it is."

"What are you talking about, Pearl?"

"Alessandra, I'm so sorry to wake you and everything, but I'm not in a good way and I really need to talk."

"If this is about *Stone Trooper*—"

"It's about Sophie, your girlfriend, my ex-to-be sister-in-law." I am aware of how crazy that sounds. I do up the top button of my coat – the London humidity is getting into my bones. My eyes are still fixed on Laura's front door as I hold my cell next to my ear in my other shaky hand. I need answers and I need them now.

Alessandra's voice suddenly perks up with interest. "Did Sophie tell you that she and I were a couple?"

"I found a photo of you two in your kitchen, and Alexandre confirmed to me that Sophie was gay."

"Don't you *dare* say anything to Sophie about us, Pearl - about that night. *Please!*" She is pleading; the desperation and fear in her voice takes me by surprise.

"So you and Sophie weren't playing some game on me? Some, 'let's screw with Pearl's head' kind of game?"

She chuckles – her laugh is laced with irony. "What? Are you *insane?*"

"It just seemed all too much of a coincidence; that I was working on *Stone Trooper*…suddenly Sophie gets involved… you coming on board at the perfect moment and then seducing me…"

"Look, can we talk about this later? I need a coffee. I can't even think straight right now."

"Alessandra. I'm sitting outside Laura's house in London and she just so happens to be - not only Alexandre's ex-freaking-fiancée - but his *present* fiancée as well. He's inside her house, as we speak. He's involved with her again. No, let me spell that out – *he is going to marry her*, she is divorcing her husband. She's all buddy-buddy with Sophie and–"

"What? Sophie hates that money-grabbing bitch!"

Did I just hear that right? "But Alexandre said they were friends."

"Sophie puts up with her," Alessandra informs me in her husky voice, all the more husky for being the morning. "She's never liked Laura. Anyway, I don't think she's seen or spoken to her for ages."

I squeal out, "But I was at Laura's house, just now, and she said Sophie was coming over! They spoke on the phone. In French, no less."

"I doubt that, Pearl. Look, I'm sleepy, can we speak later?"

"Wait! No. Alessandra…why, when we were in LA were you referring to Sophie as your 'ex' if you're still together?"

"Questions, questions."

"Please Alessandra!"

"We had a big fight – she said I was using her to get ahead in my career. All because, I was too busy to speak to her one time. That was just before you arrived in LA She told me it was over. So I had some fun with you to spite her."

"You were planning on telling Sophie about us to make her

jealous?"

"No, of course not. I'm not that dumb. She'd come after us both with a carving knife. But it made me smile inside – you know, knowing I had the last laugh. Sorry, Pearl, I have to admit…I was using you to make myself feel better. Can I hang up now?"

"No! I need to know more about Laura."

"I've never met her," Alessandra replies boredly, punctuated by a yawn.

My heart sinks. I remember Laura's words: *'He was fond of you, it's true, but he thinks you're a total loony. All that lesbian bondage nonsense - oh and your slutty past…'*

I had assumed Sophie had enlightened Laura, but from what Alessandra says, obviously not. The only other person that knew about my adventure with Alessandra Demarr was Alexandre, himself. *How did Laura know those intimate details of my sex life?* Simple – he must have told her. She was speaking the truth. He confides in her, even when it comes to me. I feel so belittled.

Belittled. And cheap.

Alessandra pipes up, "Anyway, Pearl, as I was saying, Sophie is not a big fan of Laura's. Apparently, Laura has been sniffing about Alexandre again showing real interest. Her husband has lost a lot of capital in the stock market, or is being done for some dodgy dealings tax-wise and no longer has the kind of money he had before. So Sophie thinks she's after Alexandre because of what he can offer her."

"What does Sophie say about *me*?" I ask, wondering if Sophie is suspicious of everyone who comes near her brother.

"You really want to know?"

My heart starts pounding – might as well hear the worst.

"Yes."

"She thinks you're the best thing to happen to Alexandre for years. At first, she suspected that you were like all the other women after him – interested primarily in money. But when you told him you wanted to do a pre-nup and refused to take a stake in HookedUp Enterprises, she knew you loved him for *him*."

Wouldn't everyone love him for him? "Why is she still so bitchy, then?"

"It's part of her DNA, Pearl. But if you made more of an effort, you'd find she'd be a good friend to you. She said that, too. That you didn't like her, that you still hadn't forgiven her, and that you were a hard nut to crack."

"She said all this in English? Hard nut to crack?"

"Of course not. You know how bad her English is – we speak in French."

"You speak French? I didn't know that."

"Well, Pearl – there's a lot you don't know about me. Just keep quiet about our little evening, will you?"

"Are you kidding me? Of course. Anyway, I don't have anyone to tell even if I wanted to. It's over between Alexandre and me."

"Nonsense. Latin passion can escalate or descend at any moment – he'll be back."

"That's just it, Alessandra. He broke up with me in a cold, passionless voice. And now he's seeing Laura again. Not just seeing her but sleeping with her. She's like some top model...I don't stand a chance."

"You say you're outside Laura's house and Alexandre is inside? Go and knock at the door, silly. I'm going back to sleep, Pearl. Remember, don't you *dare* tell Sophie about what happened or you'll regret it."

"Is that a Sicilian threat?"

"You bet."

Revenge is a dish best served cold. "Don't worry, Alessandra, my lips are sealed. You think I want Sophie running after me with a carving knife? Thanks for talking to me - things are a lot clearer now. Good night, morning - whatever. Sleep well."

The line clicks dead.

I take a deep breath and stand up. I have a head-rush — black stars flicker behind my eyes. Laura's front door is giving me heart palpitations. Black as the Devil himself, it beckons me and taunts me mockingly. *Come, come and humiliate yourself.*

But Alessandra's right. I need to see Alexandre face to face.

I stand at the door, once again. It is so glossy I see my warped reflection before me. A disheveled woman who is forty whole years old. No wonder Alexandre has gone back to glamorous Laura. I rap the lion's brass knocker head. The lion is saying to me, *I challenge you, go on – make a fool out of yourself, see if I care.*

I knock three times. Rap, rap, rap. My heart…pound, pound, pound.

Nothing.

I'm planning in my head everything I'm going to say: *Alexandre, please be honest with me, please…*

The smooth black door swings open. Not Mrs. Blake but Laura, herself.

I will not cry, I will not cry. Be strong, no tears, no scene…be strong.

She's standing there, looking like some figurehead on a ship; tall, willowy, in a royal blue, silk-satin dressing gown shimmering about her slim body like ripples of water. My heart sinks. She has that just-fucked look – the afternoon love-making flush glowing in her cheeks. Her hair is all mussed up. She says coyly, "Pearl, what a surprise!" Her smile is set like a plastic bride on a wedding cake. "What can I do for you?"

"I need to speak to Alexandre," I reply bravely.

"Sorry, but he's not here. He just left."

My composure melts into the damp sidewalk. "Don't lie to me, Laura. I saw him come in through this door twenty minutes ago. He's here!"

"My word, have you been spying on us?" Her smirk is victorious.

I try to stick my foot in the door. "Let me in. I need to see him, just for a few minutes and then I'll be on my way."

"Pearl, I'm not making this up. He left five minutes ago."

"BULLSHIT! I've been watching your front door. Nobody has left, least of all Alexandre."

"You don't know much about London houses, do you? This house's garden backs onto our mews house and garages. He went out the back."

"Laura, you've gotten what you wanted. Why are you tormenting me? Please, I just want to see him for—"

"God, you're a bore. Do I have to spell it out? HE. IS. NOT. HERE! Go round the back and see for yourself if you don't believe me."

"What was he doing here?" I demand, my body shaking with rage.

"Now you're being naïve. He just fucked me senseless, if you must know. You're not the only one who likes a little afternoon sex, Pearl. Now run along, I have stuff to do." She begins to push the door in my face.

And then I shout out something cruel. Something I know I'll

regret. Words spill uncontrollably from my mouth:

"I wish you'd stayed in your freaking wheel chair forever!"

The lid is firmly in the coffin now. Not only am I jilted, I am despicable. When Alexandre hears what I have just said, he'll be shocked and never want anything to do with me again.

It's official.

I'm a jealous, spiteful, malicious bitch.

Laura slams the door in my face.

I scamper around the block to see if what Laura said about a mews house and garage is true. It is. Only the extremely wealthy could afford to have their garden sandwiched between two stunning houses in one of the most expensive areas in London. The mews is cobbled – in the olden days this is where the stables for horses and carriages were but now, of course, just a mews house alone in this Chelsea neighborhood would set you back millions, let alone adjoining garages. I imagine Laura's husband, James, beavering away in the City to buy all this for the woman he's in love with, for whom he sacrificed his life – and now she is about to dump him because he's no longer rich enough for her. Does Alexandre know who he is dealing with? That Laura is as ruthless as a razor blade? Like most men who are smitten, he probably doesn't see through her sweetness and light act.

A thought suddenly rushes to my brain. Uh, oh. I just insulted her, said the worst possible thing somebody can say and she'll be out for revenge. Laura knows about me and Alessandra. All it takes is one phone call to Sophie.

The carving knife…

I call Alessandra again.

She sighs into the phone, exasperated. "What d'you want now, Pearl?"

"Laura knows about us. About…our evening," I stutter. "Just warning you."

"Deny, deny, deny. And I suggest you do the same. How the fuck would Laura *know* that?"

"Alexandre must have told her."

"Thanks, Pearl, for sharing that with him - now I'll have *him* after me with a carving knife, too."

"No, you won't – he really didn't…doesn't care. I'm history."

"I didn't know he was the tattle-tale-tit type."

"He's not. He's usually very discreet; it's not like him at all."

"Well thanks for the warning," she says grumpily. "Bye."

I amble back to Sloane Street and walk towards Knightsbridge. I have a couple of hours to kill before I need to go back to Hampstead for my suitcase and make my way to Heathrow for my flight. I get my iPod out of my bag and go through the playlist. Got it. The perfect 'fuck you' song ever written, Gloria Gaynor's *I Will Survive*. The music feels great. Powerful. Encouraging. Hell, I even feel like disco dancing along the street. I punch my arm in the air. Yes, I *am* strong and I *will* survive. I refuse to mooch about and feel sorry for myself. Life goes on and we women can be tough. I *am* tough. I'm a New Yorker for crying out loud! I can do it. I will survive, I sing out loud and I don't care who hears me, even if I'm out of tune.

Where to head now? Harrods, why not? Probably the most famous department store in the world. I'll go there and buy a gift for Daisy's mother to say thank you for my stay. Perhaps some home-made chocolates or some fancy bath salts.

I step through revolving doors, greeted by uniformed door-men and make my way through the vast labyrinth of the store to the Food Hall. There is no place like it; I could be stepping into a museum. My mother brought me to this emporium and I vowed I'd return one day. It's a work of art. This was the original part of the shop, opened in the first half of the nineteenth century. Now Harrods is comprised of seven floors and spans an incredible four and a half acres. I have never seen such opulence and grandeur where food is sold. It is like a food court at a palace – something worthy of Louis IV or some bygone monarch's banquet feast.

The black and white marble floors stretch before me like a long yawn and the imposing molding decorating the ceiling reminds you that this building is a majestic legend – a true London landmark. Hall after hall is grandly overflowing with beautifully presented gourmet food delights. My eyes and nose are already feasting. The sheer volume and selection of British and International goods is awe inspiring - artisan chocolates, lavish cuts of meat and seafood - even exotic things like sea urchin. Unusual cheeses, Dim Sum, Beluga caviar, truffle butter, pistachio and rose Turkish delights, gourmet terrines and drool-worthy patisserie - all presented in breathtakingly beautiful displays arranged behind gleaming glass counters. It is like being in the hall of mirrors in Versailles, only with food, reflected twenty-fold by mirrors set in arches, made glorious by mahogany and brass light fixtures – everything twinkling and glittering in gold.

Foolishly, I thought I could whip in and out of here, but I am mesmerized by the beauty of the place, the surreal Willy Wonka and the Chocolate Factory I-want-it-all attack. Where to begin? What to buy? You could spend a week in the Food Halls alone, not to mention the rest of Harrods. I get some exquisite French truffles for Daisy's mum, Doris, and meander towards another tempting counter.

I'm staring at cupcakes now. I need some kind of American comfort food after the Laura 'encounter.' What to choose? – Banana, Mocha, Strawberry, Rocky Road, Sticky Toffee...or the chocolate torte sprinkled with gold dust? Edible art if ever I saw it.

"Pearl, is zat you?" a voice exclaims behind my shoulders.

I nearly jump out of my skin. I see a familiar reflection in the mirror before me.

It is Sophie.

I spin around in amazement, my sneakers squeaking on the polished marble floor. A nervous guilty churn makes my stomach dip. Sophie with her carving knife...does she know about me and Alessandra?

Obviously not, because she is smiling, and for the first time her happiness seems to be genuine. Or is that just me? Now that I know she doesn't hate my guts, I can observe her with fresh eyes, devoid of judgment and suspicion.

"What are you doing in London?" she asks, kissing me on both cheeks. I inhale her usual, heady scent of *Fracas* and notice how pretty she's looking, her eyes are like pools of dark chocolate and she's dressed immaculately in a chic, navy blue pantsuit. Hand-tailored, no doubt. I know she and Alexandre get all their suits cut on Savile Row, here in London.

"I came...I...I had some work appointments," I splutter.

"What a wonderfool surprise. Alexandre never told me you were both here."

Wonder Fool. Fool being the operative word. *So you don't know we broke up? That he dumped me? That he's gone back to Laura?* "I'm leaving today," I say simply. "Back to New York."

"What a shame, we could have hooked up. Isn't zis place marvelloose? I come here to get my Jelly Belly jelly beans. Cannot get zem anywhere, you know. My little American addiction." She holds up the bag of candy. Jelly Belly – my favorites, too.

I want to spill it all out and tell Sophie my woes. I want to discuss everything and ask her about Laura; tell her that Laura warned me that she would 'top me off' in order to stop me marrying Alexandre in Vegas - but I am dumbstruck, not least by the bizarre coincidence of bumping into Sophie here at Harrods – what are the odds of that?

"Where do you go now? You want a coffee? Or razzer, in England a cup of tea, no?"

"I have a plane to catch, I need to get back to Hampstead, then get my case and catch the tube to Heathrow," I reply uneasily.

"Hampstead? Alexandre usually stays at zee Connaught."

Sophie doesn't know?? "I'm visiting a friend," I say uneasily. "Alexandre isn't with me."

"My driver, he can take you to Hampstead and zen airport, okay? Save so much time. I have a friend in Hampstead I've been wanting to see forever. We go togezzer." She links her arm with mine and ushers me through the crowds, and out of Harrods. Her embrace is warm and I wonder…was it me? Was I the one, all along, who has been spiky and defensive? Maybe Alexandre was right. Sophie has been trying to be my friend for months.

I caused all that trouble for nothing. I wish, now, I could jump into a time capsule and travel back to the waiting private jet at Van Nuys Airport.

But it's all too late.

2

The limousine is waiting for Sophie around the back of Harrods like a panther on the prowl. Or rather, a Jaguar, because that's what kind of car it is. The uniformed chauffeur opens the door for us as we slide onto the sumptuous, leather seats, and then he drives us off into the London traffic. I try to peel my gaze away from Sophie as she calls her friend, so I fix my eyes on the beautiful shop front window displays along Sloane Street (especially Harvey Nichols) as we glide through the shimmering wet streets - the traffic lights reflecting globes of color in the windows of passing cars and on the road. There is a thin haze of drizzle - bad for depression, good for skin, I think, having noticed the peaches and cream complexions of so many young British girls.

Sophie is now arranging an assortment of shopping bags and feasting on her Jelly Belly beans. She offers me a handful and I chew the mixture of flavors thoughtfully together, too afraid to speak because I really don't know where to begin. It seems she thinks that Alexandre and I are still together. *How can that be?*

Finally, she breaks the silence. "I haven't spoken to Alexandre for days - so you came to London all alone, Pearl?"

I swallow. A mélange of root beer and cinnamon swirl about my mouth. It tastes of America and I feel momentarily soothed. "Yes, I'm alone." *Is she testing me?*

"How is your wedding gown coming along? Is it finished yet?"

Oh God, what do I say? "I'm not sure," I hedge. And then I blurt out, "Do you know Laura?"

"Laura?"

"Alexandre's—"

"I don't see her anymore," Sophie interrupts.

But when I was at Laura's house Sophie called her and said that she was coming over! "Do you phone her from time to time?" I ask, the conversation fresh in my mind; Laura chit-chatting in perfect French and telling me it was Sophie who'd called.

"No, not for ages."

Oh. Strange. Someone's hiding something. Laura? Sophie? Laura, probably.

I ask, "Do you like her?"

"No, but she was in a wheelchair so I had to be nice."

"I see."

"She's been calling my bruzzer again?"

"They are seeing each other...a lot," I mutter. I want to tell her about Laura, what she said – I want to spill all the beans but stop myself. I suddenly think of Alessandra's warning once again...that carving knife... If I tittle-tattle on Laura she'll tell Sophie about me and Alessandra. Actually, she might tell Sophie anyway…I'll be in trouble, no matter what.

Then Sophie says with her mouth full, "You and me got off on wrong foot, Pearl. I'm sorry. We need to talk."

My heart begins to race but I reply, "Yes we really do need to talk. I'm sorry, too, if I've been…" I trail off – I don't know how to express myself – how much should I tell her?

"Zee last time I spoke to my bruzzer he tell me you know about me and *Stone Trooper*."

Uh, oh, here we go.

"I guess you know why I got involved?" she asks narrowing her eyes (the way her brother sometimes does).

"Not completely," I say, giving her an opening. I need to see which direction she's going to take with this conversation.

"Alessandra."

"Yes."

This is beginning to sound like some enigmatic scene in a Harold Pinter play. How much longer can I beat around the bush?

"Alessandra is my girlfriend."

I look down at my sneakers."Yes, I know."

"She tried to seduce you?"

I can feel my face burn like glowing coals, although I have been told by people I don't go red. But I feel like I'm on fire. "Why do you ask?"

"Because it's her nature…Italian. Flirt. I have a husband, you know – I can't blame her for a little extracurricular activity."

The carving knife comes to mind, yet again. "You don't get jealous?"

"Yes, but I cannot have my cake and eat it too, you know?" Sophie looks at me and throws some more candy into her mouth.

"Sorry, very rude, I eat zee whole packet. I get very greedy with this Jelly Belly. So if she flirts I'm not cross – I know you both spent a lot of time togezzer on zee script."

"Alessandra thinks you're very jealous," I venture, my heart still hammering inside my chest.

"She loves drama. She likes zee idea zat I scream and shout, you know?"

"So if she did something with another woman you wouldn't come after the other woman with a carving knife?" *Oops, I didn't mean to be so blunt. Blunt about something so sharp.*

Sophie bursts out laughing. "She tell you zat? No, Pearl. Only one time in my life did I come after someone wiz a carving knife and zat was my fazzer."

I seize this rare opportunity to find out more – my Sherlock instinct piqued. "What happened to your father?"

"He's around. He lives in Rio, I sink."

"He's *alive?* I thought he disappeared."

"Yes, he disappeared - to Rio." She's staring out the car window now – I can't judge the expression on her face.

"How d'you know he went to Rio?"

"A friend of Alexandre say she see him zaire one time."

Interesting. I change the subject. "So how long are you in London for, Sophie? How come you haven't spoken to Alexandre? I thought you two spoke every day."

"Not since I bought him out."

"He sold you his shares in HookedUp?"

"You didn't know zat? I buy but I cannot pay for it all in one go. HookedUp is worz so much money, you know? Even I cannot afford to buy in one go."

We sit there in silence both licking our lips after our Jelly Bel-

17

ly binge. Then I exclaim, "Sophie, I may as well tell you…Alexandre has left me. He's gone back to Laura. We haven't seen each other for over two weeks."

She stops chewing and her jaw drops open. I see a mélange of blues and yellows of the candy stuck on her perfect white teeth. Her usually flawless composure slumps into disbelief. Her eyes widen. She is genuinely shocked – this is not an act.

"I knew zat fucking beach was up to no good."

It takes a beat for me to realize that 'beach' means bitch.

"I went to Laura's house today. The reason I went was because…because she told me that you caused her accident, Sophie…that you wanted me dead…that you would have me killed… 'topped off'—"

"*Merdre! Poutain!* You believe I would do zat?"

I drop my head in shame and a smart of pain shoots through me – I realize, too late, I have nipped my lower lip. Tears start spilling from my eyes, "I'm sorry, Sophie. I thought you hated me. Yes, I believed her – she was very convincing. I was going through a rough patch and well…I was vulnerable."

Sophie, to my surprise, folds me in her arms and draws me close to her slim frame, hugging me like a long lost friend. Her gesture makes me shake with unbidden emotion.

I made Alexandre sell his share of HookedUp to her, and I caused him, through my nagging and suspicion, to run back to Laura. I dug my own grave. I have nobody to blame but myself.

I spill out my woes and tell Sophie the whole story, omitting only the kinky stuff with Alessandra – I come clean about everything else. She apologizes, too, tells me that she is sorry for having slipped into the *Stone Trooper* deal without warning me.

Finally she cries out in anger, "Anyway, I don't believe Laura for a second. Alexandre is crazy about you. Zaire is no way he start fucking zat skinny gold-digger beach again. No, Pearl, he loves you too much – why would he go for hamburger when he has steak at home?"

Alexandre once said that to me. I try to smile but I feel so raw inside. Raw like the steak I'm supposedly meant to be. I tell Sophie, "Laura says they're getting married."

"You know sumsing about that skinny, asparagus beach? She's a good liar."

I wipe my face with my coat sleeve. Asparagus must be the French equivalent to bean-pole. Normally I would be laughing but none of this is funny. I reply, "Laura had me fooled, that's for sure. But she could be telling the truth. Alexandre was there at her house, I saw him – it looks as if he's moved in with her."

"You spoke to him?"

"No, I just missed him. And whenever I've called his cell, his voicemail always picks up."

"You leave zis to me, Pearl. Sumzing is not right. He loves you – he is crazy about you. I know my bruzzer, believe me."

I burst out crying again. Something about having Sophie on my side when I thought she was my arch enemy stirs my deepest sentiments.

She takes her arms away from my shoulders and says, "We have arrived."

I look up from my blurry-eyed vision and see that we are in the heart of Hampstead Village, crawling along a beautiful tree-lined street where houses are like country mansions. Sophie fishes her cell phone from her purse and calls her friend.

"I get out here, Pearl. My driver, he takes you wherever you want to go and he picks me up later. We speak tomorrow, no?"

"Thank you, Sophie."

"It's normal," she says with a smile as she eases her graceful way out of the limousine. And then she turns and fixes her eyes on my face as if she is studying me. "I'm sorry, Pearl for zee names I called you once."

"It's water under the bridge."

Water under the bridge. It brings a memory to mind - when I was a little girl playing Pooh-Sticks with my brother, John; throwing the stick off the bridge upstream and rushing to the other side to catch the stick bobbing along the foamy water. The memory makes my eyes prickle again. *Get a grip, Pearl, stop the waterworks already.*

"Bye, Sophie. Thanks so much for lending me your driver."

"What time is your flight?"

"About ten twenty, I think."

"Who are you flying wiz?"

"American Airlines."

"Bon voyage, Pearl – see you in New York. Soon."

Sophie must have called the airport because when I board the plane I find I have been upgraded to First Class. The irony is not lost on me. Finally, she and I have a chance to be friends – she is making so much effort - but our friendship has come too late.

I mull over everything that Laura said about her and envision Laura clicking her slim fingers and the hot, passionate embrace that she and Alexandre must have shared, knowing that their relationship was back on course. A rush of jealousy floods through me and for a moment I feel the urge to plot some kind of Sicilian revenge on her, but then I sink back into my plush airplane seat and appreciate the fact that she knew Alexandre first. She must feel she has priority, and however strongly I feel about him is neither here nor there. It is Laura he has chosen, not me.

Traveling First Class reminds me of how my life would have continued had I been the wife of a billionaire. That word, 'billionaire' sounds ridiculous – out of my league – even out of Alexandre's league because he's just a young guy in T-shirt and jeans who likes to surf and rock climb. But he *is* a billionaire – that's who he is - and Laura is claiming him for her own because of it. His wealth is letting our love down. I think of the tree house option in Thailand and wish I had snapped it up there and then; away from Laura and her treacherous, gold-digging claws.

Alexandre doesn't love me, it's clear. He doesn't even pick up the phone anymore.

It is over. I will just have to go back to how things were before – back to The Desert. Because the only person I want is him. I cannot even imagine kissing anyone else, let alone sex.

I stretch back on my comfortable seat and close my eyes. I can feel his touch; the way he strokes my inner thigh, brushing his finger lightly against my panties which are always soaked by the time we make love because he waits until I'm begging him – screaming for him. He is always rock-hard, even when he just kisses me, even when all he does is look at me. *Stop, Pearl! Stop torturing yourself!*

"Would you like a beverage, ma'am?" I look up from my reverie and a pretty flight attendant is looking at me sweetly.

"Yes, please. Bring me a Bloody Mary with extra horseradish

and one of your best Russian Vodkas – you choose."

"Certainly."

Perhaps I can drown my sorrows, one last time, before I land in New York and start my life afresh. I have already arranged things with Daisy. She and Amy will be moving in with me. I'll be back working on documentaries and back to being the self-sufficient woman I was before.

Life happens when you're busy making plans. So true.

3

I fumble with my new apartment key, already impressed with the grand lobby and its plush décor below. I'm feeling really nervous now. It seems a lifetime away when I last spoke to Alexandre in the back yard of my brother's apartment in San Francisco. Here I am now, standing by the door of one of the 'fuck-off' farewell gifts – part of his guilt package that had him running back to Laura and brushing me off with money to ease his guilt.

Then my mind gets working…no…would that be possible? Would it have been possible that he wanted Laura back, all along, and they were in it together – that he knew about her telling me that Sophie was out to kill me? He knew that would have made me run for the hills…a sure way of getting me out of the picture….

To my amazement, the door swings open before me, and I nearly jump out of my skin. I tumble into the open gap and a pair of muscular arms catches my fall. My apartment being broken into, already, and I haven't even started living here yet? My heart is racing and I yelp at the surprise of a stranger in my new building. I trip forward in a double stumble and dare to look up at my adversary. I expect a masked robber in a balaclava but instead, I see a pair of peridot-green eyes that are inches away from my face.

"Alexandre."

"Pearl, baby."

My stomach is flipping and folding in on itself. I fall headlong into him, gasping with desire, lust, happiness and relief. But then my inner voice warns: L.A.U.R.A.

He loves another woman. *Be careful, Pearl.*

He's holding me now, tightly in his arms as he tilts my head up to kiss me. Tears are in his eyes. "Jesus, I've missed you. I can't live without you, Pearl. I need you. I've been climbing the walls."

I try to push him away. "Get off me! What are you playing at? You're with Laura now. Leave me alone, Alexandre. Why are you torturing me?"

He grabs me in his embrace, again, and presses his lips to mine. His eyes are hungry, roaming and boring into me, the green flickering like the color of lit brandy aflame. "What are you talking about? I'm not with Laura." He breathes sex into my mouth.

I turn my head to the side and hiss, "Don't screw with my head, Alexandre! I saw you enter Laura's front door today. You fucked her in the middle of the afternoon. You took her a gift in a big box. You're living with her. You're going to marry her – she said so!" The words come out in screeches and squeals. I must be waking up the whole building – not the best start to my new life here in this apartment.

To my horror, Alexander says nothing, just shakes his head as if in disbelief. I step back away from him and observe a huge bulge in his jeans and a look of libidinous need in his eyes. Laura was right, he's 'in lust' with me. He loves her and wants to be with her but he wants to 'fuck' me. His hand cups his crotch as if to adjust his massive, uncontrollable weapon – a weapon that wants to claim me and posses me. He's wearing one of his hand-tailored, made-to-measure suits. I wonder if the Savile Row tailor instinctively knows he needs to give extra space in that area – room for Alexandre's 'weapon' to flex and maneover itself.

I feel dizzy, nauseous, because my desire is as potent as his. I want to stay strong – I need to protect myself but all I can think of, right now, is ripping off my panties and spreading my legs for him. He's so good looking and sexy that I'm melting before him like the pathetic ice cream cone that I am. *Where is my will power?*

He edges closer to me, brushes his lips along my neck so I quiver with longing. I'm trying to hide my craving. He whispers in my ear "You have to trust me, baby. I don't want Laura. I haven't fucked Laura and I'm not living with her – that's crazy, please believe me."

"It's not crazy! She said so. And I saw you with my own eyes at her house!"

"Well she was talking nonsense. I just zipped by her house to drop something off."

"Bullshit! You haven't even called me, you haven't picked up your cell – you've been avoiding me!"

His voice is gentle. "I haven't called you because I knew you needed time to sort your head out. Let's face it, Pearl, you were all over the place. You needed time alone to reflect; not only those nightmares and all that shit, but on the whole Sophie issue, which I hear is resolving itself nicely. She told me you bumped into each other." He cups his large hand on my butt and I'm too mesmerized by him to move. "I didn't get in touch, chérie, because things were too haywire." He breathes into my ear and adds huskily, "But it's been hell for me; I've missed you like crazy. You're all I can think of night and day. I'm obsessed with you. I've been going around with a hard-on for two weeks. Please Pearl, calm me down. I feel like an animal – I need you – I need you, baby."

My heart is racing and my stomach's churning in nauseous waves. I'm so crazy about this man, it is literally making me feel sick. "You just want to fuck me and then go right back to Laura," I spit out. "What were you doing bringing her that massive box? A gift, no doubt – perhaps a Kelly Bag?"

Squint lines radiate from his face as if he's amused but he notices the set fury on my face and states quietly, "I was bringing Laura her books from my house in Provence, that's all. You didn't like them being there – I wanted to make you feel more at home."

"That's crap and you know it! Why didn't you get Madame Menager to just Fedex them?"

"Because the last time I used Fedex, the package, which happened to be worth a lot of money, went AWOL for three weeks. Madame Menager had put Royaume Uni on the address and it went back and forth to Romania three times – they used the first two letters, the RO. Customer service in France is a disaster -I didn't want to risk it. I needed to pop by my house – the pool's being worked on - so I picked up the books while I was at it."

"Why was it gift-wrapped, then?"

"The hotel did that. I'd bought some cashmere scarves and things that I was going to have sent to my mother, so they took the liberty of wrapping the box of books, obviously assuming it was also a gift."

I flinch and eye him suspiciously. I so want to believe him. "That doesn't explain all the information Laura has about me. How did she know about me and Alessandra Demarr? Laura said nasty things to me, Alexandre. That you think I'm a 'loony' with a 'slutty past' – she knows stuff about me that only you could have told her." I push my hands fiercely at his chest to shove him away but another rush of desire floods through me when I touch him - that chest, those abs and his smooth skin.

"She said *what*? I sure as hell didn't say any of those things. How could I say them when I don't even *think* them?"

"Well, you told her about Alessandra!"

"No, I didn't."

"Well someone did and it wasn't Sophie and it wasn't Alessandra and it wasn't me. *You* are the only other person that knows."

"This is insane!"

"That's why it's time for you to leave now, please. I don't ever, ever want to see you again. Please exit from my loony, lesbian, slutty-past life."

He holds my shoulders. There is no point trying to push him away – he's too solid, too strong, too determined.

His eyes flit about as if recalling something. "Alessandra must have said something to Sophie, maybe to rile her up, it doesn't make sense—"

"No, Sophie doesn't know - if she did she would have hardly

upgraded my plane ticket to first class. Please go now, Alexandre."

"She didn't upgrade you. I did."

"Did Sophie tell you my flight time?"

"She did, but I knew it already."

"What? How? You're spying on me?"

His mouth tips up crookedly as if he wants to smile but he stops himself. "Was it comfortable enough for you in First?"

"Yes, thank you for the upgrade, but I would have been quite happy in Economy had I known it was you and there were strings attached and that you were stalking me."

His mouth is tilted into a very subtle smirk when he tells me, "I know, it was wrong of me, baby. It's something I would never normally do – I respect people's privacy. But I was worried about you; I just wanted to know your whereabouts, just in case." He steps closer and murmurs, "Anyway, deep down inside, you secretly like me keeping an eye on you Pearl, admit it."

It's true, I do like the fact that he's been thinking about me and wanting to know where I am. But the question is, why? What does he want from me? I glare at him and say, "Stalking me - but with only one thing in mind - to get into my panties when it's actually *Laura* you want to be with." The idea that he desires me so much physically is a real turn-on. I try to hide it with my furious scowl but what's going on down south of the border is giving me away – even if only to myself.

He flings his arms in the air with exasperation. Boy he's a good actor. "I do not fucking well want to be with Laura! I want to be with *you*. I want to marry *you*. Please, baby – I'll get to the bottom of this; something strange is going on. I'll talk to Laura−"

"Oh yes, I *bet* you will."

He lays a hand gently on my shoulder and tells me quietly. "Pearl, chérie. I love you. I've missed you so much. I *love* you; *you* are the only woman I want."

I shrug my shoulder to shake off his hand and roll my eyes in disbelief like a sulky teenager.

He roars at me, "You *have* to believe me!" The neighbors would have heard that outburst, for sure.

Something about his hot-blooded anger, not only tickles me, but jolts me into action. I do want to trust him and in that split second, I decide that I have to let him hold me, at least one more time, even if he is lying. I can't stand being in The Desert. I need him, his touch, his breath on mine. I *need* to believe his lies.

I stand there weakly, succumbing to him as he unzips my jeans and puts his hand down into my panties, pushing his finger into my soaking wet opening. He scoops me up in his arms and says, "That's it, you want this as much as I do. No more games, Pearl."

He takes me into the bedroom and throws me onto the soft mattress, his massive bulge flexing through his elegant pants.

"What if I said 'no', what if I said I couldn't do this?" I mumble, only too aware that I can't resist him, knowing this whole Laura issue will have to sit on the back burner because I can't hold out anymore.

"Then I'd know you'd be lying," he rumbles, casting off his tailored jacket and unbuttoning his beautiful, bespoke pants.

I gasp at his size – his raging angry cock wants all of me – I start to frantically pull off my jeans and panties. I too, feel like an animal. I lie there thrashing about the bed - wanton like some Babylon whore, my legs spread wide. "Fuck me, Alexandre, please," I whisper – "I need you, all of you. Fuck me."

"You bet I'll fuck you." He licks his lips lasciviously, crawls between my legs, laying his naked body on top of me. He's beautiful – how I've missed this. His dark floppy hair, his lean, sexy body, his flashing green eyes wanting me, needing me. But I suddenly feel as if I've been too easy, so I close my legs – a bit late, I know, but I need to show some semblance of pretense – so I squeeze them together to try and make myself seem less like a cat in heat. A ridiculous attempt to gain back a sprinkling of dignity.

His strength overpowers me – he knows I want this as much as he does. His mouth is on mine, his tongue probing me as growls are rumbling from his throat "Don't suddenly play the chaste damsel in distress with me, Pearl. I know what you want, chérie. You want me to fuck your brains out."

He eases his hard erection between my unyielding thighs and I close myself tightly around him, still feigning the 'hard to get' female. But within seconds I'm whimpering with pleasure. He doesn't slam himself inside me, which is what I'm expecting, but starts fucking my clit. *Oh my God…*it feels out of this world. He's not even an inch in but just ramming me back and forth, pummeling me there on my sweet spot – why haven't we tried this position before? This is amazing. I'm groaning, thrusting myself at him as I sense my wetness pool with arousal.

"Alexandre, this is…wow…oh my *God!*"

His hands are clutching my hair as he fucks my clit over and over and over, groaning with each thrust, his mouth on mine, his tongue searching my tongue, tangling and lashing at each other as his cock thrashes my clit relentlessly. I always thought it ridiculous when I read about women being 'pounded' to orgasm but I think it's about to happen. The rhythmic sliding, up and down has me on the edge. I don't want to climax because this feels so fucking amazing that I want it to last forever – it's *so* hot, *so* sexy, *so* incredible - but I open my legs a touch because my body is doing its own thing. He goes in further. He hits the perfect spot and that's it. Yes, Pearl Robinson is being 'pounded' to orgasm.

"Alexandre…aaahhhh" I can hardly say his name as his mouth is hungrily all over mine. "I'm coming…oh wow, I'm coming really hard."

I can feel my slickness oozing through the core of me as spasms overtake the center of my body. He fastens his mouth on my throat and sucks, also changing the angle of his hips as the root of his erection presses into some other magical spot and I feel another wave crash through me. He pushes my thighs apart with his knees and I'm wide open – my nails scraping his back as my orgasm flutters down from its peak. He rams himself into me, filling me with his immense size and I cry out, desperate for the whole of him.

He's growling like a lion, really 'fucking my brains out' – it's true, I am no longer coherent. He's now nipping my neck, covering me with ravenous wet kisses, pumping me deep, ruthlessly – both his hands are cupping my ass tightly as he thrusts me rhythmically, bringing me as close to his groin as possible with his grip. My hands rake down his back and claw down onto his butt as I bring my legs up and wrap them around his neck. He's in so deep now, it hurts, but I'm relishing the sweet, sharp pain as he pumps his thick length into my womb.

"I. Love. Fucking. You." His mantra is almost cruel, punctuated with each thrust. "So. Fucking. Wet. So Fucking. Horny. My cock thinks about you. All…Day. Long. All. Fucking. Day. Long. Your. Wet. Pearlette. Your. Tight. Horny. Pussy. Always ready to be...Fucked. By. Me."

Our mouths are frantic, tongues lashing out at each other, licking all over, biting, sucking. This is not love-making, this is dirty, carnal sin. It's verging on painful but I want it this way. I want to feel him. To own him. Laura doesn't elicit this kind of desire from him. I do. I'm his addiction. I'm his drug.

"Why did you leave me?" I murmur as he rams all of himself mercilessly into me. "Why didn't you phone?" I push my butt up higher as my ankles close fast about his neck.

He pulls almost all the way out, tantalizingly slowly. "Because you needed to know how much you wanted me. And I needed to have you desperate for me." He's licking my tongue, speaking only between kisses which are carnal pools of frantic desire.

"I am desperate," I breathe.

He slams back into me. "I know - your body's telling me. Do you think about sex with me all day long, Pearl?"

"Yes." He pulls out teasingly slowly. Sooo slowly.

"Are you cured of your penis phobia?" He thrusts himself in really deep and hard. I groan. I feel so dominated. Then he eases a tiny way out and speeds up, circling his hips. *Oh yes. Oh yes.*

I can hardly speak but burble, "Yes, I'm over it. At least *you* override any hang-ups I have. You..." His movements are doing things to my brain, I can hardly get the words out...."You are different. You...*oh, God,* I need you Alexandre."

He slams himself all the way in, brutally. "I know you do. And I need you to need me. Are you done with your lesbian fantasy, too?"

"No, I'll never be done with lesbian fantasies," I tease.

His growl is deep with appreciation with what I've just said. "Tell me...tell me, baby, what you did with Alessandra," he asks gyrating his hips again. I can feel how thick he's getting, feel him spreading inside me even more, filling my walls.

"I kissed a girl and I liked it."

"Oh yeah – tell me more."

I raise my butt up a touch so he's in even deeper. "She licked her tongue in between my legs – she made me come."

"Like I'm coming now, baby. Oh fuck this is intense!" He rams himself hard up inside me and I feel a scalding rush of cum shoot into my womb – profound and powerful. Then he thrusts again and I sense another charge of semen burst deep within me. "Aah," he's moaning and crying out. "Jesus, Pearl, only you can do this to me. Fuck!" He's groaning as if in pain.

We remain like that for a good five minutes and then he pulls out, very slowly. I lie there, still doubled up, my butt in the air. There's a marsh between my legs – it's seeping everywhere. Slowly I stretch myself out but Alexandre's arms are wrapped about me so I can't escape.

He's stroking me gently, running his fingertips along the curve of my ass. I'm no longer being devoured but savored. "Your skin is so soft and flawless, Pearl, so beautiful. You're intoxicating...really...I just can't get enough of you."

He presses his muscular thigh into my crotch and I move myself gently up and down. At first, it feels like a small comfort after being ravaged by him but as I rub myself languorously back and forth on his muscular leg I feel desire building up again until it reaches a new crescendo – another climax shudders through me. I feel his semen hot between my satiated thighs as we both fall into a deep sleep, entwined in each other's arms.

Several hours later, my eyes spring open. Alexandre is still fast asleep but my own worry and angst have woken me. Trickles of dawn light have made the darkness fade, but it must still be very early. *Am I insane?* Nothing was resolved last night! Nothing. The fact that Laura lied to me about Sophie, telling her she wanted to 'top me off' - the fact that Alexandre must have told her about my naughty tryst with Alessandra (because nobody else knew except for Alessandra herself) – is all registering in my slow, sex-numbed brain – he really did 'fuck my brains out.' Duh! As usual, Pearl Robinson jumped into the flames without wearing a fire-proof vest.

How did Laura have that information about me? Because that bastard, who's lying beside me now, *must* have shared it with her, despite his denial. He deserves an Oscar.

I observe him as his breath rises and falls, his pecs strong and firm, the V of his sexy torso ending with his sex tool which he uses to make me weak. Anger starts to flood through me, more at myself than with him. *Why did I let him have his way with me last night without talking things properly through?*

I get up and tiptoe to the bathroom. That's right! My suitcase is still outside the door (I hope) – everything was dropped (including my mind) when I saw his green gaze and his drop-dead gorgeous body which, I hasten to add, had broken into my apartment, no less! *Pearl Robinson, you are a disaster!*

I pee and wash my hands before going to find my abandoned case which I wheel inside. I go back to the bathroom and run the shower faucet. So preoccupied was I last night with the vision of Alexandre and my lusty appetite, that I didn't even have time to appreciate the lovely and sleek modern furnishings of my new apartment. It's all cream and white with soft carpets and smooth silk curtains. It looks like a five star hotel – a place where you wouldn't call home but where you'd lounge about in pure luxury wishing it were yours. It is too perfect to call home – too sleek. The bathroom is all pale Italian marble with his and hers wash basins and a massive mirror. Uh oh, inspection time. I have definitely lost weight through nerves, despite my Jelly Belly binge.

I jump into the hot, steamy shower and lather away at my hair and body with some delicious vanilla-scented shampoo and body wash. Did Alexandre organize all this? As I'm exiting the shower all wet, there he is. He's been watching me like a Peeping Tom. I know because his boner tells me so.

"Beautiful. Just beautiful," he says running his tongue along his lower lip. "You've lost a little weight, though."

"I guess you were so busy fucking me you didn't notice that last night," I remark, bitterly angry with myself, knowing that I'm going to give into him all over again.

"Oh, I notice everything Pearl. Everything. Like how tight and wet you were last night. How much you needed me inside you. Bend over."

"No! I won't."

"Don't be disobedient. Bend over. I just want to see how much weight you've lost."

"Alexandre!"

"Bend over and touch your toes."

Here we go again. A pool of desire gathers in my stomach. *In for a penny, in for a pound.* I bend over. Actually, the stretch to my backbone after the hot shower feels good.

He comes up behind me and I feel his erection press up against my ass. His thumbs part my butt crack and he gets down on his knees. I sense his tongue lashing in great sweeps up and down and then flickering at my entrance and the soft hair on his head tickling my inner thighs. I can hear myself moan involuntarily - he's got me again.

He stands up. Then the slapping begins, his cock walloping my opening. He's guiding it with his hand – I can sense it teasing me. He pulls away. Then suddenly, I feel a hard slap right in my hot spot with his palm. It stings. I cry out in shock.

"What are you doing?"

"A little spank, that's all. You hurt my feelings, Pearl, when you ran off at Van Nuys Airport."

I'm dreaming again. Please no. Please don't say this is all a goddamn dream and that, in fact, I'm still fast asleep on the plane in First Class. "Pinch me," I tell him.

"What?"

"Pinch me hard. I want to know I'm not dreaming."

He pinches me on my Venus lips and it hurts. Almost. But seconds later, I feel the urge. The urge to be claimed again. "I need you, Alexandre," I pant, sticking my butt out further.

"I know you do. Hold on to something. I have to fuck you again, Pearl."

I'm still doubled over and I hold onto the edge of the bathtub. I'm sore inside, yet I still want more. What is *wrong* with me? Why am I such a push-over?

He cups my breasts with both hands, kneading and playing with my nipples. I can feel desire shoot through the back of my molar teeth – all connected – my groin, my mouth, my nipples. I jut my ass out towards his erection. With one hand tight around my waist he pushes his cock inside me but just an inch. I can hear my wetness ooze about him and I cry out like the little slut that I am. Even if I have to share Alexandre with Laura I'd rather do that than not have him at all. I'm so hooked on him and his body parts – I can't deny him. He's my drug.

And he knows it, too.

He starts with shallow thrusts just sliding in an inch or two but it's so huge that even just a little of him is a stretch. Then he takes it all the way out and slaps it on my clit, fucking my clit so it's rubbing it up and down. Then he jabs it at my entrance again without entering. I'm screaming now.

"Ssh, baby, we don't want the neighbors to hear."

He pushes inside me again and tweaks my nipples between his thumb and index finger, rhythmically pumping me but still hardly entering. Then he rams it all the way in. Hard. Then pulls back out. Again, just the tiny thrusts. I'm whimpering. He's unpredictable – I don't know if I'll get the whole plunge or not. And then, as if by perfect osmosis, just as I bring my own hand up to pressure my clit he thrusts once more all-in, deep from behind and I feel myself coming in a burst of unbelievable pleasure, his thick cock pushing out against my walls, filling me with tingling spasms as I contract all around him like one of those fly-eating plants, sucking him in, eating him whole. He stills his movements and I really sense his swelling inside me, which makes me come even harder. Then I feel his own release, hot and quiet as he groans gently with hushed arousal, his fingers exploring my butt, snaking them up around my waist which he grips harder as he bursts inside me.

"I love you, Pearl. You're my treasure. I love you and I always will." Then he cries out with another hard thrust, "Fuck you make me come hard – can't keep away from you. Gotta keep fucking you for the rest of my life. Is your wedding gown ready yet?"

My legs are tucked beneath me on the couch and Alexandre's head is in my lap. He thoughtfully stocked the refrigerator for me before my return and we're sipping freshly squeezed orange juice. He knew exactly when my plane had landed. He has had my every move monitored since I last saw him. How? Through my cell phone, he now admits. Duh. It was Alexandre who bought me that Smartphone – it's as good as a GPS; I should have thought that might happen, although assuming he had lost all interest in me, it hadn't occurred to me that he'd be tracking my movements with modern technology.

I've been trying to make sense, all morning, of what is going on between us and I'm still confused. For hours we've been talking things through, about Sophie, about Laura, about the fact that he left me broken-hearted for two weeks believing it was all over. Now he says he wants me to return to his apartment and leave this place to Daisy and Amy. He iced me out, now he wants all of me back. I'm still recovering – still assimilating what has happened. I'm not ready for this. Well, I am; all I've been day-dreaming about is getting back with him – but I still don't trust him a hundred percent. Maybe not even seventy-five percent.

I plump up the cushion behind my back. "Is that *really* true, what you say, that you followed me to Laura's through my cell phone?"

"Yes. But I got there too late – I did a quick detour to my hotel to pick up Laura's box of books but I wasn't fast enough - you'd already left."

"There I was, watching you, sitting on that park bench listening to heartbreaking lyrics by Patsy Cline and thinking we were over and that you were back with Laura for good."

He threads his fingers through mine. "And I thought the same. She told me you'd had a talk and that, as far as you were concerned, we were finished."

I want to scream. *She had me fooled and tried to do the same to him!* "And you believed her?"

"No. That's why I'm here now. I knew in my heart you still loved me."

I throw my hands in the air. "You're so cocky! I wish I was that sure of myself. There *you* were, all cool, calm and collected and I was a friggin' basket-case!"

"Not cocky, just confident. I thought, if I can fuck Pearl just one more time, she'll remember how much she needs me." His lips flicker into a subtle but wicked smile.

I shake my head and raise my eyes to the ceiling. "So unbelievably cocky! By the way, Monsieur God's Gift to Womankind, I'm not done with this conversation yet. I still have quite a few more questions. I mean…I'm sorry, Alexandre, but *someone* must have told Laura about me and Alessandra Demarr. You swear it wasn't you – then who *was* it?"

"I have no idea."

I take a long sip of juice and say coolly, "Wouldn't it just be easier to tell me the truth?" I make a mental note to myself that next time I want information I should hold back the sex. I have zero bargaining power now.

"Look, baby, I swear I don't know, but everything that Laura told you is bullshit. I can't believe—"

"Believe it! Don't you fucking dare," I snap, "doubt me again when it's my word against Laura's. She lied to you, *too*. I should have recorded the conversation at her house with my Smartphone. I should have—"

He presses his lips to my temple. "Okay, calm down, I believe you. But why would she say all that when it just isn't true?"

"She wants you back, Alexandre."

"Well, I don't want her back."

I finish my juice and ask, "Why were you in London, any-way?"

"I was curious as to why *you* were there. I wondered what you were up to."

"I don't believe that for a second. You could have simply phoned me and asked me straight."

"I was forcing myself not to call. Trying to let some time pass – you needed a break. Feel it. Suffer a little so you realized how much you missed me." A faint smile touches his lips. *He knew what he was doing. He was being calculating.* This man knows me too well!

I pout. "You could have just come and gotten me."

He shakes his head. "Sometimes pursuing something you want is the fastest way of losing it. I learnt that a long time ago. If I had chased you relentlessly, Pearl, I could have lost you for good. You needed time to reflect and sort yourself out."

I observe him cautiously. I so want to believe this. *Is he telling the truth? Or is all this a crock of horseshit?*

"Why else were you in London?" I grill.

"Business."

"Not true. HookedUp didn't have any meetings or Sophie would have said."

"I told you, I have other projects in the pipeline."

"Like what?"

He hesitates. Glugs down all of his orange juice in one go, and says in a flat voice. "Don't ask me about my business, Pearl."

"Don't ask me about my business, Kay. My God, can you hear yourself? You sound like Michael Corleone!"

"You regret meddling between HookedUp and Sophie. It won't happen again. From now on, what I do is my concern and you, chérie, need to keep your pretty nose out of my business affairs."

I bite my tongue. It's true. I got myself into a real pickle with Sophie; my imagination running wild. I still can't work out, though, how Laura would have private information about my sex life. Is Alexandre lying to me? Does he want us both?

"Why was Laura wearing a silk robe and told me you'd just had afternoon sex?"

He bursts out laughing. "She said that? I suppose I should be flattered that two women are fighting for me but—"

"I'm not fighting for you. If you want her, go! Go on...fuck off out of here and fuck that skinny bitch for all I care. But you have to choose—"

He laughs even harder and I scowl with fury. I stand on the couch, now, kicking him with my bare foot. "Fuck off!" I scream, realizing that I've said the word fuck way too many times. "Go on, go back to her if that's what you want, but my *'pearlette'* is off limits forever. Do. You. Understand?"

He grapples me and pulls me back down on the couch and pins me beneath him again.

"No! Alexandre, I'm sore."

"That's just how I like it so you can spend the day hobbling about, feeling like you've still got my cock inside you."

"You're disgusting! Obsessed with fucking. Obsessed!"

"Look who's talking – you can't get enough of me."

The arrogance! I pummel his head with a cushion and the next thing I know we are at it again, this time he's rolled underneath me and pulled me on top of him, slipping himself inside me - I find myself riding him – my anger boiling (even though I'm smiling) but because I have control and can dismount any moment, I take a long, deep breath and decide I can use this to my advantage. Yes, I have control! Now is the time to ask some more questions. I ride him for a while until he's really aroused and then slow down.

He scowls when I stop and flexes up his hips. "Keep going baby, it feels incredible."

I mustn't let him win this round. It's my turn to take the reins. "When you left Laura's house, how did you leave?" I test him.

"What do you mean?"

I freeze my movements. "Which door?"

"Out the back."

"What back?"

"Through the garden, through to the garage."

"Why did you go to the garage?"

"What is this, *Homeland?* Why are you cross-questioning me?"

"Why did you go to the garage?" I repeat, punctuating my question with a thrust.

"Because I keep my Aston Martin there."

"What! You have stuff at her house?"

"My Aston Martin is not 'stuff' – it happens to be a 1964 DB5, the same Bond car, I'll have you know, that featured in *Goldfinger* and *Skyfall*. Anyway, the last I heard, it wasn't Laura's

42

house but *James's* and Laura's house. Yes, I keep my car there, for now. They have the space – they borrow my house in Provence for summer vacations, I use their garage from time to time, what's the big deal?"

I relax into him for a moment and go back to my stallion ride. I feel sore but then I drag my sleepy eyes over his body and get a renewed rush of desire. Christ he's handsome. His wide chest is smooth, warm, his biceps chiseled and strong, and the cords of his forearms flex as he holds me around my waist, making me feel petite and feminine. His dark hair is mussed up about his face and when I lift up my butt and plunge back down on him he groans, biting his beautiful lower lip, red and lush. He grabs my ass and starts pumping from underneath.

"Not so fast, cowboy," I scold. "I'm sore, remember."

I lift myself almost off him and rest my body forward so just the tip of his crown is inside me. I tease myself with just the big satiny head of his cock and no more, all my nerve endings are gathering in a sensuous dance at my aroused entrance. My eyes flutter and I keep my rhythm as he groans beneath me. I pile cushions behind his head so he's in the perfect position to suck at both of my nipples, pleasuring each one in turn, flicking his tongue over the puckered areolas. My clit's rubbing up and down on his taut stomach with my rhythmical, almost horizontal movement, while his erection pushes in and out just a couple of inches inside my wet hole. Mixed with the tit sucking it's driving me crazy with desire… I plunge hard back down and that's it… I start coming in both places - a deep vaginal spasm mingles with a massive clitoral orgasm slapping against his hard abs, pulsating through me. This is a Mighty Big O and I start screaming. How I love the fact that every time I come, Alexandre's button is also pushed. It's impossible for a woman to come on command – our bodies just don't work that way - but men are different; at least Alexandre is. My excitement always gets him hot and he, too, is crying out my name, his release intense – there seems to be no end to the semen inside him.

He starts kissing me, his tongue probing, pulling and sucking on it - he breathes into my mouth, "Pearl… Pearl, forever. You're mine forever, please never leave me baby, I'm so in love with you."

"Me too," I cry out. "I love you, Alexandre," as another wave rolls right through the core of me making me clench and contract with unbelievable tremors.

9.8 on the Richter Scale, this one.

4

It strikes me that I have a real problem. We both do. Alexandre and I are hooked on each other sexually. I think back to my marriage with Saul. He was completely faithful to me.

Yet I was in The Desert. If Alexandre is not being faithful and he's cheating on me with Laura, what do I do? Which would I rather be… in The Desert with a faithful man or in the flames with a cheater?

Cheating Flames…Alexandre?

Safe but Lonely Desert…Saul-type of man?

My head is opting for The Desert but my heart…

Not to mention my nether regions…

Because maybe the twain cannot meet. Maybe the sex-god, Mr. Good-Looks-Charmer only comes with the cheating strings attached.

It has been a week now. Alexandre wants me to move right back 'home' he said, (his place) but I have managed to resist. I'm still in my new apartment. Daisy and Amy have moved in, sharing the second bedroom. I have managed to keep a modicum of autonomy. Because a little voice inside my head is warning me to be cautious. All it has done is make Alexandre even keener.

Because of my insistence, the wedding and the gown are on hold. I want to hear it from Laura's lips that there is nothing going on between them and find out how she knew private stuff about me. Alexandre is on probation. The southern part of my body (the Deep South) may be foolish but I, the cerebral tough nut up north (the Rocky Mountains) am not.

My brain, at least, must stay intact. For the moment I have told him it's just Sex, nothing more. No marriage, no living together officially, until this Laura nonsense gets sorted out. The only problem is that she isn't answering my calls nor replying to emails and snail mail letters. I want to ask her why she's pretending that they're together if they aren't.

I have also tried contacting her estranged husband, James, although rumor has it that he has slinked off to the Cayman Islands. Alexandre, too, tried to contact him but he won't respond. Did Laura feed her husband the same story and now James hates Alexandre's guts? For good measure, Alexandre's precious, classic Aston Martin (how men love their cars) has been moved – collected and driven by his driver, Suresh, over to his house in Provence. That was one of my demands and he obliged without flinching.

Alexandre swears that he won't see Laura again, not even as friends, and that all connection has been severed for good. Still, I am biding my time. In my head, I have moved our marriage to St. Valentine's Day. It will still give me my white winter wedding but let me sort things out. I'm not telling Alexandre about my secret plans. Let him teeter on the edge – let him be the one to feel insecure for a change. I have thought long and hard about this. I imagined that if I ever got Alexandre back, I'd snap him up, rush to the altar just to seal the deal, but I want this marriage to be secure. I really do need to clear up the Laura issue – be one hundred percent sure.

A marriage is for life, not just for Christmas.

To my surprise, I'm enjoying being the Sex Only woman. I feel liberated – free. I hold the cards. I have control…

Except, of course, in the bedroom. Alexandre still seems to have jurisdiction over my body. It has a mind of its own as if it were a marionette - he being its puppet master.

To think that I spent eighteen years without anyone being able to give me an orgasm and he can just ease them out of me, every single time, like falling drops of rain. It's a miracle.

Work is better than ever. I am still in contact with Sam Myers via Skype and have decided to keep the HookedUp Enterprises fifty/fifty deal going with Natalie – even with feature films. If a good movie script comes in, I'll take it. But I will not get so emotionally involved again, and I certainly won't tamper with any script, nor have private meetings with movie stars.

Natalie and I could have changed the name. After all, Alexandre severed any connection to HookedUp Enterprises by bowing out gracefully and handing the business over to us. We can buy him out over time – although, luckily, no money had yet come in before he and Natalie did their 'sweet' deal so, in effect, we are just buying options, rather than anything that exists. The features can help us budget our documentaries which, bit by bit, are gaining more recognition. Not to mention the favor Alexandre is granting us: HookedUp Enterprises gets free advertising on his social media site. Another reason to keep that name.

While I'm busy doing a spurt of cleaning, organizing, chucking out the old and in with the new, Laura calls. Finally. About time. Now I can get on with my life – my plans; get a few facts straightened out. I can tell, right away, by the tone in her voice that she's feeling triumphant.

"Hello, Pearl," she purrs in her upper class British drawl. She sounds like Cruella De Vil. Perhaps if she got her hands on Rex, she'd turn him into a fur wrap. "Sorry I haven't got back to you but we've been busy."

We've.

"Laura, stop trying to pretend that you and Alexandre are an item. I'm not buying it."

She groans. "God, I hate that American expression, 'buying it'. You lot should really learn how to speak properly. You've got *us* now infected with your way of speech - all your inane TV shows…going up at the end of perfectly normal sentences as if they're questions when they're not. Saying cute instead of sweet, warranty instead of guarantee, kidding instead of joking. Next thing you know we'll be calling our knickers panties."

"Speaking of panties, Laura, stop throwing yours at Alexandre. It's over between you two and it has been for three years.

You're acting like some deluded fan who won't take no for an answer."

"Ooh, Pearl, I can see your claws are really out for the kill."

"You bet they are, Laura. Just keep away from Alexandre, okay?"

"How can I keep away from him when he won't keep away from me?"

"Stop bullshitting me, Laura."

"I think you'll find out in time, Pearl, that you're the deluded one, not me."

"I want to ask you a few direct questions and I'd like direct answers, please."

Silence.

"Laura? Are you still there?" I ask between gritted teeth.

"I really don't think I owe you a thing after you insulted me. Do you know what it's like being in a wheelchair? To imagine never being able to dance again? Or sail. Or even walk. Can you imagine that?"

"I apologize - I do, for insulting you at your front door. It was a gross, unkind thing to say and I'm glad that you are no longer in a wheelchair, but it doesn't give you license to lie to me. Pretending that Sophie was out to kill me. Lying about you and Alexandre, telling me that you were sleeping with him again and getting married and—"

"What makes you so sure that's not true, Pearl?"

"Because Alexandre swears it's not true, that's why."

"He'll swear his father just 'disappeared,' too. He's a good liar, Pearl. Anything to get into your 'panties' - as you so vulgarly call them."

I can see this conversation is going nowhere, fast. "Why did you lie to me about Sophie?"

"For your own good."

I sit on the edge of my bed, kick off my shoes furiously and hold the phone closer. "Something tells me, Laura, that you are so *not* concerned about my welfare."

"Listen, it's only a matter of time until Alexandre and I are back on track. It was kinder to nip things in the bud between you two - sooner rather than later."

This woman is something else!

"You don't give up, do you?" I spit out.

"Alexandre and I are meant to be together. One day, you will accept that. Really, Pearl, give up. I'm stronger, mentally, than you are. I'm like a Rottweiler with a bone. You'll see. Soon, you'll be so exhausted by this whole ordeal that you'll be handing me Alexandre on a platter, relieved to be out of it. Do you really want to go into battle with me? Do you *really* want to find out what I'm capable of?"

"I don't take threats lightly."

"Oh, please, don't get me wrong – this isn't a threat. Oh no. This is a friendly warning."

I lean against the headboard. Maybe this conversation will be longer than planned. "Where's your husband?"

"James is indisposed right now. He's having a holiday."

"Why isn't he returning Alexandre's calls?"

"You know how it is, Pearl…sometimes people just go AWOL. Bit like Alexandre's father…just slipped off one day never to be seen again."

"What are you telling me, Laura?"

"I'm not telling you a thing. You're a bright girl…summa cum laude and all that – I think you can work it all out for yourself. Especially with your penchant for super-sleuthing." She bursts out into a demonic cackle.

"Speaking of sleuths, Laura, how did you know about me and Alessandra Demarr?"

"Alexandre told me."

"No, Laura. You know that's a lie. Tell me the truth."

"You are a bit thick...I'm amazed you passed any exams at all."

"Just tell me, Laura, I need to know."

"Well, because I don't *need to know* what you're up to anymore, plus I really couldn't give a toss now that I've got Alexandre's attention back...well, I'll give you a clue."

"I'm listening."

"I really shouldn't be divulging my secrets."

I sigh into the receiver.

"Alright, but this is just between you, me and the gatepost."

I claw my nails into a cushion.

She whispers, "I'll give you a itsy, bitsy, little hint...does your phone have trouble shutting itself off or stay lit up after you've switched it off, or does it light up even when you aren't using it at all?"

Yes, I think. All of the above, which surprises me because it's new. "My Smartphone. But how? You've never had my cell in your possession."

"As I said, you're a bit slow on the uptake. You're so 1972, Pearl. So Watergate. But I suppose it makes sense for you, at your age, to be locked in a time warp. Anyway, must dash. Lovely chatting."

"Wait! That means you've hacked Alexandre's phone too? Maybe even Sophie's...hello? Laura are you there? Laura!!"

In a frenzy, I go online and look up cell phone hacking. The British newspapers did it, so why couldn't Laura? Especially with all her money and contacts.

I read hungrily:

Cell Phone Spying: Is Your Life Being Monitored?

It connects you to the world - but your cell phone - anyone from your boss to your wife could be monitoring your every move.

The same modern technology that keeps you on the move and in touch with everyone could also be your road to ruin – without you suspecting a thing.

Long gone are the days of simple wiretapping when all you could fear was someone listening into your conversations. The new generation of cell phone spyware provides a lot more power. Eavesdropping is easy. Your calls and text messages can be monitored – systems can even be set up so the spy is automatically alerted when you dial a certain number. Anyone who can perform a basic internet search can find the tools and figure out how to do it in no time.

Even more worrying is what your phone can do when you aren't even using it.

Location – simple surveillance.

A service called *World Tracker* lets you use data from cell phone towers and GPS systems to pinpoint anyone's exact location any time – even with the phone switched off – as long as the person has it on them.

I think of Alexandre – knowing I was at Laura's and when I would land in New York – upgrading my plane ticket. But he had my phone in his possession so that makes sense. It hadn't occurred to me that I could be a technology target of Laura's. Scary. I read on:

All the spy has to do is log onto the website and enter the target phone number. The site sends a text message to the phone that requires one response for confirmation. Once that response is sent automatically by your phone the spy is locked into your location and you can be tracked. The response is only required one time – after that, you, the cell phone owner, can be monitored – pinpointed on a Google map, without even knowing it.

Eavesdropping.

So once that person has been located they can also be spied upon. **Even if you are not talking on the phone, the eavesdropper can still listen in to conversations.**

Dozens of programs are available that can turn any cell phone into a high-tech, long-range listening device, unde-tectable to the average person. A phone's microphone can let the listener hear any conversation within earshot. The program can be installed from afar – the spy does not even have to come into contact with your cell phone. Once your number is dialed it taps into your phone's mic and can hear

everything going on. Your phone won't even ring and you will have no idea that the listener is virtually at your side.

It is now also possible for the spy to recover your deleted text messages and last dialed numbers – even deleted contacts.

I sit there stunned. My cell, that nice new Smartphone, and my old one – especially my old one (lost with my handbag) with even more unprotected technology - have been unwilling traitors to my every move, my every word. My phone, a recording device even when switched off? Laura could have practically been in the bath with me and Alessandra; been privy to our bondage madness, heard everything about my night with the footballers, not to mention all my intimate text messages and phone calls to Alexandre and Daisy! Maybe she's been in on my emails, too. And if she has me tracked, who's to say she hasn't done the same to Alexandre, or anyone she chooses?

I'm horrified, yet relieved. Alexandre has not lied to me. He did not betray me. Laura is psychotic. And dangerous. *Dange-air oose*, as Alexandre would say.

Anything I say, I do, can be used against me. Not in a court of law, no – the woman is breaking every ounce of the law, what she is doing is highly illegal. But her knowledge is her weapon. There's only one thing to do. Take my phone to some techie-genius to be swept clean of her spyware and get a new chip not registered in my name. And phone Alexandre – let him know that his ex is a total nut-job. Speaking of techie-geniuses, how come Alexandre, himself, didn't catch on to the fact she was hacking my phone? He must know all about that sort of stuff. How come he didn't guess?

All that Laura was saying about her husband, too? Being AWOL. Has she topped James off??'

I need to be careful. She's not only jealous, bitchy and determined…

She is terrifyingly dangerous.

I take my phone to a specialized shop and the man confirms that yes, it looks as if it has been hacked. He restores the factory settings, changes the chip so I have a new number and warns me to watch all text messages coming in which could be new attempts at breaking into my conversations and messages.

As I'm opening my front door, my landline is ringing. It's Alexandre. His voice sounds shaky and very apologetic. "Your cell isn't going through," he lets me know in an agitated voice.

"That's because I changed my phone number. It had been hacked. By Laura."

"I gathered."

I chuck my coat on the hall table in fury. "What? You're not surprised?" I shout out. "Why didn't you warn me?"

"Because I didn't put two and two together until it was staring me in the face. I was being very blind, Pearl, and I'm sorry. I'm so sorry about Laura."

"She's been listening to my conversations! Maybe yours, too. I don't trust my cell…even now after I've just had it swept clean. And you – you've been tracking me too – I don't like it, Alexandre, I don't like it one bit."

"I feel safer when I know where you are, chérie. I just want to look after you, know you're okay. Listen, baby, I have to take a trip – at least a week."

"What about Christmas?"

"I have an emergency; I have to see my mother."

"Oh my God, is she okay?" I think of my own mother – *please don't say it's the Big C.*

"Physically, yes, she's fine but...well...we have a family emergency."

"Is Sophie alright? Elodie?"

"This has nothing to do with Sophie. It's just between me and my mother. Something's come up."

"What? What's wrong?"

"When we're married, Pearl, I'll tell you all about it."

This mysterious and enigmatic comment leaves me speechless. Suspicion nips at my heels.

"Pearl, are you still there?"

"I don't understand, 'when we're married.' Is this some kind of moral blackmail to speed up the wedding?"

"No."

"Then what are you saying something like that for?"

"When we're married we'll be a team."

"We're a team now, Alexandre," I say, hurt. I slump onto the chair and take off my sneakers.

"Not quite. I need to know...look, I don't want to discuss this over the phone."

I'm rendered silent, still trying to digest this weird conversation. Laura calling, telling me she finally has 'Alexandre's attention' and Alexandre's mother who isn't ill, yet has a mysterious emergency. *What* emergency?

"Look, I'm flying to Paris in a couple of hours."

I wait for him to say more. Wait for his invitation. He says nothing.

"Christmas?" I ask.

"I'm in a real mess right now, a real bind. I'm sworn to secrecy."

"Christmas?" I repeat, my heart pounding with disappointment and anger.

"Baby, of course you're welcome to come for Christmas in Paris but…"

"If there's a 'but' involved, I don't think I want to," I reply tentatively, my throat swelling up.

"Yes, there is a very big but."

I take a deep breath. My eyes are prickling with tears. I had imagined Christmas here, in New York, both of us alone with Rex. If his mother were ill of course I'd understand, but this…this is beginning to sound like some strange excuse. "What's going on?" I croak through my wooden throat.

Alexandre's voice sounds as pained as mine. "Something I have to sort out. I don't want to lie to you, Pearl, so please don't ask me any more questions. Just know I love you and want to marry you the second you say yes."

"Why would I want to marry someone who has secrets from me? Someone who's hiding something?"

"It's a Catch 22, isn't it?"

I try to stop my voice from breaking. "It certainly is."

"I love you."

"Are you going to London, by any chance?" I ask, not wanting to hear the answer that I'm dreading.

"Please don't ask me any more questions - I don't want to lie to you."

"I take that as a 'yes.' So you're going to London," I state flat-
ly.

"Look, I have no choice."

"We always have a choice, Alexandre."

"External forces are trying to pull us apart."

"Laura."

"Yes.

"You're going to see Laura?"

"Please, Pearl, don't make this harder for me than it already
is."

I hang up. There is no more to discuss. I don't want to humiliate myself, scream and cry down the phone. All I know is that he
will be seeing Laura again after he promised not to. Her phone
call...she knew she had him back. She was right; *I'm* the deluded
one, not her. For whatever reason, whatever hold she has over
him, he just can't keep away from her. And he's not even offering
to explain why – everything shrouded in some big, enigmatic
secret. Well, fuck him!

This time I know it's over between us, once and for all.

5

Christmas zipped by, Alexandre spent it in Paris. Anthony came to stay (Bruce went to his parents in Napa Valley because his father was ill). Here, at my new abode, it was like one big slumber party. Daisy and Amy, Ant and I all snuggled together in our two bedroom apartment, Ant on the couch and Amy in her special Wigwam in the bedroom which was a gift from Anthony. It was fun.

We watched endless children's movies which we loved, particularly the *Toy Story* trilogy. Embarrassingly, I found myself weeping in *Toy Story 2*, identifying with the toys being abandoned by their owners. I still have all my old teddies; I never did have the heart to get rid of any. It feels to me that only yesterday I was a child, playing tea parties and doctors and nurses the way Amy does now.

She, Ant, Daisy and I all played cowboys, too – a toy gun and western outfits came along with the wigwam kit, although Amy refused to kill any Indians – a politically correct tomboy. Christmas is all about children and Amy had a ball.

I kept waiting for Anthony to slip into his old sarcastic, jaded demeanor but he didn't. He was adorable and very loving towards me. I am so glad the troubled part of our relationship is history.

The troubled part of a relationship….namely, Alexandre. He called on several occasions and each time my brother picked up and chatted merrily away, but never handed over the phone and told Alexandre that as long as he had anything to do with Laura I was not interested in seeing him. Alexandre didn't push it; he just seemed pleased to have news of me. He has been flitting from Paris to New York to London. I keep half expecting him to be waiting outside my door but it hasn't happened.

I guess he has made his choice, after all.

And that choice is Laura.

Made all the more complicated by something I have been feeling for two whole weeks. Swollen breasts, sleepiness, occasional vomiting and a strange longing for pickles.

Perhaps my old teddies will get unpacked, after all.

Yes, I'm pregnant – at least that's what a home pregnancy test has confirmed. I called my gynecologist and booked an appointment for next week. Meanwhile, I thought it was time to pamper myself, so I also booked a massage.

The Ayurvedic salon is not what I had imagined. Daisy recommended this place to me – a friend of hers comes here on a regular basis for soothing massages. Daisy's friend had described in detail *a warm herbal oil massage designed to bring nourishment to the tissues, deep relaxation to the muscles and calmness to the mind.* Hmm…sounds perfect. However, this place seems like less of a beauty parlor and more of a doctor's office. I am given a form to fill out with my medical history – *Jeez, all I wanted was a relaxing massage with oils!* But because the book I'm reading on my e-reader has me hooked, I remain in the waiting room patiently; in fact, happy that I have this peaceful excuse to devour my novel.

Finally, a large woman in a white coat brushes out of her office and says a warm goodbye to the lady before me. She smiles and ushers me in. She's Indian and dons a happy, friendly face with cheeks like ripe apples.

"Come in, Ms. Robinson, sorry to keep you waiting."

"No problem, I caught up with some reading."

"Please sit down. Let me see your medical history," she says, and I hand her the piece of paper.

She adjusts her spectacles and peruses it with great interest, although I'm not sure why – I'm your pretty average type. No allergies, no epilepsy, no addictions – except, of course, for sex with a particular Frenchman, if you count that. Right now, you could say I was going 'cold turkey.'

"Now, what can I do for you?"

"Well, I…um…I came here for a basic massage."

"Nothing is basic about our massage therapy, Ms. Robinson."

"Oh, I see. Please call me Pearl, by the way; I hate formalities."

"Pearl – what a lovely name. Tell me, what's troubling you? Are you feeling tired, sluggish, depressed?"

"Yes to the first two things you mentioned. Depressed? Well, I would say I feel more anxious that depressed."

She says nothing, just nods her head as if to say 'go on'.

"I'm pregnant, for starters."

"Congratulations, that's wonderful news." She beams at me, her sparkling white teeth are set off against her coffee-colored skin.

"Thank you. Well, yes." I want to explain to her that I'm not with the baby's father; I want to burst out crying, fling my arms about her ample shoulders and unleash my inner turmoil, but I chew my lip instead, and fight back any impending tears.

"Well, of course, you know that *any* kind of massage therapy is out of the question for you right now, don't you?"

I'm stunned. Who is this woman? *I just want a goddam massage, lady!*

"But why? That's why I'm here."

"Well, perhaps it's divine intervention – you don't want to lose your baby. How many weeks are you?"

I think back to the rampant, sex-fueled night with Alexandre when he practically pierced my womb he went in so deep. I can't be sure if that was the qualifying moment, there have been so many since.

"I think about five weeks. I'm not sure – I just did a home pregnancy test this morning."

We discuss my periods, dates, medication and so forth for a good ten minutes. I'm wondering why I'm offering all this information about myself to a massage therapist when she informs me, "I run this Ayurvedic practice but, you know, I'm just as much a doctor as I am a masseuse."

"No, I had no idea. So you don't practice regular medicine here in the States?"

"Ayurvedic medicine is not recognized officially in this country but where I come from – Kerala in southern India – well, it is an important part of our culture and taken very seriously. But I am also a qualified GP. My mother was a doctor and also my grandmother; all of us GPs with a particular interest in preventative medicine."

"But I have nothing to prevent," I venture, still confused as to how I got myself into the doctor-ish situation when all I wanted was a freaking massage.

"I see here that you are forty years old."

"Yes."

"With a history of two miscarriages – one D&C," she says, reading my notes.

I remember that awful time; when I went in for an ultrasound and they discovered the baby had no heartbeat. I had been carrying about a dead fetus for two weeks and they had to operate immediately. "Yes, I had a D&C," I say, suddenly profoundly grateful that I'm now pregnant, that God has given me another chance even if I am to be a single mother forevermore.

"How many times have you had sexual intercourse with your partner in the last few weeks?"

"Er...none."

She nods with approval. "Good. You must abstain from sex for the first three months of pregnancy or you risk suffering another miscarriage."

Well, that will be easy now that Alexandre is with Laura and I can't even look at another man, let alone bed down with one.

The doctor continues, "Any penetration is dangerous for a woman of your age with your medical history. You will not find this written in any textbook and most modern-day doctors would poo-poo this idea but, believe me, old wives' tales are very often true."

I stare at her bemused. *Abstain from sex?? What has this got to do with my herbal massage?*

She goes on matter-of-factly, "No penetration but you can do other, non-invasive sexual practices. No massages, least of all with powerful oils that can upset the body's hormone-balance. You must not even indulge in reflexology; too much stimulation. Some doctors believe abdominal massage is good as it gets the blood flowing. I do not, unless it is very gentle and with your own hands – do not go to a massage therapist for the first three months or you could lose your child. You're forty; this could be your last chance at pregnancy, you need to take all the precautions you can."

I eye her suspiciously. Is she some kind of quack? "I've never heard of this before. It seems so extreme."

"Once, my dear, people thought it was extreme when they were advised not to smoke and drink whilst pregnant. Believe me, I have been in this business all my life, since I could walk and talk – I have breathed it – every single member of my family, the men included, are doctors. We have picked up a few tips over the years." She waggles her head in a figure of eight.

I observe her warily but I'm also fascinated by this information. My mother would have loved this woman – she hated conventional medicine.

"Now, what I'm going to prescribe for you, Pearl, is simple. One baby aspirin a day. This will safeguard you against any premature clotting. Stay off caffeine, alcohol and away from second-hand smoke - eat plenty of fresh vegetables and protein, but you probably already know all that. No heavy exercise at the gym, no jogging."

"Is swimming okay?"

"Swimming is perfect but don't train for the Olympics." She smiles. "Folic acid in a multi-vitamin, B6, B12 and omega 3's," she states briskly.

"I already bought all that at the pharmacy, and fish-oil tablets."

"Good. I'm going to give you a painless saliva test to see your progesterone levels and if they are low I'll prescribe a completely natural progesterone cream. Progesterone is responsible for creating a healthy environment in the womb by creating and maintaining a healthy uterine lining. If more people used this treatment a lot of miscarriages could be avoided. All you need is a pea-sized amount of cream on your finger which you can rub into a different area each time, just once a day - somewhere the skin is thin; your breasts, face, upper thighs. It's completely natural, no synthetics, no harmful ingredients."

She sticks something into my mouth to do the saliva test. My mind wanders off to my baby-to-be - that is, if it can survive the next couple of months up until the first trimester, the most precarious. Will he be blond or dark? Will she have Alexandre's curvy red lips and his crooked smile? Will she be proud like him? Will he break hearts like his father...

"Oh, and one more thing," the doctor says assertively. "Try to keep your cell phone calling to a minimum. Radiation levels are harmful and can impair fetal brain development. Nobody will tell you this and few people want to listen but−"

"No, you know what, doctor? I think it would be a great idea to dump my phone, once and for all. It'll be safer for both me and the baby."

Alexandre may have been stalking me through my cell but I am stalking Rex. I miss that dog. I can't break our bond. On my way back home, I get off the bus at Central Park South and walk into the park, listening to Michael Jackson sing *Ben*, the best love song ever written about an animal. But instead of 'Ben,' I sing along with the word, Rex.

I know Sally's schedule – she and Rex will be somewhere near the big bronze Alice in Wonderland statue, chit-chatting with her dog owner friends discussing their 'children's' behavior and comparing notes. Will I be doing the same soon? Only, with a human child, not a four-legged one? I guess I should join prenatal classes and discuss breastfeeding options and which is the best brand of diapers.

Maybe I'll be coming to this spot, myself, watching my child climb on Alice. Unlike most sculptures, children are invited to climb, touch and crawl all over Alice and her friends. In fact, through the decades, thousands of hands and feet have literally polished parts of the statue's bronze surface completely smooth. I observe Alice now, sitting on a giant mushroom reaching toward a pocket watch held by the White Rabbit. Peering over her shoulder is the Cheshire Cat, surrounded by the Dormouse, Alice's cat Dinah, and the Mad Hatter and yes, I see Rex and Sally not far off, just behind this landmark, Rex sniffing a fellow mate.

Sally loves to pass by here every day. With her shocking pink pigtails and punk rocker outfits, Sally is an eternal child. Alexandre found her walking dogs with one of the dog walking companies that roam the Upper East Side. The handlers typically walk ten dogs at a time all leashed, making sure their right hand is free for picking up dog poop with wads of newspaper stuffed in their back pocket. Sally makes three times the money, now, being Rex's personal nanny.

"Hi Sally," I shout, rushing over to Rex to hug him.

"I wish you'd come home, Pearl," Sally grumbles with a sad pout. "Alexandre is a bit mopey without you there."

"Really?" I ask, thrilled to know he may be suffering a little (obviously not enough, though, to stop seeing Laura).

"Yes, really. He's always on the phone doing business – doesn't smile much these days, his temper's short; he seems to have lost his sense of humor."

"Have you seen Laura?"

"No, who's she?"

I try to sound casual but fail miserably. "Do you ever hear him speaking to a woman on the phone – you know, sweet-talk."

"The only person he's been talking to more than usual is his mother. I know it's her because he has one voice for his mom and one for Sophie. You know his 'mom voice' is super-protective – it's very cute. Not that I understand French but I can hear the tone."

"No lovey-dovey talk with other women, then?"

Sally shuffles her big biker boots along the muddy grass. "No way! He obviously misses his precious Pearl. Sometimes I hear him say so to Rex, discussing how lost they are without you. Not that Rex can talk, but you know, I think he understands. And the other day, Alexandre gave me a whole bunch of photos of you – I was asked to drop them off at the framers. Like I said, he's either working or moping about you all day long. Rex is sleeping in his bed now."

"You're kidding?"

"I know! Alexandre snuggles up with Rex everywhere. He's now allowed on all the couches, even the bed. Since you've gone all Alexandre wants to do is be with his dog."

"Has Alexandre been traveling lately? To London?"

"Yes, he went to London last week."

"I see." I am now reminded of my mission. To forget about Alexandre for good and let him go - move on with my life. He has Laura now – he can't have us both. *Be strong, Pearl.* "Oh, Sally, I have something for you." I bring out my Smartphone and hand it to her. "A gift for you. It's already unblocked."

She jumps up and down and her pigtails swing as if in celebration. "Wow! Really! But this is like, brand new – this Smartphone is the best!"

"It's a great phone. It has advantages. You can keep your gloves on when you dial a number – not all Smartphones let you do that. Handy here in New York with the cold winters."

Sally's Cheshire Cat smile is spread across her whole face. "This is the greatest gift ever."

"Don't let Alexandre know I was asking about him."

"Okay, sure."

"And if you hear any information about Laura, pass the word along." *Oops! I have just broken my own resolution to put him out of my mind.* I add hastily, as if to excuse myself, "I just worry about him, that's all."

"Of course. You have my word this is just between us."

Sally, Rex and I meander about the park for a good half hour before I wend my way back home.

I am cell phone-less and it feels great. After all, once upon a time we humans made dates with people, arranged a time in advance and turned up. We couldn't cancel at the last second and flake-out when a better deal came up. We were responsible people, once. We could spell: see you tonight, not C U 2 nite. We had attention spans of more than five minutes at a go. We painted, sketched and wrote in notebooks, not just flicked like mindless idiots through our Facebook and HookedUp pages, worrying about what everyone else was doing and living vicariously through them. Yay! I am no longer shackled-down with invisible chains to my social-media addiction!

It's a wonderful feeling with no cell to know I am not being spied upon nor stalked. I feel liberated and brain tumor-free. Most of all, I feel protective of that tiny bundle inside me; not that there is much evidence; no more swelling than a large bowl of pasta or rice wouldn't do. There is life within me and it feels incredible, especially as I am so in love with its maker, despite Alexandre being a heartbreaking bastard, I will still love everything about his future offspring…

Because deep down inside me (call me a clueless fool), I feel there must be some mistake – he cannot be lying to me, he does love me.

Yet – I need to get a grip - all the evidence is there, clear and sharp as crystal – he still can't give up Laura.

A week has passed by. Sneaking off for my secret Rex *rendez-vous* has become a regular habit. If I can't have Alexandre, himself, I can feel close to him through his beloved dog. Today I've arranged to take Rex alone.

I meet Sally at the entrance at Sixty Forth Street by Central Park Zoo. Rex is there waiting, all excited. Funny how Labradors and Labrador mixes wiggle the middle of their torso when they wag their tails. He's ready for his tour around the park.

I kiss Sally hello and give her a one hundred dollar bill. "Have a nice breakfast."

She shakes her head; her Cerise-colored pigtails swing in surprise and her wildly plucked eyebrows, which seem no more than painted curves, shoot up. "Pearl, this is way, way too much."

"I don't have change," I lie, wondering if she has caught onto my not-so-subtle bribe. It's good to have Sally on my side, to get snippets of information about Alexandre, know where he's going and when he'll return. "Treat yourself to something delicious. I'll meet you back here in an hour and a half."

"Are you going to the Central Park Paws event this morning?"

Only dog-mad Sally could know about such a thing as Central Park Paws. "No," I answer, "but tell me more, I'm intrigued."

"Well, Central Park Paws hosts regular events for dog owners in the park. Today is Monthly Bagel Barks – it gives dog owners the chance to meet, talk and have breakfast while the dogs enjoy some off-leash playtime. It starts in fifteen minutes until nine o'clock."

"I'm so sorry, Sally, am I robbing you of your meeting? We can go together if you like."

She looks at the hundred dollar bill and says, "No, it's okay, I've always wanted to go to The Carlyle for breakfast …well, thanks so much, Pearl. Have a nice walk."

The Carlyle – where Alexandre and I had that dreaded breakfast when I hadn't been honest with him about wanting to do a documentary about HookedUp and he lost his temper with me. This is the third time we have split up and this time I fear it's for good. It still doesn't make sense – he doesn't strike me as a person who would lie but the evidence is there – he can't keep away from Laura. She has some kind of emotional hold over him, no matter how in love with me he claims to be. I want him so badly but this time I must keep my resolve.

I wave Sally good bye and Rex and I go into the park. It is covered in a blanket of fresh, untrammeled snow and looks like a fairy-tale; the sky a clear, icy blue. Some pale crystal flakes flutter through the air – it's snowing, but only just.

We start wending our way across the twisting paths and buried grass towards Bethesda Fountain to the other side of the lake, now frozen, near to the woods and where I can confidently unleash Rex to run free and sniff about. I love New York. Here in Central Park, you are allowed let your dog off the leash before nine a.m. and again after nine at night. Not that I would brave Central Park at night alone – just in case. I let Rex loose; he's so well behaved that I don't have to worry about him escaping, unlike Zelda, the beautiful Husky of my childhood years.

We walk at a fast-paced clip, my thermal boots squeaking on the powdery snow, my huge, floor-length overcoat brushing against itself, whooshing and shuffling in muffled silence. Hardly anyone is around, just a few other dogs and people walking with purpose as if they are going home after an all-nighter or cutting through the park to work. It's still only seven thirty.

"Stop it, Rex," I scold, as he pees against a lumpy, half-melted snowman with a drooping carrot for its nose. I take the carrot between my gloved fingers and push it further inside its head.

"There we go, Mr. Snowman, you'll last a little longer."

I zip along swiftly in the direction of the woody grove – New Yorkers walk fast – no meandering ever; you can get mugged that way. I wear eyes in the back of my head. This part of the park is remote. When I hear footsteps behind me I am aware of what a risk-taker I am. Rock-climbing, trapezes, going with two football-ers to their dorm alone and dating a man too young for me with such a rampant sexual appetite he desires more than one woman to satiate him; he'd date us both simultaneously if he could get away with it. When will I ever learn? The footsteps are male, booted, tough…Holy crap! I spin around, my fists in balls and call Rex over to my side. I need to clip him back into his leash to show the world I'm a woman with a black Pit-bull mix…DON'T MESS WITH ME!

It's HIM. No less dangerous than a mugger. He's dressed in a long military coat that looks as if it's from World War One and big, black boots. His hair is damp and ruffled from the snow-flakes, his dark eyelashes sparkling with moisture, his curvy lips red from the cold, tilted up into his signature crooked smile. He looks delicious, sexy, mysterious. Uh oh.

"Pearl, stop!" Alexandre rushes up to me and grabs my arm forcing me to stumble into him. His breath is on my face, hot mist clouding the tiny space between our mouths. He has the 'I'm going to fuck you' look written all over his face and I know I'm in trouble.

"What do you want Alexandre?" Stupid question. I know what he wants.

"I can't bear this any longer, Pearl – please." He starts kissing my eyes, my nose and the animalistic groan deep within him makes my stomach flutter. I know what will be beneath that military coat. A big, huge, rock-hard Weapon of Mass Destruction.

"Christ, I've missed you."

"How's Laura?" I hiss from my tightened mouth. My white, steamy breath is like a dragon's; no less furious.

"Please let's not argue. Please, chérie, I'm going crazy without you. I need you."

"You just want me for my body, Alexandre."

"That's not true. I need you, baby. I need—"

"You can't have your cake and eat it, too."

"You're the only cake I want, I swear." He takes my gloved hand and pulls me towards him. "Come over here, we have to talk."

"We can talk right here."

"Too public, please baby."

He draws me behind him towards a large elm tree and pins me up against the solid trunk. "I have to kiss you."

"No."

But he starts with his trademark wispy kisses on my eyes again, on my icy cheeks and then my temple. I quiver all over and can feel my panties moisten. "Leave me alone, you bastard. How did you find me anyway, now that I don't have my phone?"

He breathes in the scent of me. "I have ways."

"Did Sally sell me out?"

"No, annoyingly Sally is on your side." He slips his black leather-gloved hand through a small opening in my coat and around my waist. Then the other hand. I can feel him un-glove himself and his warm fingers are tracing their way about my bare flesh. My skin tingles. He starts a familiar journey down the back of my butt cheeks but I slam my behind against the tree, trapping his hand. He was inches away from knowing how wet I am, and how I long for him inside me.

"Ouch, tigress, that hurts."

"Take your hand away, Alexandre."

"I know that you secretly want me, chérie, but as you wouldn't let me see you, I thought I'd better come and claim what's mine wherever I could - and it happens to be here in Central Park."

"Get it through that arrogant, ego-inflated head of yours that I do not belong to you! I am not your soul mate, nor your *media naranja*. You have all that already with *Laura*."

"You *are* my soul mate, my *media naranja*, my wife-to-be, my everything, Pearl. You're Rex's mother, too. We're a family."

Little does he know there's more family on the way. "You ruined and destroyed all that by seeing Laura again!"

"How many more times do I have to tell you that I don't love Laura? I don't want her - haven't for years and certainly not since I met you. The truth is, I don't even *like* her anymore."

I bellow at him, "Love and like have nothing to do with it for you. You covet her because you can't bear to give up any of your women. You're like a cock with his hens. You *are* a cock! One big walking, talking, cock! You have a Weapon of Mass Destruction which you go around using at every opportunity!"

He strokes a loose tendril of hair from my cheek. "I swear, believe me, it's been tucked away, unused except by my own hand since I last made love with you."

"You haven't 'made love' with me for ages, you *fuck* me! 'Fuck my ass off' 'fuck my brains out' as your expressions go."

"Come back and live with me again and we'll be making love again...just...I go crazy when I see you...this *diet* of sex - of us not living together is making me go insane so the last few times we got together I felt like a beast."

He takes my hand. "Feel it. Feel how hard it is. All I can think of is your voice, your smile, Pearl, your face, your lips, your ass, your tits and most importantly, your soul - your essence, your very being. I can't live without you, chérie. Every waking moment, every sleeping second I'm dreaming of you, Pearl, I'm so crazy about you, it hurts."

"Then fucking stay away from that asparagus stick bitch, Laura!" I yell, remembering how Sophie had described her as an asparagus.

Rex comes bounding over and jumps up. My screaming has alerted him and he starts to bark at his master. "You see?" I screech - "even Rex is on Team Pearl. He knows what a prize jerk you are. A lying, two-timing jackass!"

"Look, I'm dealing with Laura—"

"*Dealing* with her? You are unbelievable. Unbe-fucking-lievable!" I try to break away from his devouring gaze which is swallowing me whole.

But he has my wrists in a clasp so I can't escape. Christ he's sexy.

"I swear I haven't lied to you. I swear I've been faithful – I haven't touched Laura – please trust me, Pearl. Please have faith."

"Then why have you been seeing her?"

"I can't tell you. But trust me." He breathes into my face seductively – he smells of apples and sweetness. "I was just protecting someone I love."

"Someone *else* you love? How many of us *are* there, Alexandre? How many more women have you got hooked on you with your panty-melting antics?"

"I'm sorry, chérie. But I had to see Laura – I had no choice." He looks down at his boots. "And I'm afraid I'll have to see her again."

His words stab my heart. *I'll have to see her again.* I shout out in a jealous rage, "What is it that Laura has that I don't?"

"Something I need from her. Once I get it, I'll never go near her again, I promise."

I try to struggle free. "You are quite something, Alexandre Chevalier. Wow! You really win the prize for being a French, macho SHIT-head!"

He keeps hold of my wrists. "Please, baby, trust me. I can't say more, just trust me." He pushes his soft lips onto mine and kisses my closed, bitter mouth. He begins to lick me very gently and an unbidden low moaning sound escapes my throat which I know is my downfall. He pushes his wavering tongue inside my longing mouth and parts it. My jaw drops open. Even through his thick military coat I can feel his erection pressed up against my thighs.

"Hey, you two! No indecent behavior in public!"

I open my eyes from my reverie and say a little prayer to St. Lucy. Thank you, Santa Lucia, for saving me; for shining a light on this situation and showing it up for what it is…madness. It's a police officer and now he's making his way over towards us, half smiling as if he was kidding about 'indecency' but I take this opportunity. I slip from underneath Alexandre's clutches and dash towards the uniformed stranger.

"Bye, Alexandre. Rex! Come boy, come!" I start galloping at full pelt in the direction of the East side.

Rex runs behind me, following at racing speed. Rex has chosen me over his master and I feel triumphant.

I don't look back.

Daisy and I are sitting on her bed with our legs tucked under us while Amy's playing with her teddies in her wigwam.

"It's just my body he wants, Daisy, nothing more. Laura was right; he's in 'lust' with me."

"Nonsense, he wants all of you."

"All of me *and* all of Laura. He wants her for…I don't know what…and me…just to fuck."

"Rubbish. Look, Pearl, if all he was after was a sexy body…well… I don't mean to sound harsh and you do have an incredible body and you really are beautiful but…well…if all he wanted was a body, he could flick his thumb through any Victoria's Secret catalogue and pick off any top model he wanted – well, anyone who Leonardo di Caprio hasn't already claimed, that is. With his money and looks Alexandre could, literally, have any *body*. But he's chosen you."

"I suppose you're right. It's true, he could be going out with a supermodel. A supermodel who wants world peace and plays chess, to boot. He could get anyone. Sometimes…no - not sometimes, often - I wonder what he sees in me."

Daisy rolls her eyes with irritation. "Stop sounding so poor-me and buck up, woman! He sees your good heart, your soul. And you may not be a supermodel but you look bloody amazing for your age. You have a better body than most twenty-five year-olds, and a beautiful face – sometimes you remind me of Grace Kelly. It really pisses me off when you start all that, 'I'm just an average-looking girl next door' nonsense. It's bollocks. Plus, Alexandre feels at ease with you, likes to hang out. You both love dogs."

I suddenly think of Laura (Cruella De Vil) calling Rex a 'creature' and it makes me seethe. "Alexandre swears nothing is going on with Laura and that I should trust him."

Daisy sucks in a lungful of air. "Well, I'm obviously not the best person to discuss this with after what Johnny did to me. And to Amy. I trusted him implicitly – I don't think I'll ever be able to do that again with any man."

"At least he wants you back and he's groveling."

"But I don't want him back now. How could I live with that uncertainty again?"

"What about Amy?"

Daisy looks over at the wigwam. Amy is muttering to herself in different voices and playing 'tea party' inside. "That's my only concern. Amy loves her dad, obviously, but at the same time it's no good if we're unhappy together – that's no good for her at all."

"You need more time to think it through. Let Johnny wallow in his misery a bit, it'll do him good. Make him appreciate what he's lost." I realize I sound like Alexandre – that's exactly what he said to me.

"Coming from you, the eternal forgiver, that sounds tough."

"Well, some men deserve the cold shoulder, now and then. If you're too nice they walk all over you."

"Actually Pearl, I have a confession to make."

"Really?" A gamut of possibilities runs through my mind. Perhaps she's been having private conversations with Alexandre and has been holding out on juicy information.

She looks at the wigwam and whispers, "About Zac."

"Zac, the surfer? The good looking one we met on the beach?"

Daisy looks down; her face flushes pink. "We kissed."

My jaw drops open. "You are *kidding* me? Daisy – that's so exciting…"

"It gave me confidence – made me realize I was still attractive."

"Are you kidding? You're gorgeous. Especially since you've lost all that weight. He should be so lucky."

Then she squeals quietly, "But wait. There's more!"

I laugh. "You sound like one of those infomercials…'but wait, there's more.'"

"I shagged him."

Shag - British for 'fuck'. I scream, "No!"

Amy pokes her head out of the wigwam. "Why are you shouting, Auntie Pearl?"

"Nothing, honey. I thought I saw a spider but I was wrong."

"I like spiders. I would never kill a spider."

"That's because you're an angel, sweetheart. Don't worry, I don't kill them, either."

Amy slips back inside her wigwam and continues her tea party.

Daisy whispers, "I haven't been able to get him out of my mind since."

"I'm not freakin' surprised. He was gorgeous. When did this happen? You're such a dark horse, Daisy."

"That day when you three all went on a walk in the woods. Remember? When I said I'd stay behind? Zac popped over."

"Sounds like he did a lot more than just pop over."

"Well, yes. It started with a kiss and then…well, I thought, 'I'm on holiday, what the hell.' I didn't mean it to go so far but my hormones took over, I couldn't resist him."

"And? Was it worth it?"

"Let's just say that he woke up a certain part of my body that had lain dormant for a long while."

"You were very brave to just *go* for it like that."

"Like I said, I was on holiday - I felt reckless. As far as I was concerned it was a one night stand…I mean a 'one *day* stand'…but he had other ideas."

I'm still grinning at this gossipy news. "Like what?"

"He told me he wanted more. Well, I left him hanging - you know, it wasn't exactly the right time in my life to be jumping into another relationship. When a woman doesn't give a damn, it makes a man all the more interested. I told him I wasn't ready for a relationship."

"*Relationship?* You'd even consider Zac as *boyfriend* material?"

"He's gorgeous, Pearl. And he's a really sweet guy. And not dumb either – he's interesting. Yes, I see potential there."

"But… but… he's a *surfer* - the non-committal type - he'd drive you nuts."

"That's what your dad's like. Zac is more demonstrative."

"Really? What did he demonstrate?" I laugh at my silliness and wait for a detailed description of the nitty-gritty.

Daisy replies in a serious tone, "Nothing like 'absence making the heart grow fonder.' He wants me to think about moving to Kauai and living with him."

Stunned doesn't even begin to describe how I feel. "You'd consider leaving New York? Living in *Hawaii?*"

"You bet. I mean, it's so beautiful there, so peaceful. A great place for a child to grow up. You get a tropical life but it's still part of America – the best of both worlds."

"Are you sure it wasn't something he just *said* – the way guys do sometimes. Empty promises and all that?"

"We've been in touch by email. No calls. I told him not to call – I don't want to upset A. M. Y."

A little voice pipes up from within the wigwam, "Mommy, I know you're talking about me."

"Just saying how pretty you are, Amy," I shout out. "My God, she's bright for her age."

Daisy whispers, "He's invited us to stay with him at his house. A three month trial period, he suggested."

My mouth hangs open. "I can't believe I'm hearing this. A surfer with *plans*?"

"Well, he said it. It was his idea. Maybe not every surfer is as flaky as your dad when it comes to relationships."

"And you're *considering* it? Seriously? What about your practice? What about your job?"

"I'm self-employed, I can go anywhere. I could start up something there. I may earn less out there but the cost of living will be so much less than New York City. I mean, Amy and I wouldn't move in with him straight away. I think that would be foolish. We could get something small nearby. See how it goes first. It would be an adventure – a life change. I'd keep my autonomy. Then, if it didn't work out with Zac it wouldn't be the end of the world and if it did, well…hello? Book Two of my life."

"What about Johnny?"

She lowers her voice to an almost inaudible whisper, "Johnny can fuck right off."

"Really?"

"The only reason he wanted us back is because Lady-love Phoenix has gone back to her husband. He had the perfect life with me and Amy and he blew it. We can't be left-overs. Anyway, don't worry, I won't do anything rash. But I am weighing things up." She clears her throat. "And what about you, Pearl? D'you think you'll have the willpower to stay away from Alexandre when he's still expressing undying love for you?"

"This time I have to, Daisy. I have no choice. I can't be left-overs, either."

"I just don't get it. *Why* is he still seeing Laura?"

"He says he needs one more thing from her and then he'll never see her again."

"Is that code for one last goodbye, d'you think? One last shag?"

"That's what I fear but he's been taking his time about it – this Laura thing has been dragging on for weeks."

"It must have been painful for you not spending Christmas with him."

"I had an amazing Christmas here with you and Amy and Ant."

"Yes, but still. Have you spoken to Sophie, by the way?"

"Yes, she called the other day. So strange. She asked me what was going on with Alexandre. She asked *me*."

"But surely she must *know* if it's to do with their mother - this big 'emergency' Alexandre was talking about."

"Exactly, that's what I'd presumed. But no. She's as much in the dark as I am. That's why I'm beginning to think this mother emergency thing is a fig leaf of an excuse to keep seeing Laura."

"But what you told me – the stuff Sally the dog walker said. It sounds as if he's miserable without you. None of this makes sense."

"Maybe he's miserable because he can't make a final choice and it's ripping him apart. I'm so glad you're here to protect me, Daisy, or I know what he'd do. He'd be at my door wooing me with kisses and flexing his huge great Weapon of Mass Destruction until I succumbed. He knows how weak I am, how I can't resist him.

"You're really hooked on him, aren't you?"

"I'm head over heels in love with him. I have never, ever felt like this about anybody."

"Are you going to let him know you're pregnant?"

"No. I want to know it's *me* he's choosing if he finally makes his mind up. If he knows there's a child involved he might come back to me just for that reason. It has to be me, and only me he wants."

"Did you tell Sophie about the baby?"

"No. I can't trust her not to tell him. You know how close they are."

"I wish I had a crystal ball, Pearl. I wish I could offer great advice but I've screwed up with you on more than one occasion. I was just as suspicious as you were about Sophie and if I'd kept my bloody mouth shut maybe you and Alexandre would be married by now."

"And what? Be divorced ten minutes later because of Laura? Having a ring on my finger probably wouldn't have changed a thing. Maybe he's like all those ex French presidents and aristocratic types who have a wife and also a mistress at the same time – maybe that's what rich French men do."

Daisy frowns. "He didn't strike me as that sort. I still can't believe he's with her. I mean, he swears to you that he hasn't touched her – why would he say that if it weren't true?"

"Because, as you know more than anyone, men can be very convincing. Listen, some women fall in love with serial killers and have no idea. I have obviously fallen for a pathological liar who can't keep it in his pants."

6

Alexandre felt as if he had been sliced in two. This whole situation was a fucking nightmare. He had never imagined that Laura could do this to him - have this hold on him just as everything seemed so perfect with Pearl. Crap timing - that was for sure.

He sat in his parked car, watching as snowflakes drifted across the windscreen... waiting, his heart pounding fast...with rage. He hadn't done anything like this for a long while; hadn't got into any fights for years because he knew what he was capable of. Anger and excess energy had been building up steadily over the past few weeks and this fuck was going to get it – he deserved it. He'd show that fuck, once and for all, that you just can't go through life treating people like garbage, especially women. Jim was his name. Probably thought that, because he made a killing on Wall St, he was above it all. He needed to be taught a lesson.

Alexandre's eyes were fixed on the man's front door. It was still decorated with a crown of holly, the imposing white brick house boasting expensive Christmas lights; tasteful, not overly done. Must have cost a mint, this place; Mystic, Connecticut was not cheap. He imagined the man's wife and 2.2 children, perfect and with no clue to the monster that lived within their loved one. Alexandre wouldn't damage him, no. He wouldn't do that to a man with kids but he'd scare the living shit out of him. Make him pay. In more ways than one.

He smiled to himself as it struck him that he'd never let onto Pearl that he was a black-belt master in Taekwondo. He hated people who boasted about their prowess at martial arts or sports. But after his father, he swore nobody would ever have the power to hurt him again physically. He remembered his teacher, Sophie's first serious boyfriend. He started to train her, and then Alexandre took an interest. The man was a real grand master, a genius; had been trained in Korea as a child. Alexandre remembered the mantra he had been taught, 'I shall be a champion of freedom and justice' and 'I shall build a more peaceful world.' Justice – that's what he would set right tonight. And as for a more peaceful world, Alexandre would ensure that this fuck, Jim, made his contribution to help abused girls in need.

Alexandre noticed the front door open. Fuck, there he was, that little shit. Just seeing his enemy made the thigh muscles in Alexandre's leg twitch. Those legs that had been trained to kick like a weapon; break a concrete block in two – even if he hardly trained anymore, it was second nature, his leg could fly up and smash any opponent in the head, knocking even the strongest man to the ground without even trying too hard. He'd have to control himself, though – he could kill, just with his thumb on someone's pressure point. Peace before combat at all times – except now, this bastard had it coming to him for nearly twenty years.

Alexandre briskly eyed his opponent's cocky way of walking and could see straight away that he was brawny – yes, he had a footballer's shape, but an ex-footballer who'd had too many lunches on his big fat banker's budget. Good, just as he'd been told – the man was going out alone. His family would still be inside watching TV. His contact had told him as much, that Jim liked to go out to a particular bar down by the Seafront on Saturday nights, usually coming home about ten thirty.

Alexandre watched as Jim got into his SUV and snailed out of the driveway. He waited a beat and when the vehicle was far enough ahead of him, he started his car and drove cautiously behind. He thought about people feeling repentant - how it was only possible to forgive someone when they were truly sorry for what they'd done. That's why his father had ended up dead – because he could never admit culpability, could never say he was sorry. That's all it would have taken, that one word beginning with S to save his life – but the shit couldn't even say it.

So he'd ended up electrocuted in his bath, the electric appliance zapping him until his body's spasms jittered like a live wire. Finally, like a huge wet fish he lay silent, his reign of terror over for good.

Jim parked his car near the bar. Alexandre did the same and swiftly got out, calmly walking over. Luckily, nobody was around; a couple had just gone inside the bar. Alexandre stepped up beside his target, grabbed the man by the shoulders and stuck the pistol into his back.

The man tried to spin on his heel but he was locked in a vice.

"What the fuck?"

Alexandre murmured quietly, "I've got a gun pointed right into your spine. If you don't do as I say, I'll pull the trigger and if you don't die you'll be paralyzed for life."

"Who the fuck are you?"

"Your shadow. Now get back into your car – we're going for a little drive. Don't fuck with me, this gun has a silencer. I'll pull the trigger, walk you over to the water and throw you in. Nobody knows I'm here, nobody has seen me. Nobody will hear a thing. You'll be fish food."

The man flinched and swallowed hard. Alexandre could smell his fear, the man was a coward. Bullies are always cowards.

"Get in the car, Jim."

"How d'you know my name? You're accent…are you like… one of those Romanians, the guys from the mafia? Look, I already said I didn't want to do that deal—"

"Shut the fuck up, Jim, just get back into your vehicle. If you do as I say, I won't kill you. If you fuck with me, I will. You're driving by the way."

"You must have me mistaken for someone else."

Alexandre pushed the gun in his back a little harder. "I don't think so. It's payback time, buddy."

The man let himself be bundled into the driver's seat and panted with fear. He had tears in his eyes and sweat dripping from his brow. Alexandre carefully got into the back seat, keeping the gun pointed at his spine – maintaining the pressure close so there was no doubt he meant business.

"You know, this country's gun control laws really need to be revised. Where I come from, you have to be part of a sporting club or a hunting club to get a gun license. They don't let any

Tom, Dick or Harry go around with arsenals of lethal weapons."

The man stuttered, "Where are you from?"

Alexandre replied quietly, "That would be telling. Now start the car and drive."

"Where are we going?"

Alexandre's gloved hand pushed the weapon harder into the man's back making a dent in his cashmere overcoat. "Somewhere nice and quiet. Don't try anything smart, remember. This baby is still nuzzled right on your spinal cord.

Jim squeaked, "I swear I won't try a thing."

"So you live here just on weekends?"

"Weekends, holidays. I work in Manhattan."

"Yes, I know. You do well?"

"I'm proud of my capabilities, yes."

"Capabilities…hmm, that could be disputed. How much money do you earn a month, Jim?" Alexandre already knew the answer to his question.

The man's breath hitched. "It depends. You know, on bonuses and stuff, but I make a good fifty grand a month."

"That's a lot of money."

"Yes, it is."

"It's how much I make every thirty minutes, more or less."

The man sniggered uneasily as if he thought Alexandre was joking. He wasn't.

Alexandre went on in a low voice, "I don't like people telling others how much money they earn; I think it's tacky. But I thought you might be interested so you understand who you're dealing with. So you understand that, not only could I have you killed at any moment, but right now, I have an alibi. I have three people who can testify I am *not* here now… with you. That is, should you get any smart ideas. Should you want to call the cops at a later date or tattle-tell on me. You see, I am way, way richer than you are. And you know what money buys, don't you, Jim?"

Jim nodded.

"It buys power," Alexandre whispered.

"What do you want from me?" the guy asked edgily.

"I want you to make a donation. Not much at all. I'm going to be really fair. All I ask is that you donate two month's salary."

Jim squealed, "I can't give you a hundred thousand dollars just like that! I don't even know who you are!"

Alexandre replied calmly "Oh, I think you can, Jim. Here's the thing. I'll make you a deal. You give me the names and phone numbers of all your rapist friends who were there that night – when was it, yes, about eighteen years ago. All those assholes who violated a beautiful young woman called Jane Doe, and I will give you a ten percent discount."

"You're nuts. Completely nuts."

Alexandre poked the gun into the man's back even harder. "You're absolutely right. I'm so nuts, I'm capable of killing you."

"I can't even remember who was there."

"So you admit what you did?"

Jim wailed, "She wanted it, man. We were all drunk. She was asking for it. I can't even remember that far back."

"So all these years have gone by and you've never felt a drop of shame or remorse?"

"What would you have done? A naked chick with her legs splayed open...ouch, that hurts!"

Alexandre released the pressure of his middle knuckle just under the man's ear lobe and spat "Okay, your choice. A hundred and fifty thousand, then. Or you die here tonight."

"Okay, okay, I'll give you names and take the ninety grand discount option. How do I know you won't kill me anyway?"

"Because I'm a man of my word. And right now that's all you've got. I want the payment wired tomorrow."

"Tomorrow's Sunday," Jim squeaked, his voice like a terrified boy.

"I'll give you until Wednesday. If it doesn't arrive I will hunt you down, Jim, do you understand? You can hire bodyguards but I am a very patient man. I will wait quietly. Silently. You will never know when I might strike. It could be years from now, it could be days. Do you want to live that way? Constantly in fear?"

The man's breathy response was weak. "No."

"Do you want your wife and kids to know who you are, what you did?"

He shook his head pitifully. "Where am I to send the money?"

"To young girls who have been abused by men like you – I'll give you the details. Men who thought their actions held no consequences. Now, pull the car over, right here."

They were on a remote beach miles from anywhere. With one hand still holding the pistol, Alexandre handed Jim a bit of paper with the bank account number of the charity he had set up. "Now, you have a choice. We are going to get out of the car. You can either strip naked and walk home in your bare feet in the snow or we can fight this out, man to man. Whichever you choose, the donation will go ahead as planned." Alexandre chuckled facetiously. "Hey, don't look so glum, it'll be tax deductible – the fact I need you to make that donation means I'm not going to kill you now."

"You have a weapon!"

"I'll put the gun in the trunk of my car. We can fight it out weapon-free just using the tools that God gave us. Or, Jim, you can strip naked and walk home."

"I'd catch hypothermia, are you crazy?" The man began to wheeze.

"That's just what I thought you'd say."

"Give me a break, man!"

"Oh I *am* giving you a break. You'd already be dead if I weren't such a reasonable man."

"This is crazy. It was nearly twenty years ago. What kind of fucked-up vendetta is this?"

"The Sicilian kind. You know, if you'd just said one simple word beginning with S and showed some kind of remorse, some kind of feeling for the woman you hurt, I would have felt so much more compassion for you."

"Jesus! I'm *sorry*, okay."

"Too late, Jim. I know what kind of person you are. The kind who thinks he's the master of the universe, the kind whose ego gets the best of him. Now find those numbers of your friends in your Smartphone and tell me their names and any extra details you have. Here, you can write them on this piece of paper." Alexandre got out a scrap of paper and handed the man a pen from his coat pocket.

Jim was shaking uncontrollably but managed to scrawl down some names.

"If none of this makes sense, if these names are false or you happen to be playing any kind of game with me, remember, I know where you and your family live. I also have your New York address. I know where you work. I know everything about you, Jim. Give me your cell phone."

"Why?"

"I said we'd leave all weapons behind. I leave my gun, you leave your phone. Get out of the car…slowly."

Jim opened the car door and exited carefully. A gust of icy wind blew into the vehicle. It was crisp outside and pitch-black. Alexandre quickly got out, too; he noticed the man's large shoulders were shaking. "Hand me your phone," Alexandre said quietly. His breath was making steam in the frosty air.

Jim handed over his cell. Alexandre's black gloved hands took it and he proceeded to frisk him all over; just in case the guy had two phones, or even a gun or knife on him. But he was clean.

Alexandre said, "Now hand me over your car keys."

Jim obliged. Alexandre took the Smartphone, then threw it with the gun into the trunk, took off his long coat which he chucked over the back seat, closed the car doors, zapped them locked and pocketed the car keys. "We're both weapon-free now." He smiled.

"You still have my car keys, man!" Jim replied with a sneer.

"Come and get them. Come on, you're a big man - throw me one of your best punches and you can have it all. Me, the car keys, your car, your phone – even the gun."

Jim eyed him suspiciously and rocked from one heavy foot to the other as if weighing up his options.

"Come on, you pussy," taunted Alexandre. "If you're the big, bad money-maker, Wall St. master of the universe footballer, come on! Show me what you're made of! Come and get me."

Jim launched himself at him, flailing his fist as it caught the air because Alexandre ducked and side-stepped so fast. Jim swung again and Alexandre dodged to the left. A third swing had Jim's punch meet the edge of his SUV and he shouted out curses then shoved his bashed hand in his mouth to ease the pain of his bleeding wound. He then pushed his feet on the side of the car to give himself momentum and threw himself at Alexandre smashing hard into his torso, but Alexandre didn't fall. Alexandre simultaneously elbowed his adversary in the face and drew up his knee sharply into Jim's crotch – Jim stepped backwards, buckling up in pain as he cupped his testicles protectively.

"You need to lose weight, you rapist scum," shouted Alexandre.

Then it happened so quickly: Alexandre moved his body with fierce momentum as his leg swung in a semi-circle landing like a bolt of lightning on Jim's head. Jim toppled over instantly, groaning in agony. Blood was pouring from his ear.

Alexandre bent over to check the damage. "You'll live. That was for Jane Doe. Remember, the money. No fucking about. You might want to warn your rapist buddies to have their money ready, too. Two month's wages, each one. They would be advised to give a little extra as a bonus just so I know they're showing good will; call it a heartfelt apology. In fact, I'll leave it to you, Jim, to collect the money. Within a few hours, I'll know who they all are, what they all do for a living, how much they earn, so no bullshit." He gave the man one last kick in the kidneys. "Have a nice walk home, scumbag."

Jim was moaning in pain hunched into a fetal position, the icy ground was blotched red with his blood. He moaned, "You can't leave me to walk back, it's freezing!"

"Leaving people lying like garbage when you're done with them? You'd know all about that, wouldn't you, Jim?"

Alexandre zapped Jim's SUV unlocked, got in and drove off. In his rear-view mirror he saw Jim get up and collapse on the ground again still cradling his groin. Alexandre sped off back to his own rental car. He'd rented it in a false name, just in case. Jim couldn't prove a thing and he'd be an idiot if he tried.

He parked the SUV, took the gun out of the trunk, leaving Jim's cell phone inside and the keys on the windscreen wipers, changed vehicles and screeched off back in the direction of New York. He smirked to himself about the gun. The 'gun'. It was one of those cigarette lighters – pretty convincing, but if you pulled the trigger all that happened was that an orange flame ignited. Alexandre laughed out loud and then turned on the radio. It was that song again. The one Elodie kept listening to: *Little Things* by that boy band, *One Direction*. It was uncanny, as if the song had been written especially for Pearl, *the dimples on her back, the crinkles by her eyes* – the lyrics spoke of a woman's insecurities but how the guy loved her despite her faults, even *for* her faults. A beautiful song....

Pearl...fuck he missed hanging out with her; it was driving him crazy. He could feel his cock expand, now, just thinking about her face, her peachy ass. He had in his mind's eye her soaking wet pussy and he could almost taste her, just thinking about it. So sweet. Always trimmed and neat, always tight and hot, and always, always ready to be fucked by him. Nothing in the world gave him more pleasure than making Pearl come – nothing. No woman had ever desired him as much, and that was the biggest aphrodisiac of all.

Jesus! His cock was rock hard now and it ached. He thought of that last time when he had her moaning as if she had a fever, squirming on the bed beneath him. He loved the way she was always so vulnerable; tried to act like a tough cookie but always gave in, in the end.

Except for now. Lately, she was being really stubborn. He wanted to fuck that stubbornness out of her, make her scream his name. He'd have to get her alone without Daisy there. Damn Daisy, always hovering about, and Amy, too – even worse. He could hardly just barge into the apartment with a five year-old there, even though he still had keys. His mind ticked over, thinking of ways he could get Pearl alone, whisper into her ear, push her up against a wall and kiss her so she couldn't…wouldn't want to get away. His heart was beating like a drum out of rhythm, imagining how he would fuck her again, how he'd tease that little pearlette, prize open that glistening oyster with his big hard cock. He needed to control the beast in him, though. Needed to sweeten her up a bit more before he pounced. He *had* to have her, had to fuck her…Jesus, this was torture.

His cock was flexing and throbbing. He stopped the car and pulled over. He unbuttoned his jeans. He freed his cock from its prison and it sprang through his boxer briefs, rock hard and wet with pre-cum. It was huge, even he realized that. He knew the size of men's dicks in general – seen them in the gym - he knew he was big (the only decent thing he had inherited from his father). Girls had told him all his life, too. More than once, he'd been too much for them to handle – he'd even scared some women away on occasions.

He let the car seat go all the way back and relaxed into it. He thought of Pearl now, kissing Alessandra Demarr and he gripped his hand about his pulsating phallus and squeezed hard. Ah, that was better. He moved his hand up and down his smooth length, with images of Pearl's wet pussy and her mouth sucking his cock flitting like photos through his brain. He imagined the two women kissing and wished for a second he had been there, too,

not enjoying a threesome but just to be a fly on the wall –
because a threesome would have hurt Pearl. Not in the moment,
no, she would have been turned on - but afterwards – she was
too sweet, too easily wounded. Other men had screwed her over
enough for several lifetimes – he wouldn't go there. She was too
vulnerable to experiment with. Besides, he'd been there, done
that - had his fun with threesomes in his late teens; they weren't
all they were cracked up to be – two's company, three's a crowd.
He didn't like it when women felt hurt or jealous from feeling left
out, which is invariably what happened, at some point, when
there were three.

And right now he, ironically, found himself in this situation
of *three* with Laura right there in the middle. He knew how poor
Pearl's heart was bleeding, but what could he do?

He thought of all the women that had come and gone over
the years. *Come* and gone. There had been too many to count.
How he was taught – no *trained,* by a professional - how to make
love. How to really get a woman turned on. It was Sophie's co-
worker, Hélene, the one who pulled his sister into the game when
she was seventeen. Sophie worked with her for years. By the time
Alexandre got to be broken in, the woman was thirty - Alexandre
was fourteen. His hand was moving fast, now, remembering his
first fuck-orgasm, how mind-blowing it was for him as a skinny
teenager and how he feared his penis might explode with pleasure.

He and Hélene needed each other. It had been the perfect
symbiotic relationship. She taught him everything about the art of
sex. *Because never forget, great sex is an art...* How to take his time,
how to wait until she was really wet and never enter her too early.
She taught him that if he had to use lube then he must be doing

something wrong. She explained how women want to be told sweet nothings and dirty talk but nothing too crude. To be dominant, but never aggressive...to hold out until the woman was begging for sex, take his time; it wasn't a race – that if the man could be patient he'd get paid back double-fold by her passion.

She explained to him that many men were fools...so obsessed with the chase that they lost focus. Forget the chase, she said. That's 'old-school.' Don't end up with a woman just because she says 'no' to you or plays hard to get. Just because she says no doesn't make her any more special. Look into her soul, her eyes. Don't judge a woman by her past. A woman in love with you, she let him know, was a woman who would be sexy as hell. And loyal, too. Loyalty, she said, was like a sovereign coin - never abandon family...never abandon those who truly love you.

Hélene told him how all women were different; there was no blueprint and how he must pay attention to the girl's whole body not just her orifices and breasts. Stroking and caressing – foreplay was imperative. Any man could 'stick it in', she said - and don't be fooled into thinking you were good in bed - women were good at faking orgasms. She'd warned him about this on countless occasions.

She drummed it into him that the woman must always come first – well, he'd got that wrong once or twice with Pearl. Fuck, with her sometimes, he couldn't control himself - even just one of her kisses could drive him wild. No woman ever had gotten him as horny, no woman could hold a candle to Pearl in the sack. Why? Even he couldn't explain. Was she the most beautiful woman he had ever dated? No. But she had something, something irresistible. The smell of her skin. Her flavor. Her humor…her sweetness…her smile.

An image of Pearl's tits flashed through his head – couldn't put a pencil under those. No – too pert. Her ass, her tits, her face, her wet pussy – which was his very own little private pearl, his pearlette - her lips, those big blue eyes….

He groaned out loud and felt the spurt of his climax pulsing through him. Fuck, his cum was all over the seat. But it wasn't enough – he needed the real thing. He couldn't stand it anymore – the minute he got back to New York he'd have to fuck her.

Fuck her till she screamed.

7

Here I am in the kitchen again, eating ice-cream. They say just as much ice-cream is sold in the winter as in the summer months, and I believe it. Daisy and Amy are fast asleep. That will be me, soon....a single mother with my child...although, I suddenly remember...Daisy and Zac – wow, that came out of left field. She may not be a single mother for long. I have mixed feelings; delighted for them but...well. Time will tell if he's good enough for her.

My ice-cream reverie is interrupted by the sound of the front door opening - I forgot to lock it with the safety latch. A rush of adrenaline surges through my body but then I remember... Alexandre still has keys. I pray it's him and not some armed robber, although Alexandre is just as dangerous, in another way. I go to grab the first thing I can think of for protection; a kitchen knife – just in case it really is an intruder. No, that's dangerous; it could be seized from me. I see Amy's cowboy gun lying on the kitchen table, snatch it up - it looks quite realistic - and tiptoe quietly down the hallway towards the front door. It isn't a thief. Well, it is. A thief of my emotions…Alexandre.

There he is….gorgeous as ever.

He turns on his heel and observes me with wry amusement stealing across his face, ready with my toy gun.

"Sorry, baby," he whispers, "I didn't want to wake anybody so I thought I'd slip through the door quietly."

I should be furious but all I can think is, *what took you so long, I've missed you.* My heart is racing with left-over fear of thinking I was being broken into, and renewed fear of being broken in-to…my body being broken into. No sex, the doctor forbade it. I keep saying this mantra to myself in my head. Despite all this, desire is circling me like Cupid with his arrow and I'm only too aware of an aching need for Alexandre to hold me.

Until I remember the L word.

I'm wearing pajama bottoms and a thin cotton tank top and his glittering green eyes stray to my swollen breasts. A low rumble comes from deep within him like a lion about to devour his prey. He doesn't say anything, though, but I can see the rise and fall of his chest – his heart is also pounding. His desire for me is palpable and I sense the familiar tingle between my legs.

"You need to leave, Alexandre." My voice is weak, laced with yearning. My sexed-up pregnancy hormones are not helping one bit.

"I need to hold you, baby. To breathe you in." He comes to-wards me. I'm still grasping the gun and his half-cocked smile breaks into a grin. "But I think you'd better put that gun down, don't you?"

In a moment of foolishness I grip the handle even tighter and wave it in front of me.

He grins, "Love the toy gun. You and I have more in common than you can possibly imagine."

But I'm not smiling back. "I mean it, Alexandre, you need to leave me alone and stop torturing me this way."

His smile fades and he says sadly, "yes, it *is* torture – you're right. I just can't go on like this – I can't stand it anymore." He slumps against the wall and slides down so he's sitting on the floor. His big boots drip with melted snow on the polished parquet wood. Tears are welling in his eyes. I've never seen him look so vulnerable and it's breaking my heart.

I set Amy's gun on the hall table and sit down opposite him. He holds his dark ruffled head in his hands. He's wearing the long World War One overcoat. He looks so handsome, like a movie star – the Hollywood legend kind, the kind they don't make anymore.

"Why are you doing this, Alexandre?" I speak in a whisper because I don't want to wake Daisy and Amy. "Why can't you stop seeing Laura?"

He looks up at me and a tear falls down his cheek. I want to hug him but perhaps this is all part of his little-boy-lost act, the act that makes dumb women like me swoon and lose all reason. Talk about Hollywood. This guy's a good actor.

"My plan was to come here and fuck you, Pearl. But I can't play that game anymore. It isn't fair on you."

My heart starts thumping like an oil well. What's worse than him wanting to use me for sex? Not wanting me at all. A lump gathers in my throat. "What's going on, Alexandre? Why are you…practically crying?"

"Because all I want in the world is to be happy with you and it doesn't seem possible."

"But that's your choice, Alexandre. It's *you* that's putting up all these barriers. All I want, too, is for us to be together but I can't be in a relationship with three people. You have to choose – me or Laura. You simply can't have us both."

"That's why I keep asking you to marry me, baby….despite Laura. So you'd be my wife and you couldn't testify against me."

I flinch. "What the hell are you talking about?"

He temples his hands over his nose and lets out an exasperated puff of air. "I literally don't know what to do! With all my money and influence…yet still, she has me beat…I swear I don't know what to do."

"You're being so obtuse and enigmatic, right now, I'm completely lost."

"Please come here, chérie – I need to hold you. I swear I won't do anything. I won't even try and kiss you. I promise."

I tentatively shuffle my behind over to his side and sit close to him. He puts his arm about me, his fingers squeezing me tight. He smells of the night air and his Alexandre elixir that weakens me every time. I stroke his head and he sighs, closing his wet eyes and biting his lips…perhaps to stop himself from actually weeping. I'm dumbfounded by his demonstration of emotion and understand now that it is for real. I lay my head against his shoulder and we just continue sitting there on the floor in silence with only the sound of our breathing between us.

Finally I say, "Why?" I don't even know what I am referring to but 'why' seems like a good thing to ask.

"Remember I told you I was protecting someone I love?"

"Yes," I say bitterly, conjuring up a host of ex girlfriends. Or is he talking about Laura, herself? The idea of him loving someone else sends a wave of jealousy to course through my veins and circle my stomach.

"I was talking about my mother," he says in a grave tone.

I exhale with relief but then ask, confused, "What on earth does Laura have to do with your mother?"

"Laura's threatening her."

"What? *How?*"

"Laura has something that belongs to her, something incriminating, something…Look, Pearl, I've already said enough. I made a promise to my mom that I wouldn't ever say a word and…" His eyes tighten as he starts chewing his lip with worry.

"Your mother did something and Laura has evidence?"

"I knew if I said anything you'd pick up on it straight away. I've revealed way too much, I need to go, I—"

"You can trust me. I don't care what your mother did, or what you did – I love you," I plead. "I would never say a word. Never."

"Please come back with me tonight. I need you in my arms, baby. I need to sleep with you. I've been going crazy without you."

I take his head in my hands and say, "Look me in the eyes and tell me the truth."

He nods.

"Have you had sex with Laura since you've been with me?"

He fixes his gaze on me and I feel sick for a moment. The dark flecks in his green eyes flicker with hesitation. Can I bear what I'm about to hear?

"I swear by my mother, by Sophie and Rex and all those who I love. I swear by you and the moon and stars, I have not touched, nor even kissed any woman since I met you, least of all

Laura."

The relief I feel right now is indescribable. I search his eyes for clues – he's telling the truth, I'm sure of it. Now it's my turn to well up. A hot tear rolls down my cheek.

He continues, his mouth pinched, "I despise Laura. She's trying to ruin my life. If it were just *my* life she wanted to butcher, I might be more forgiving, but she's threatening my mother. And you."

"Me?"

"I know you, Pearl. I know that if you don't spend the rest of your days with me you won't be truly happy. I don't mean to sound conceited saying that but deep inside me, I feel exactly the same. If we can't be together we'll both go through life half dead. Without you, I feel my flame has been snuffed out. I function on auto-pilot. Without you I am half the person I should be."

I take his chin in both hands and tilt his mouth towards mine. I run my tongue along his upper lip to ease the tension in his angry mouth and we kiss gently. To my surprise, he's not ravenous for me but just returns the kiss sweetly. Innocently, even.

He breathes into my mouth, "If I can't marry you, Pearl my life will be running on empty."

"I want to marry you more than anything," I whisper back. "I love you. I can't be without you, either."

"Will you come home with me tonight and we can talk?"

"If you promise to tell me the whole story. If you promise to trust me. I don't care *what* you've been hiding from me," I say honestly. "What hurts me is that you've been hiding it."

"If I tell you everything, will you promise to marry me, Pearl? No more running away?"

For some reason, his request causes a rush of adrenaline to

stream through my body. Fear? Excitement? Panic? This is it. I've been running from him, using every excuse. But I can't run anymore. I need to trust him, to show my loyalty. I take a deep breath and reply, "I promise."

Alexandre gets up onto his haunches and lifts me up, cradling me in his arms as if I were a baby. His eyes stray to my pregnant breasts again. But I don't care if he has sex on the brain - I want him even more than he wants me. I can feel my nipples pucker with desire, my breathing's shallow. He sets me down and kisses me lightly on my temple. I grab my long overcoat from the hall closet, my Birkin bag and slip into my thermal boots. I can't get back to his apartment fast enough.

"You're coming just like that? In your PJ's?" he asks, surprised, yet eyeing up my ass with a look of lust.

"I think we've both waited long enough, don't you? I just want to be back in your bed even if Rex *has* taken it over."

He laughs. "You've heard, huh?"

"Yes, Sally told me."

"I've been lonely. Missing you like crazy."

As I'm scrawling out a note to Daisy so she doesn't think I've been abducted, I say, "Are you going to tell me everything, Alexandre?"

He nods.

"*Everything* about Laura?" I ask again, double-checking that this isn't a trap of seduction to get into my panties (or PJs).

"I promise. Let's go."

106

The whole time I have been in my new apartment it has felt like Limbo and, now back at Alexandre's, I know I've come home. We're sitting on one of the huge white couches in the living room, snuggled up with Rex. I'm keeping the bedroom at bay, for fear of letting desire get in the way of my mission; to find out everything I can. If Alexandre doesn't come one hundred percent clean about this insidious situation with Laura, which has been eating into our relationship, then I will give up for good. This is Make or Break time and I think he senses that.

My eyes stray to the bald patch on the wall where my engagement gift was; the Jim Dine painting of the big red heart that is now hung in my new apartment, and I feel a wave of sadness. So much time has been wasted because of our own fears. It has all boiled down to trust. I have not trusted him; not trusted his judgment about Sophie – of course he would never have put me in danger; of course he knows his own sister. And now, he has been keeping secrets from me for fear I might abandon him, or worse, report him for whatever wrong he or his mother has done – that I would betray his family.

I lie back with my head in his lap as he strokes my hair, the soft touch of his long fingers caressing me, making me remember that I belong to him and nobody else.

"I'm breaking my promise to my mother but if I don't tell you, I know that our lives will be ruined. I'm trusting you to keep this to yourself, take it with you to your grave, Pearl."

"I swear." I make a cross sign on my heart.

"You know what I told you about my father? That he disappeared?"

I hold his hand to let him know that I'm on his side, no matter what he tells me. "Was it a lie?"

"Yes. Not all of him has disappeared – that's the whole problem."

"What do you mean?" *This is sounding really crazy.* "Sophie told me that he had gone to Rio - that he'd been spotted there."

"That's what she still believes. I told her that a friend of mine had seen him there. This friend doesn't exist, of course. My father's dead, Pearl."

"Did you kill him?"

He says nothing for a beat and then answers in a cold voice. "No. My mother did. No, let me be completely honest here. She didn't just kill him, she murdered him."

I try to sound unemotional. I don't want to spook him away. "Was Laura witness to the murder, then?"

"No. It happened when I was only nine."

"Well what does Laura have to do with it? Even if you told her, she has no proof!"

"Oh, but she does. She's got proof that he's dead. And he has never been declared dead. No death certificate, nothing. Officially, he's still alive. And there are some people still wondering where he is. His brother, my uncle, for one."

"I don't understand – how does Laura *know* he's dead?"

"He was lying peacefully in his bath. Ironic that. Some of the only times when he was being truly peaceful was when he was wallowing about in warm water. My mother had bought him his favorite Scotch. She was plying him with it so he was completely relaxed. She'd had enough, and knew that the only way to be free of him, once and for all, was to kill him. He'd threatened her that if she ever left him he'd hunt her down and kill her – then search for us, too." He looks at me and hesitates.

I absorb all that Alexandre has said. It sounds crazy but you read about these people and see them on the news often…the nutters that shoot their families down, killing each and every member, or massacring them in a stabbing frenzy before doing themselves in, too. I squeeze Alexandre's hand. "I empathize, Alexandre. I really do. Please go on."

He stares into space as he reels off the story in a monotone, hardly stopping for breath. "She had the electric heater plugged into the wall with the extension cord. She'd planned everything. When he was lying back with his eyes closed she came into the bathroom with the pretense to top up his drink and threw the heater into the water to electrocute him. She was even wearing rubber shoes and gloves just to take extra precaution."

I gasp. What a scene that must have been. "Did he die instantly?"

"I don't know. My mother had assumed she could pretend it was an accident but there were huge burn welts where the water level was. It was obvious it was cold-blooded murder. She had to think on her feet. Had to get rid of the evidence – there was no way she could pass it off as an accident."

"So then what happened?"

"Luckily, she had some French doors in her apartment that led onto a balcony. She unplugged the electricity, drained the bath, hauled him out, little by little, and rolled him into bed sheets, wrapping him like a mummy. Then she pushed him off the balcony in the dead of night. Once she was sure nobody had woken from the thud of the body landing on the ground – she was two flights up – she dragged him to the car. Amazingly, nobody saw her, or if they did, they never said a word. The neighbors hated him anyway – even if they'd seen something they would have probably been relieved. She managed to haul him into the trunk of her car."

"That must have been hard. Was he tall and strong like you?"

"No, my height comes from my mother's side of the family. But still, it was no mean feat. She drove to the countryside. When she found an isolated place, miles from anywhere, she made a bonfire and set him alight."

"Oh my God. Nobody saw? No farmer or anyone?"

"She doused him with gasoline – he went up fast."

"I still don't understand what Laura has to do with all this."

"Not everything burns, does it?"

"There were remnants?"

"My mother waited for the fire to burn all the way down but there were two things left over – his teeth and bits of his hip replacement, both identifiable through medical records. There was the titanium part of the fake hip and a ceramic ball bit that didn't burn either. They have identification numbers, not on the parts themselves, but from the factory where they make the prosthesis. These are kept by the hospital on a register with the name of the patient and the date of operation, in case of problems like breaking or premature loosening. They can be traced back to their source. It's the same with teeth and dentist's records - a common way of identifying corpses."

"How the hell did Laura get her hands on those?"

"Years ago, I found them in my mother's house in a drawer when I was looking for something – I put two and two together; that's how I knew he was dead. I'd always suspected, anyway, because I knew if he'd been alive he would have hunted her down. Anyway, I had a long talk with my mom and she told me the whole story. I've kept it a secret all these years; I never even told Sophie."

My nose is prickling with tears as Alexandre's voice sounds as if it's about to break at any moment.

"But what on earth was your mother *doing* with all that evidence? Why didn't she chuck it all in a river or take it out to sea?"

"That's the multi-million dollar question, but she had a reason, crazy as it was. Having the remnants, she said, reminded her that he was truly dead – that he could never harm her again.

Anyway, I took away the bits of evidence and took them to Provence with me – I didn't want my mother having them in her house, in case her husband found them. But at the same time, I didn't throw them away because I didn't feel it was my right to if they were so important to her. I was an idiot. A fool. I should have taken it into my own hands. Instead, I hid the teeth in a multi-volume Encyclopedia. Call me a heathen but I'd cut out the centre of one of them and placed the evidence inside. Nobody looks at Encyclopedias anymore with the internet and Wikipedia – I thought they'd be safe there. And the titanium bit of hip was wedged behind the book. Laura knew exactly what it was because she, too, had a hip replacement a couple of years after her accident. And I'd mentioned to her once, years ago, about my father having had one – tried to assure her that they worked."

"She discovered them?"

Alexandre looks down at the floor ashamedly.

"But even if I found that stuff, I wouldn't know that they were *body parts of a dead man*. How did she *know*?"

"When I started dating you, Laura became obsessed. I didn't realize this, of course, until just a few weeks ago. I thought we were friends, I had no clue that she wanted me back, that she was still in love with me. Although, when 'love' is that warped it's hardly a word I'd use to describe her feelings for me. Basically, she became obsessed, possessed - and will stop at nothing to get me back."

"I still don't understand. How did she *know* for sure that those things were parts of your father?"

"You've been her victim, as I have. She had my cell phone hacked, too. Really dumb of me to not have caught onto that, especially in my line of business. A joke, really. I think she must have been in on a text message or conversation or even an email to my mother — we've never mentioned the murder in a call or message but Laura's not dumb. Who knows? She's a smart woman — she put two and two together. I've never admitted a thing but she has all the evidence in her possession. With forensic labs the way they are these days — medical records; all it takes is one call from her."

"When did she get her hands on all this?"

"When she and James were there last summer."

"You didn't notice it missing?"

"No. I wouldn't have thought to look. I'd pretty much for-gotten all about it, actually."

"If she's had everything since the summer why has she waited until now to tell you?"

"Good question. She must have thought things with you and me would die down - fizzle out. It didn't, she tried that stunt pretending Sophie was responsible for her accident, which nearly did the trick to split us up, but when she saw that you and I were back together, she pulled out all the stops."

"What does she want, exactly?"

"She wants you out of the picture and for me to marry her."

"But that's *insane*, especially as you don't even love her."

Alexandre closes his lids as if locked into a deep thought and continues in a grave tone, "The truth is, after her fall she was never the same person. I did understand why, though, at the time. Shit, your whole life changes after an accident like that. They said her head wasn't damaged in the fall, but when I think of it now, I think they were wrong. I'm convinced something changed in her brain. She was so sweet before, so loving and fun. After the accident…well, I didn't spend much time with her afterwards, we didn't see each other for a couple of years, anyway, so it was hard to gauge—"

"But I thought you two were bosom buddies."

"She left me immediately for James. Said I couldn't look after her properly, that I was too young and she needed stability. What she really wanted - even I wasn't stupid – was someone who was rich enough to take care of her. That's why I worked my ass off – determined that HookedUp would be a financial success. I became driven with the idea of proving that I, too, could look after her, could be wealthy enough to take care of her. Not just her but any future relationship – any future girlfriend or wife. I felt very proud – I still do. I'm old-fashioned in that respect. I'm the type of man who wants to be able to support my partner financially."

"Well, why didn't you both get back together as soon as you'd made all that money?"

"By that time, I'd become good friends with James and I just wasn't in love with Laura anymore. They came to stay in Provence and stuff. I genuinely had *no idea* she was still into me, until recently. I think the second you came along she became competitive and wanted me back. At first, she was convinced you and I would split up, but the moment she heard about our marriage she went wild with jealousy."

"What about James? How does he feel?"

"He still hasn't returned my calls. He got busted for dodgy tax dealings and is in financial straits. That made Laura nervous. I don't think she loves me at all, really, I think she loves my bank balance. Plus..." he hesitates.

"What?"

"James can't have children and she's fixated on the idea of getting pregnant. She wants me to father her child."

A stab of fury seizes my heart making it skip a beat. "Jesus. Why can't she pick on a single man? Why *you?*"

"I know."

"So she's blackmailing you, then?"

"Exactly. But in her warped brain she believes it's for my own good and we'll live happily ever after."

"Where has she got the evidence hidden?"

"She says it's in a safety deposit box and if anything happens to her, any accident or mishap, she has instructed her lawyer to open the box and its contents with a note revealing everything."

"What a monster!"

"Tell me about it."

"But that's insane! If you don't love her, how could she have a happy life, even if she did get you back?"

"As I said, I think some chip in her brain went doolally when she had that fall. The girl I dated would never have done this. Her behavior is totally irrational. I just didn't see it before because James was always about. He's a good guy. We've done some Aston Martin and Austin Healy rallies together, he's a nice man. It's crazy what she's playing at." Alexandre buries his head in his hands and lets out an exasperated sigh.

"So her idea is to have the evidence sitting in that safe deposit box forever, blackmail you throughout your 'marriage' so you'll never leave her or else your mother goes to jail?"

"Yeah, that's more or less the plan she's got up her dirty little sleeve, although she's not coming out and saying it directly. She pretends it's for my own good, just in case the evidence got into 'the wrong hands', she says."

"That's terrifying. I mean, if she were to get run over by a bus tomorrow, out comes that goddamn safe deposit box."

"Exactly."

"What are we going to do?"

Alexandre smiles at me. "Thank you, chérie, for using the word 'we' - although that's why I've been so secretive - I didn't want to get you involved in this mess."

"Till death do us part. For better or for worse. We may not have said our vows yet, Alexandre, but I'm with you one hundred percent, whatever your decision."

He puts his arms about me and holds me close to his chest. I feel his slow, strong heartbeat. His voice is low and quiet when he tells me, "I love you, Pearl."

I breathe him in. "I was so scared you wanted her back, that you were still in love with her – all those parting, 'goodbye' gifts you gave me; the Porsche, the Mercedes, the apartments—"

"It was never goodbye, baby, not for a second. You needed some space to sort out your head. We needed to be apart for a little, but goodbye? Never." He smiles and I notice the roguish dimple on his cheek makes its signature mark. "I knew I'd see my pretty Porsche again and that we'd be vacationing in that apartment in Cap d'Antibes. You and I are forever, Pearl."

I bite my lip just thinking about how it could have been. The agony I would have suffered. "I was scared that everything we had was a fantasy, a figment of my imagination."

He kisses my temple. "I'm sorry I've put you through all this. I kept thinking I could reason with Laura, make her see sense – that's why I saw her face to face, but she's being impossible. Inflexible. I just don't know what to do."

"What does your mother say?"

"She wants to have it out with Laura – she's furious."

"So your mom's husband has no idea about any of this?"

"No. Not a clue. He's a very straightforward guy."

"But if he loves her why would he care what she'd done? It was self-defense."

"That's *you*, Pearl. You think that way. But other people are more wedded to the law. A lot of men don't get it. They don't understand what it's like to be bullied, day in day out, to be humiliated, threatened and abused. My step-father's a great guy but he just wouldn't understand. Besides, it's one of those things she should have come clean with straight away when they first met – maybe he would have forgiven her, but she didn't dare test him. And if she let him know now what she did it would look as if their entire marriage had been a lie all these years."

"Do you believe Laura when she says she has it all in a safe deposit box? Maybe she's lying."

"Maybe she is, but I'm not in a position to risk it, to call her bluff. My mother's life is on the line, or at least, life imprisonment which would amount to the same thing for her."

"I thought France was lenient with crimes of passion."

"I'd rather my mother didn't even spend one minute in a jail. So many years of her life were hell and finally she's found happiness. Plus, this is all my fault. If I'd just bloody well left the evidence with her and hadn't meddled with it all, we wouldn't be in this mess."

I look at my watch and then stretch my arms in the air. "We should go to bed. It's three a.m. Let's see if either of us comes up with a brain-wave in our dreams to sort out this fiasco."

"You dream a lot, don't you?"

"You have no idea."

"What have you dreamt about me?"

"There was one dream in particular that had me squirming with pleasure," I tease, remembering the Johnny Cakes March with the sexy spanking session.

His eyes light up. "Oh, yeah, what was that?"

"It's my secret."

He gives my wrist a small squeeze. "Come on, tell me."

"No, but I will tell you another secret, if you like."

"I'm listening."

"I'm pregnant – you and I are going to have a baby."

He kneels before me and gathers my hands in his, softly kissing each finger. His eyes are brimming with emotion. "You've made me the happiest man alive, Pearl. If I could jump over the moon, I would. And as far as secrets go? That's the best damn secret I've ever heard in my entire life."

8

Waking up next to Alexandre is pure heaven. We dozed off, intertwined together like ivy, last night, listening to each other's heart beats, soothed by one another's breath. I fell asleep, dreaming of ocean waves. His smell…it's intoxicating, and I was reminded of how much I had missed him. The idea that I have spent so many nights alone is heartbreaking. All those wasted hours. When we needed each other - when we could have helped each other. Perhaps that's what an engagement is all about. A test to make you stronger. Although I doubt any other couple has endured what we have – unwittingly putting each other through such turmoil.

I observe him now, his lids closed in deep slumber, yet beneath the sheets another story is being told; a huge penis, smooth as alabaster, proud as the Washington monument, is puckering up the bedclothes with its rock-hard stance. I don't want to wake him but I can't resist. How I've missed that core of him. I've dreamed of it, come in my sleep thinking of it.

I nestle my head on his stomach and let my tongue flicker on the end of his crown. It's bigger than my dreams had allowed me to remember. I nip the rounded end of it and he groans quietly. Then I guide my tongue down his length in semi darkness under the sheet. I take one ball in my mouth and suck on it languidly. I can feel his arms now stroking my hair. He flexes his hips up a notch and I hear him say, "Oh fuck, oh wow, I've missed this." My tits are alive with desire, my nipples aflame with sensation and I need him to play with them. I wriggle up the bed until I'm straddling him.

I lean my breasts over his erection, take it in my hands and tease my nipples with its smooth head. Holy hotness, I'm wired like an electric cable – everything is connected and desire shoots through me in pulsating tingles and spasms. My breasts have always been sensitive but lately, since pregnancy, even a breeze of cool air can get them excited.

Alexandre's eyes spring open, "Jesus, Pearl, your tits… I need to fuck those beautiful big, pregnant tits."

When I told him last night about the Indian Ayurvedic doctor I thought he'd think she was a quack but he said, 'old wives' tale or not, I'm not going to be the one to put it to the test'. He swears, even if I beg him, that he won't penetrate me. I wonder how long I can hold out, though.

I suck on him, then move my body up a bit and swirl his cock about my nipples again, mewing softly with pleasure. The wetness of my saliva makes them pucker into tight, dusky-red buds; I re-position myself and rub my clit against Alexandre's muscular thigh as I continue teasing my nipples. I start moaning – from my head to my tail bone, this feels amazing.

"Fuck, your pussy's soaked," he murmurs, thrusting his leg at me, keeping up the pressure.

I rub against his solid thigh, back and forth, and he pushes it hard against me so my clit is getting a real massage. I continue teasing my nipples, slapping them now, using his penis like a whip. He starts rubbing his leg rhythmically against me; I graze his erection round and round in circles on my nipples, taking it in turn with each one, as I feel the build-up and I start coming hard – a series of long, slow convulsions and spasms explode inside me, my nipples harder than bullets, stimulated beyond imagination. I'm letting out moaning wails with every sweet spasm.

"That's right, baby, let your little treasure come on me – I'm going to keep you coming for the rest of your life."

I collapse on top of him, my afterglow alight like burning embers, and after a few minutes of relaxation, he rolls me over gently, straddling me without any of his weight. I see his taut stomach ripple with lean muscles and his huge cock nestle itself between my tits. He pushes them carefully together, almost enclosing his hard shaft. I take over, pressing my breasts tightly around him and he begins to fuck my chest, his balls rubbing lightly against my skin, his cock pressing hard against my breastbone, the tip almost reaching the hollow in my neck every time he pushes northwards. I keep my breasts squeezed together, putting the pressure on his thick, long length.

His movements are languid as if he's really making love to my breasts, his eyes transfixed on my swollen boobs, his sex mantra punctuated by thrusts. "These. Hot. Horny. Tits. Making. My. Cock. So. Fucking. Hard. My. Seed. Exploded. In. Your. Hot. Pearlette...Fucking. You. To. Pregnancy. So. Fucking. Sexy." He groans. Scorching, creamy cum starts spurting on my face, my tits, my neck - shooting out like a fountain. He's crying out, "Pearl, baby, I love you." His orgasm is super-intense – I can tell he's charged with passion; his face twists as if he's in pain.

He stills as his climax slowly fades, his cock flexing in spasms, and then laughs out loud and shakes his dark head of hair, "Fuck, that was fast."

I smile. "For both of us."

"Did you notice something? We didn't even kiss. We were both so hungry to release weeks of sexual build-up and tension, that we haven't even said hello properly."

I laugh, and run my finger over my sticky breasts, scooping up a taste of him and popping it into my mouth. "Powerful stuff this," I remark. "It can make a woman pregnant."

His mouth flicks into a broad grin. "Hang on, chérie I'll get a towel." He kisses me lightly on the nose, goes to the bathroom and comes back with a damp washcloth. He gently wipes his sea of pleasure off my chest. "I just want you to know something, Pearl…"

A panic of fear sweeps through me; a twisting, chilling knot in my solar plexus. Another secret? Something else he's been holding back?

But he laces his fingers through mine and whispers in my ear; the soft wind of his breath sending shivers down my spine, "Of all the women I've ever been with, you are the most spectacular, the most beautiful, the *most* in every, single way."

The knot unfurls and my heart feels as if it will explode with happiness.

"And I'm not just talking about sex. I'm talking about love, chérie. I love you, Pearl. Even in the days when I was happy with Laura, I *never* felt so serene, so at home with her as I do with you.

I have never experienced this deep, bottomless ocean of love with anyone but you. It's almost as if it hurts, there's so much love bursting inside of me."

"Semen bursting inside of you," I joke, but then immediately wish I hadn't made less of what he has just shared with me, opening his heart up the way he has. I tighten my grip on his hand, "I feel that bursting love, too."

He takes a loose, sticky tendril of my hair and parts it away from my face. He lifts his head from my ear and his crooked smile seems thoughtful as he squints, honing his gaze on mine. "We both need a shower, I think."

I enter the steamy shower with Alexandre. It is almost like a little room. It is all tiled in white mosaic, including the built-in bench The heat suddenly gets to me and I sit down. He's standing before me; my eyes are level with his beautiful, muscular ass. He is like one of those Greek statues but so much better endowed – oh yes, this art is more exquisite than you would see in any museum, his sculpted thighs, his taut, flexing gluteus maximus, the glorious V that runs from his waist to the core of him – the core that has me light-headed, that has created the living seed inside of me, the tiny being that belongs to us both.

"He holds my hand as the hot water rains from above. "Are you okay, baby, you looked a bit dazed."

True. I am in a daze. This is real. We are together and in love. We are going to have a baby. "I'm fine, I just get a little dizzy in the mornings."

Alexandre lathers up his hands with some lavender body wash and begins to cleanse my shoulders very gently, moving his hands softly about my breasts and under my arms as he lifts each up to massage me. This is crazy…his soapy hands softly kneading my breasts is turning me on again. I am like a hormone machine. I don't know if it's because that crazy Indian doctor forbade intercourse that I have it constantly on the brain, or if it's my pregnancy playing havoc with my body parts, but flashes of Alexandre claiming me, pumping me with heavy thrusts into my wet hole has me squirming. His penis has hardened with every one of his gentle strokes and his fingers gently tug on my nipple, shooting tingles directly to my pulsating clit. I grab his butt and pull him close to me, nipping softly on his balls as the water falls on my face and breasts like a cascade. Just the pressure of water is doing things to me, let alone the vision I have before me – the veritable piece of art that is my fiancé.

"Alexandre," I moan into his thick, hard cock, licking the un-der-shaft with long sweeping strokes of my tongue.

"Pearl, oh yeah, baby." He's holding my hands, his legs astride to lower the height of his body so he is at the right level for me. My lips nibble his length and my tongue flickers all over the enormity of his smooth, dreamy cock. Not even Michelangelo could have created a penis so beautiful as Alexandre's. I think of riding him, how he fills up my walls, pressing all the right places which effortlessly brings me to mind-blowing orgasms every time, and just the memory of it makes my core pulsate, swelling with needy desire.

"I need you to fuck me, Alexandre," I breathe into his groin.

"Not a chance, until these three months are up, baby."

I take some body wash on my hand and begin to lather his balls, tracing my fingers up the crack of his butt, exploring the dips and valleys of his solid boulder of an ass. I turn him around so it's in my face. Water is cascading over us and I let all the soapiness rinse away before I part his butt with my fingers. I begin my tongue's journey from his swollen, hard sacks up his crack, lashing my tongue up and down. I can hear his low moans beneath the rush of water. There it is, that scar. Once, I asked him how he got it and he wouldn't tell. I kiss him there, now – licking the old wound with all the love I have inside me. Then I trace my tongue up and probe his hole – only a woman beside herself in love would do anything so intimate. I hear a low growl emanate from deep within him. His right hand is on his erection now, fisting it into a tight vice.

"Come on my face, Alexandre. Come on my lips, come all over me, baby." I guide his body back around so I can see his glorious cock as he slides his hand up and down from the huge crown to the root, his long fingers gripping tightly about himself. All I can think of is it inside me, fucking me, slapping itself on my clit when it withdraws, then ravaging me with hard, ruthless, pumping thrusts. I'm aching, tingling, delirious with the space that is between us. I need my fiancé inside me.

Alexandre's tongue runs along his parted lips, his green eyes hooded with pleasure as if he is thinking exactly the same thing...fucking me...owning me...ripping through the core of me with his relentless virile masculinity. The fingers of his left hand are in my mouth and I suck them, imagining my mouth is my man-eating Venus; that his fingers are his cock - I pull them in, my lips a vacuum. I also cup his balls with my hand. My gesture makes his hips jerk – his hand jacks his cock back and forth at a feverish pace.

"Pearl," he cries out as cum starts spurting everywhere like the Trevi Fountain.

Rivers of white-hot cum snake over my still seated body as the water washes it away. Alexandre catches back his breath, gets down on his haunches and takes my face in his hands. He starts with a flick of the tongue and I moan into his mouth, opening my lips letting the kiss go deeper, tongues tangling and probing together, sending direct hits to my clit. I see his penis harden and I whimper at how horny I feel. I want that between my legs. His kisses brush my jaw, my neck and then my breasts. My legs splay open in readiness and I cry out–

"Please, I beg you, fuck me!"

He sucks each nipple in turn, and I throw my head back in ecstasy. He turns on the hand-held shower and directs the water at my ready, horny vulva and the power of the spray has my juices oozing with excitement. I jut my hips forward to meet the tingling pressure on my clit and jerk with spasms of pleasure, feeling I could come at any moment. Every bit of my body is alive with sensation. Then he holds the shower head away and nestles his face between my thighs – his hair tickling my flesh as he begins his slow, languid tease. He doesn't touch my clit with his tongue, no, the water has already made it super-sensitive. He avoids it, flicking and wavering his hot lips everywhere else so I am moaning and begging.

"Please, Alexandre."

"See how wet you are for me, baby? When I fuck you your tight pearlette is like a welcoming haven for my cock, clinging onto it like a tight glove, contracting around my cock - never wanting to let me go." Then he slips his magic thumb inside my glistening hole, slowly lingering there until it finds its way to my lush Garden of Eden - my G-spot.

"I *never* want to let you go," I scream out, tortured by pleasure.

Every part of me is clamoring for attention. Just as I thought it couldn't get more intense, Alexandre starts sucking at my nipples again, his thumb still inside me. The familiar electricity sparks my connected inner-wires – tits, clit, mouth, all quivering in unison, building up to the Mighty O. With his other hand he presses my clit with his flattened fingers, gently rubbing in small circles – his thumb on the nub of my G-spot, the pressure on my clit, his tongue on my tits – it's as if there are three Alexandre Chevaliers all at once… as if I'm in the sexiest threesome in the universe. I arch my back and push out my hips, moving my ass up and down, pressing hard against his fingers.

"Alexandre!" The force of his touch – his lips on my tits, his thumb, his fingers, has me coming in a rush of frenzied contractions. I hold his head to balance myself - I feel as if my whole body could detonate with bliss and pleasure-pounding gratification. "Aah…Alexandre," I scream out like a banshee.

Half a minute later, I feel weak; my orgasm has sucked all the life out of me as it pounds its way to a plateau, and finally calms itself like a gentle heart beat.

Alexandre turns off the faucet, cocoons me in a warm, larger-than-life towel, and carries me to the bedroom. He lays me on the mattress like a sleeping baby and says, "You rest, my angel, I'm going to make us some breakfast. You need your strength as I'm not done yet, certain parts of my body are aching for more of this. Call me a beast…I am…I can't get enough of my pregnant fiancée. After we've eaten, I'm going to tease you into another orgasm, but this time we're going to come simultaneously."

He pats me dry with the towel – I see his erection is full-on again. Hearing me scream, watching me climax so intensely has gotten him hot once more. We are both insatiable. I lie there, feeling very pregnant and yes – still horny as a rabbit in spring.

How does he know I want more? As if he can read my body. I cannot believe I am so wanton. And I know Alexandre. His Latin blood has been bubbling away. Aware that his seed is inside me, growing every day, makes him want to claim me whole – possess me even more. Never have I been so turned on. Never have I felt so ravenous for sex.

And *never* have I wanted a man to own me. Until now. I ache for that wedding ring to be planted on my finger. I want Alexandre's hard cock inside me whenever he wishes it. I need to be dominated by him. Enjoyed by him. I want to be a vessel for his pleasure. Forever and ever. *Does that make me crazy?*

A revelation strikes me. This is the first time I have really truly been in love and wanted to put another person's happiness before my own. Everything else has been a dress rehearsal.

This is it. Now. This is the final act. And I'd better not blow it.

9

We sit on the bed eating breakfast – the usual mouth-watering selection of *patisserie,* freshly squeezed juices and fruit. No coffee for me, at least for now. I know that a woman in her twenties could probably guzzle down whatever she chose, but I have to be vigilant; this could be my last opportunity to be pregnant – I shouldn't take any risks, even with something innocuous as coffee.

Alexandre brushes the back of his hand along my cheek. "Thank you, Pearl, for letting me forget about my quandary for a while."

I kiss his hand. "I know. Sex and sleep are the only two temporary cures."

"Every time I wake up, I'm okay for a few split seconds, and then I remember the mess I'm in."

"*We're* in," I correct. "We're in this *together.*"

"I wish you weren't involved in this fiasco. My mind spins in circles all day long; I just can't come up with a solution. Laura's threat could cause havoc. My uncle, my father's brother – if he got wind of this…he's never believed my father just disappeared; he's always been suspicious. If he knew about this, he'd be down on my mother like a ton of bricks."

I feel so bad for Alexandre – the searing regret he must feel at not having destroyed the evidence when he had the chance. "It's in a safe deposit box in the bank, right?" I ask.

"That's what Laura says."

"We have two options: to steal it back or to *make* her give it up." I take a long swig of apple juice.

"She won't, there's no way. Even if, hypothetically, I gave her everything she wanted, she'd still protect herself; still wrap up her blackmail like a neat burrito."

"Then we must steal the evidence. Well, not *steal*. It doesn't belong to her in the first place."

"It's in a vault in the bank. I may have a bit of money and can pull some strings but I'm not Tom Cruise in *Mission Impossible*. Nor can I pay anyone to do it for me. The job's too…too bloody difficult."

"Not do a robbery in that way, silly."

He stares at me and shakes his head. "No way, Pearl. Don't even think about it. I already said I didn't want you to get involved."

"I'm already involved. Look, Laura and I don't look that unalike. Well, she's taller and skinnier than I am but we're both blonde, both have blue eyes."

"What about I.D?"

"Steal her passport, or we can make a duplicate."

"You've been watching too many thrillers."

"Alexandre, you're ridiculously wealthy; now's the time to really *use* some of your money, your clout; pull some of your weight. I'm sure you can work something out – you have all kinds of people on your payroll."

His crooked smile makes the dimple in his cheek stand out more than usual. "*Now* look who sounds like Michael Corleone."

I reply seriously, "We have to *do* something. She's going to want an answer sooner or later, you can't stall her forever."

He sighs and stretches his long legs out. He's half dressed but his feet are bare. I never tire of looking at those elegant feet. He leans his head against the headboard of the bed and mumbles in a tired voice, "But I don't want to see her again."

"You'll have to. At least to get your hands on her passport. Or do you have a connection at the British Embassy?"

"I don't work for the MI5, Pearl."

I take another long swig of juice. Thinking about all this is making me thirsty. "Then you need to swipe her passport and find out which bank holds the evidence. Then find the safe deposit box key."

He raises his eyebrows. "And then you'll go personally to the bank masquerading as her?"

"It's the only thing I can think of. If I get arrested, though, you'll need to find me the best attorney in the world. O.J. Simpson's lawyer would be perfect," I joke.

He shakes his head. "It's too risky."

Another idea flashes into my brain. "Laura hacked our phones, you need to hack hers; get all the info you can – keep us abreast of what's going on."

"That part will be a piece of cake." He squeezes my wrist as if he's afraid I'll run off and do something crazy without him by his side. "Pearl, I don't want you to put yourself in the middle of this. You're pregnant, this is insane – there has to be a better way. In fact, *no* – there's no chance I'll let you do something so crazy."

"Then hire someone. Hire an actress to be Laura for an hour or so." I bite into another mouthful of croissant.

"If the impersonator got caught she'd let the cat out of the bag, though."

"That's why we'd need to keep who we are a secret – not show our faces. Pay the actress in cash. Half up front, half later."

He chuckles. "This is beginning to sound like some crazy suspense movie. Worse, a Woody Allen film that could go laughably wrong."

I don't say anything but in my mind I think, *what Alexandre's mom did was pretty nutty.* Not the killing part, so much. I can see how that could happen in a state of black desperation, fearing for your life - but not getting rid of every scrap of evidence? Not such a bright move.

As if Alexandre can read my mind he says, "I know it seems as if my mother did something really dumb but for her it was a reminder that my father was dead and gone, that he couldn't hurt her anymore."

I bite my lip. "I understand," but I think to myself secretly, *what a nut-job family I'm marrying into. And, worse, what a mad person I must be, myself, to identify with a murderess as much as I do.*

"Tell me about your father," I probe – a question I have been trying to ask for ages without any definitive answers.

"I think you can read between the lines."

"Alexandre, I am going to be your *wife*. I need you to open up to me, to share your pain and your past. I shared mine with you."

"True," he admits. He takes a deep breath as if he needs an

extra dose of oxygen to remember the worst. "The scariest thing about my father was that he wasn't always a monster."

"I figured, or your mother wouldn't have stayed with him so long."

"They had a connection – very physical. He was extremely handsome. She was sort of… hooked on him."

I don't respond but I can imagine. After all, Alexandre is his son.

"He was witty, charming, very charismatic. Clever, too. He could walk into a room and everyone would pay attention. People wanted to please him, be loved by him."

"But he was violent."

"Not at first. They had several happy years. He was Bipolar, you know, what they used to refer to as 'manic-depressive.' Everyone is affected differently. Some Bipolar people lead almost normal lives and are pussycats; never show an aggressive side at all. Others…well. When my father was nice he was great, very loving. But when he was in a manic state, he became a complete monster."

"A real Jekyll and Hyde?"

"He was violent and very sexual if he drank. Drinking sent him over the edge."

"And that's when he sexually abused Sophie?"

"Yes."

"And you, too?"

Alexandre lowers his head and nods. Pain is wavering between us, filling the room. "That's when Sophie knew she had to take me away. She could deal with him – but when he started on me, she lost it. That's why she stabbed him in the groin. She was outraged that he could sink so low."

I lay my hand on his. "It must have been hell for you, I'm so sorry."

"I blanked it out mostly. The same thing happened to me as to you…just blacked my mind from the whole ordeal."

But I know what he is telling me is not completely true. Muscles have memories. When we first started spending nights together, when Alexandre was fast asleep, I would cuddle into him in the spoon position, me behind. A couple of times he woke in a panic, elbows and knees crashing everywhere, flailing his legs and arms about. Someone edged up behind him still means only one thing: sexual abuse. My heart aches for him so badly. What happened to me was horrific but at least it wasn't *betrayal* of the first degree.

"Didn't your mother realize what was going on?" I ask, tears pooling my eyes.

"She was in total denial."

"Does that make you angry?"

His face is impassive, although his calm demeanor doesn't fool me for a second. "I was too young at the time to be angry. But Sophie still feels bitter towards her. She has tried; gone through God knows how much amount of therapy, but Sophie will never be able to *truly* forgive her. That's why I've never let on to her about the murder. I couldn't trust her a hundred percent."

"Just awful to have that treachery come from your own father. I can't even imagine." I bring Alexandre's hand up to my face and rest my lips on his long fingers.

He frowns and says, "Have you noticed that whenever they deal with incestual abuse in films or novels they always have a *step*-father or *step*-brother? Never blood parents or blood siblings. Why? Because it's such a taboo topic that nobody wants to talk about it, let alone believe it. It's such a shameful subject. I've felt shame all my life. Illogical but that's how it is for victims, I don't need to tell you that."

"I know," I say quietly.

"But you know what, Pearl? I'm not the only one. Believe it or not, there are lots of us out there. More than anyone would dare to imagine. Fathers fucking their daughters and sons, brothers, uncles, even mothers doing it to their sons. And within wealthy, privileged families, too – this disease isn't a class, race or monetary issue. It's happening all over the world even in nice, tidy, middle class households."

I know that he's right, although it seems impossible to accept, but it's a vicious, insidious truth eating into society, ruining many people's lives - sometimes forever.

"Why wasn't your father on medication? Lithium or something?" My question seems redundant, ridiculous, but Alexandre is discussing this, finally. He is trusting me with his dark, buried secrets and opening up. I know how painful that is.

"Oh, he *was* on medication at the beginning, but pride got the better of him. He felt he didn't need it, that he could fix himself. Of course, he couldn't. When he came out of the manic episodes he could never explain why he'd done what he did, and he'd always feel guilty, sad and remorseful. My mother always used to end up forgiving him."

A spike of fury stabs me in the heart. How could she do that? Forgive such a monster? But I remain calm. Alexandre loves his mom, however sick she makes me feel. I ask simply, "So what tipped her scales finally?"

"The violence. He was raping her, repeatedly. His condition got worse and worse. He was beating her up, continually. Broken ribs. Nose. You name it. That's when she decided to leave. She tried, once, but she ended up in hospital. He said if she tried again, he'd kill her next time. And us, if he found us – we were in hiding by that point. That's when my mother hatched the plan to get rid of him, once and for all. But deep down inside? She's still in love with him, even now. The good side of him. She kept the teeth and stuff to remind her that he was dead but she also has photos of their happy times in a secret box in the attic. She sneaks up there, sometimes, when my step-father's out of the house, or she pretends she's spring cleaning."

"Pretty screwed up, huh?"

"You bet."

As much as I hate her for what she did to Alexandre by not protecting him, I do identify with Alexandre's mother. Falling in love with someone you think is the perfect man and then he turns? That must be hard. What would I do if Alexandre suddenly changed his colors? Women all over the world face this predicament, especially if they have kids. It's easy to spot an abusive man as an onlooker, but when he is living with you every day and you love him? Not so much.

I look at my fiancé and wonder. What would I do? Because the truth is, Alexandre's dominance turns me on. It's only in small ways that he demonstrates it and he has never, ever made me feel scared of him physically, but I do enjoy being beneath him (no pun intended). I know it's crazy but being submissive makes me feel sexier and relieved that I don't have to make all the decisions – he can take command. But it also causes me to feel frustrated with myself, as if I'm putting the clock back on women's rights by a hundred years.

We sit there in silence. I know this must be the first time he has really opened up to someone about his past. He's been carrying this all on his own shoulders. No wonder he has been so protective of Sophie. She's the only one who has been through hell and back with him. She truly *knows* him. I think of how understanding he was about what happened to me, horrified that I'd even considered that it had been my fault.

I get the feeling that he is all talked out. He's revealed so much about himself, laying his wounds open to the elements. It's time to change the subject. I slip my hand under his T-shirt, maneuver myself so my head is on his stomach, look up at him and say in a soft, seductive voice, "I had an erotic dream about you when I was in Hawaii."

He narrows his green eyes that seem to be twinkling with amusement. "Oh yeah, you mentioned you had a little secret. Tell me about it."

"I dreamed that you were spanking me."

He gives me a wry, wolfish smile. "And?"

"I woke up the next morning, soaked between my legs, nursing a post-orgasm after-glow. After-shock, more like. Pretty high on the Richter scale, it was. The truth is, what you did in the dream really turned me on."

He licks his lips. He's the wolf and I'm Red Riding Hood. "Is this an invitation?"

"I'm curious," I whisper stroking his navel.

"You girls have been reading too many erotic novels. You think you want it but, in reality, it would freak you out."

"I might. I might love it. I did in my dream."

"Because it was a fantasy, baby. Some women fantasize about being raped but would be horrified if it happened in real life. I don't need to tell *you* that, of all people."

136

"I enjoyed my little adventure with Alessandra, though."

"Because she's a woman. You knew you were equals in strength. Neither was the *dominante*."

"Oh, I don't know, she wielded that little whip with *panache* and relish," I joke, remembering that mad evening of lesbian bondage as if it only happened yesterday, although I realize now that she really did take advantage of me. She sensed that I was weak and vulnerable and honed in on me.

Alexandre's eyes scan me from head to toe and settle on my breasts. I know this conversation is turning him on, even if he won't admit it. I add, "I'm just curious, that's all, about a little BDSM."

"So am I."

My eyes widen. "Really?"

"Of course. But I would never *act* on it."

"It wouldn't mean that you were like your father, Alexandre. Not if it's consensual and both parties are up for it."

He runs his fingers along my collarbone. "I wouldn't dare, Pearl."

"Why not?"

"What if I liked it? What then? What if I got a taste for it and it took me over?"

"It wouldn't."

"Don't be so sure," he tells me with a dry smile. "I might develop an addiction for putting you over my knee. Whipping that wet little pussy of yours. Whipping it, then sucking it, then fucking it."

I can feel moisture flush through my hot kernel.

"Enough of this conversation, chérie, it's dangerous. Although, I have to admit, it's a good distraction from our dilemma." He rests his hands on his huge hard-on. "And you've got me in the mood again."

"To fuck me?" I purr, stroking him through his pajama bottoms, feeling that comforting ridge that never lets me down.

"No, baby, you know the rules."

I squeeze him a little. "But my gynecologist said it was fine to have intercourse! Only if I was spotting was it risky. She said−"

"I don't care what she said. I'm going by the Indian woman's advice. Delicious sex comes in many forms; it doesn't have to involve penetration. It's like martial arts - training with your hands tied behind your back − your footwork gets better, so do your kicks."

"Do you know anything about martial arts?" I ask, running my hands along up his solid thighs − he must have gotten those sinewy muscles from some kind of hard training.

"A little." He winks at me.

"By the time we have sex I'll be desperate."

"You'll be like a virgin on our wedding night. I'll fuck you then. When *is* our wedding, by the way?"

"It's a surprise. Just make sure you don't double-book. Keep your calendar open until the end of February, at least."

"From now on, chérie, you *are* my calendar. You take top priority."

"What about your business?"

"We're going to be even richer."

I raise my eyebrows. "What have you got brewing?"

"You disapprove of video games so I won't tell you."

"*Video* games?"

"You see, I knew you wouldn't understand."

"Okay, tell me. You know I'm not a video game kinda girl but

I do respect the creative process that goes into them."

"As well as that side of things, I'm not selling HookedUp to Sophie, after all. She simply can't afford to buy me out – she pulled out of our deal at the last minute. We might both sell at a later date – strike while the iron's hot. You can be a lady of leisure if you like, Pearl."

I feel relieved that the family business hasn't broken up because of me. I think back to our other conversation, fondle his cock and say, "If you spanked me, Alexandre, tell me how you'd do it."

He strokes his thumb languidly over my lower lip and I suck on it, letting my teeth graze across the ball of his thumb, flickering my tongue on his shiny square nail. He takes my other hand and presses it against his erection.

"See how hard you get me, Pearl, lying against me with your pregnant tits, those nipples like silk bullets? But you're wrong if you think I'd spank a woman with my child inside her."

"Please, just humor me. Just pretend. Tell me how you'd do it." I walk my fingers under his PJ's and squeeze his penis, feeling the throb of it in my fisted hand.

"I'd bend you over my knee with my arm over your shoulder so you were locked into position and couldn't wriggle away. With my right hand I'd stroke your hot little pussy-pearlette, tickle it, tease it until it was glistening wet. Until it was begging me for more."

I run my tongue along my lips and stroke the length of his smooth erection, softly. He bucks his hips up a little so I can roll his pajamas down, and I hear his quiet moan.

He talks on in his deep voice, "Once you were really aroused, I'd bring my flat palm down hard on your ass with a stinging slap.

It would shock you, might even hurt you a little, but it would also make you want more. Then I'd tap your hot, juicy little pearlette so gently, letting my fingers dip inside."

I grip him harder and begin to jack his cock up and down, concentrating on the crown of it, teasing the bulbous tip.

"Then I'd slap you again, this time the tips of my fingers would land on your pussy. You'd be moaning for more. I'd plunge my fingers inside. Then slap you again with my other hand. Then stroke you softly. You'd be going crazy because my rhythm would change. You wouldn't know if you'd get the tease or the slap. Then I'd throw you on the bed and fuck you so hard from behind while your own fingers played with your clit. I'd ravage you like an animal. Bad boy style. Play the ruthless, selfish bastard. Girls like that. Pump your pussy until it was numb. I'd fuck your ass off, thrusting in and out till I came really hard deep inside you, emptying all my seed. Then I'd pull out before you had a chance to come."

He's really rock solid now and I'm soaked hearing him describe this particular brand of torture, my clit pounding with arousal.

He's grinning now, enjoying this game. "You'd be confused, chérie. Almost in pain, but wanting more. I'd leave you there for a few minutes. You'd spread your legs begging for me to come back."

I lick my lips. "Yes, I would."

"I'd spank you once more, just so you'd know who was boss. Then I'd turn you over. I'd fuck your clit with the tip of my cock till you screamed. Then I'd enter you again. You in the missionary position. But really slowly and gently, this time. I'd cup your ass with my hands tightly so it was all mine, bringing it as close to me as possible. I start a slow fuck, hauling your peachy ass up towards me with each thrust. My pubic bone would be rubbing on your clit, or I'd change my position so the root of my dick would massage your clit - and my cock would be pressing against your secret places, those places that drive you wild. I'd keep my motions as rhythmical as a metronome, the thing musicians use to keep the beat…"

I feel I'm about to come just listening to his description.

"Come here, Pearl," Alexandre grabs me about my waist and maneuvers me so I am above him, my Venus on his face, my butt in the air, doggy style. He flickers his tongue up beneath me, lapping at my opening - he's groaning. "Fuck you're wet," he murmurs.

We commence our 69. I wrap my lips about his steel rod and start sucking the tip and then put as much as I can into my mouth, sucking in like a vacuum, riding my head up and down, letting my mouth fuck him as if I were mounting him. It's hard to concentrate because his tongue is doing magical things to me, also sucking in a vacuum, drawing out my juices.

My eyelids flutter – I'm entering another realm. "Alexandre…"

His hands are clamped on my thighs so I can't escape – not that I want to. He's pulling my groin closer to his face and taking me whole, fucking me now with his tongue. Then with his right palm, he brings it up between my legs and cups my mound, keeping the flatness of his hand hard against my clit and rubbing in small circles. His tongue lashes at me from behind as I relish the pressure of his hand on my clit…aah…Incredible.

I compress my lips around his broad length and fist my hands about the root….there's too much of him to fit in my already stretched mouth. I can feel him thicken…

"Jesus, your wet, sweet-tasting pussy is driving me wild," He groans. The throbbing expansion of him inside my mouth is giving me all the clues I need…he's going to come any second.

I grab his hand and push it even harder against my clit and start coming in a powerful rush. His hand is moist from my oozing and I slap my groin into his palm, my mouth trying not to leave his cock – I need to keep the pressure up. He needs me but my orgasm is making me selfish. "Aah, baby, I'm coming so hard," I cry, releasing my own hand from his.

Whorls of bright colors spiral in my brain as intense spasms crash through my core. I tighten my lips about him and he's coming too, spurting inside my mouth. I swallow eagerly, sucking it all in.

"Je t'aime, Pearl," he groans. *I love you.*

"Moi, non plus," I scream out, aware I'm quoting Jane Birkin in the song and what I've said is mad nonsense…'me, neither' is the translation.

He pushes my legs further apart, holding his tongue flat against me as my aftershocks fade slowly, my orgasm riding on its vibrating plateau. Alexandre can read my body like a memorized book – he always knows what to do, always senses when I need extra pressure or when I need stillness. It's as if he has studied the art of lovemaking somewhere along the line. He knows when to fuck hard and when to be gentle. When to be a pirate, and when to be a gentleman. Right now, his tongue is motionless – just what I desire. As my climax shimmers like the glistening pearl he tells me that I am, I collapse my face into his crotch, licking all the droplets of cum from there and his solid thighs. Whoever imagined that carnal lust could be so beautiful…

I am totally spent.

10

Two days have passed and I still haven't been back to my apartment. It feels good to be at work knowing that 'home' is at Alexandre's place with him - that at the end of the day, I have my partner waiting for me. Finally, I can concentrate when I'm at work – doing something else other than obsess over lost love. Although he and I still have a lot of making up to do for lost *time*, or should I say, 'making out' to do. Like teenagers freshly fallen in love, we can't get enough of each other.

I think back again to the way I behaved, crawling out of that toilet window at Van Nuys Airport and it feels as if it was someone else, not me. I don't think I had fully appreciated the toll that the rape had on me; the memory flooding back in such detail – gang rape – being abused, used and made to feel like trash, as if I had no importance in the world whatsoever. People imagine it's the physical violation that is so devastating, and although it's true, it is nothing to what goes on inside your brain. I had hidden it deep in my subconscious, but it was still there – the feeling of worthlessness that ate into my psyche every single day for eighteen years. And whatever anybody says, however hard they try to assure you, deep down inside is that feeling of culpability - even if you know, logically, that it's nonsense.

No, I don't think I took it all on board and the effect it had on me. Remembering everything brought me back to that moment, that night. It made me vulnerable, a pawn for Laura. Had I not been in such a sorry state, I don't believe that I would have been so naïve, so blind – making rash, foolish choices based on nothing but fear. I have always prided myself on being astute and on the ball, but I was like a helpless beetle that had been flipped over, flailing my weak legs in the air. My armor was on my back, not on my underbelly where I needed it most.

Or perhaps the way I handled things with Alexandre was a subconscious desire to continue punishing myself because I didn't believe I deserved better. Alexandre said so at the time; that I was using Sophie as an excuse to run from him. It was only when I felt I'd lost him completely that I could see the situation for what it was. Me – all alone for the rest of my life. Back in The Desert. Thirsty for love. For sex. For self-worth. I'd lost the one thing that was true: Alexandre.

Alexandre *gives* me that sense of self worth. Having a man be so intimate with you, telling you that your private parts are 'sweet' and 'delicious' is a real gift. Few men do that. Few men make you feel really special and treasured. Yes, I am hooked on the orgasms he feeds me every day, but it is the intimacy, the connection that gives me those orgasms in the first place. He is accepting every part of me, even the 'dirty' bits that he finds beautiful. He finds my vagina so beautiful he calls it my 'pearlette' – because for him it is a little part of me – a little part that is like a jewel. Yet for me those 'bits' caused such inner turmoil for so many years making me feel I was bad and unworthy. Alexandre has restored the faith I once had in myself before that dreaded event.

As he once told me, 'the biggest sexual organ is your brain' and he is, little by little, convincing me that I am precious – that I count in this world. Being sexy is all about self-confidence. It's all a question of how you feel inside. Alexandre took my dull nub of a diamond and he polished it until it began to shine.

I have even given nicknames to my vagina: Venus, V-8 – that's how confused I've been about sex and my own sexuality. Like a little girl not being able to call it by its real name. Both ashamed and amused, all in one. Tittering about its naughtiness like a child in the classroom with a secret joke. Too fearful to come out and say the real word. Vagina. There, I said it. Was that so difficult? God gave females vaginas yet I was subconsciously shameful of having one because of what it brought me. That rape left me ashamed of having a vagina, of being a woman.

Sex is not everything but it is, literally, the core of us. We are born from sex. The world lives on through sex. We can feel ecstasy through sex.

Or misery.

And I never want to return to that place again.

It's all abuzz at HookedUp Enterprises today. Natalie is putting the final touches to our documentary, *Child Traffick – Red Light*

Alert - (a double entendre on traffic lights and the red light districts in the sex industry). It's looking great. Well, 'great' is not exactly the best word to use with such a heartbreaking topic – let's just say, the film is brilliantly put together. We have already sold the rights in ten countries and it has been entered into several competitions. I have high hopes for this film.

I'm in my office sorting through paperwork when Jeanine, our receptionist, buzzes me.

"Hi Pearl, Natalie wants to come and see you, are you free right now?"

"Absolutely," I reply, curious as to why she's paying me a visit – usually we meet in the editing room.

Ten minutes later, she bursts through the door, looking stunning, as usual, yet with a girlish restlessness about her which I haven't noticed before – Natalie is usually so composed, such a 'grown-up'.

"Hi Natalie. You look amazing – like ten years younger or something." I rake my eyes over her outfit: tight jeans; not Natalie's usual attire.

"Or something," she says with a laugh. "Do you want to hear the good news first, or the good news second?"

"The good news second."

She sets her tablet on my desk and plunks herself in my swivel chair giving it, and herself, a little spin. Boy, is she in a good mood. "Actually, I can't make up my mind which is better," she gushes.

"Tell me either way, the suspense is killing me."

"Okay. Firstly, your fiancé has started this foundation for us – a charity."

"Oh yes?" I ask with curiosity. *How come he never mentioned this?*

Natalie goes on, "It's called the Jane Doe Foundation. It has been set up for sexually abused girls and young women. Because of all our research and experience with the girls we've met through our project, he thinks HookedUp Enterprises is the perfect vehicle, although I have been sworn that HookedUp Enterprises will never be mentioned at any time. The Foundation is financially independent.

"I guess I shouldn't be surprised. He's rich; he can afford to give money away to worthy causes – good for him."

She nibbles on a pen lying on my desk. "No, that's what's so cool. This isn't his money but has come in from four, other, private sources."

"Jane Doe, you say?"

"That's right. Because abused girls are handled like Jane Does, identities unknown, or treated like they haven't got a name; they are victims, not just because they've been abused but because so many people don't even know who they are. Or worse, they don't care."

"Jane Doe," I repeat. "Was that his idea?" Natalie has no clue about what happened to me all those years ago. Primarily, ours is a working relationship.

"Yeah, not even I could have come up with such an original name."

I raise my eyebrows. Is she being sarcastic? I study her expression.

"No, really, I think the name is cool," she says, tapping her legs eagerly as if she's ready to talk about her other good news.

"Who are these benefactors?"

She beams at me. "Anonymous."

"And they all came in together with the money? At one time?

Or was this charity set up a while ago and this is the first we're hearing of it?"

She's still grinning. "It was set up, oh, I think less than a week ago."

"And we are to distribute the funds as we see fit?"

"That's right."

Revenge is a dish best served cold. What has Alexandre been up to?

"Do you want to hear my other good news?" Natalie asks, impatience dancing in her eyes.

I blink to concentrate on what she's about to say. "Yes. Yes, of course."

"I'm dating someone new."

I give her a cheeky smile. "Hence the sexy jeans?"

"You like my new look?"

"Any look suits you, Natalie," I say, trying to get Alexandre and his Robin Hood shenanigans out of my head. I wonder how he did it. The coincidence is too much. Four benefactors, Jane Doe…

Natalie jiggles her boot. She's wearing heels. "Aren't you going to ask who it is?"

"Let me guess. That lawyer guy you saw last year that you kind of liked?"

"No-o," she sing-songs.

"That doctor who your friend, Gail, wanted to send you on a blind date with?"

"Not even close."

I throw my hands in the air. "Okay, I give up." Natalie swore she would only ever date a man who earned a six figure salary. With all the commotion with her aunt after Hurricane Sandy, I'm amazed she has even found time to date anyone at all. In fact, this is the first time I have seen her so giddy with happiness – she deserves it after the Sandy aftermath and all that she has been doing for her family.

"A firefighter," she says and then laughs. "I know…not what you expected." She gives the chair a three hundred and sixty degree swivel.

"Probably not what *you* expected, either," I joke.

"He was cleaning up the devastation where my aunt used to live. Broken gas pipes, et cetera – the place was dangerous, you know. He told me to clear off. Then we got talking."

"What's his name?"

"Miles. After Miles Davis."

"I'm so happy for you," I tell her, trying to hide my surprise.

"You don't think I'm crazy?"

"Are you kidding? They're the bravest, coolest bunch of people in the world. Not to mention…" I trail off.

"What?"

I try to suppress a grin. I think of Alexandre in his firefighter get-up and a sexy-memory frisson runs up my spine.

"You have such a dirty mind, Pearl."

"Well, let's face it - a guy in uniform? A *firefighter* in uniform is every woman's fantasy."

"Well, I have to say…" she arches a neat eyebrow.

"You *haven't, you didn't?*" Natalie and I rarely talk about anything other than work. But she's in the mood to reveal all, obviously.

She widens her hazel eyes. She looks like a little girl who's had way too much candy. "He was very apologetic. I went to his house for dinner and he hadn't had time to change. I flung myself at him."

"I bet you did. So what does he look like? No, that's wrong – I should be asking you if he's kind and caring—"

"Imagine a young Denzel Washington with a bit of Wesley Snipes thrown in."

"Very nice, indeed."

"Miles is a sexy cocktail, alright."

"Yeah, you look a little tipsy," I joke, "that's for sure. How old is he?"

She sighs. "A little younger than me."

"Join the club. So is this serious, like *relationship* serious or just….exercise?" I ask.

"That's what's so crazy. At the beginning I thought it was just for fun but he's like…so sincere, so genuine. I think I'm falling for him."

"Does he know that?"

"No way! I'm not like you, Pearl. I don't wear my heart on my sleeve. I'm playing it cool. You know, not always available. Making sure he knows he has to book an evening with me way in advance. No last minute dates."

I think of my rock climbing date with Alexandre…so last minute. Boy, was I easy. "Poor guy," I say making a face, "You've probably got him pining for you."

"That's the idea."

"You're such a catch, Natalie. I bet he feels he's in over his head."

"I don't think so. He's very confident and pretty cocky."

"Well, he's met his match in you."

She giggles. Natalie never giggles. "Am I that bad?"

"You can be pretty formidable."

"Is that what your father said about me?"

"No, Not at all."

"The truth is, there was no way I was going to move to an island in the middle of nowhere and leave New York – it would never have worked out with your dad."

"I know. My dad got that. Speaking of moving to Hawaii …no, never mind." I walk over to the window and look down at the street. People are rushing this way and that, buzzing about in the post-holiday sales.

"What? I hate it when you do that – give me half a secret and then take it away again."

I turn around. She's still swiveling in my chair. "How do you know it's a secret?"

She glares at me playfully. "I can tell by the look in your eye."

"I'll tell you when it's a sure thing."

"See? There you go again, Pearl."

I hesitate. Would Daisy mind me telling Natalie? No, she wouldn't. I say, "Well, okay. It looks as if Daisy might have something going on with someone she met there."

Natalie claps her hands. "That's fantastic! Who is he?"

"A surfer dude. But very cute."

"You see, there was no way I could be part of that world. I guess I'm a city girl at heart. About your dad – I've been feeling a little guilty, you know, like I was a bit unfair to him. I didn't call him because I didn't want him to think we were…you know…still on. But I realized that I was being a bit cold."

"He'll live. He knew you'd never settle in Hawaii. You don't want some zen hippie like him, anyway – that's not your style."

"A New Yorker born and bred - that's me."

"Exactly. My dad wouldn't last more than three days here."

"Can you envision Daisy there, though?"

"When she came to visit, she was like a duck to water. It might be just the thing for her and Amy."

Natalie's smile fades. "What happened to Johnny – she doesn't want to get back together with him?"

"He's repentant." I feel my hackles rise on Daisy's behalf. "But he's too late."

"Hell hath no fury like a woman scorned," Natalie chirps.

I've heard her quote that before. Shakespeare? No, the Restoration playwright. "Congreve, I believe?"

"You're a poet and you don't know it," she replies, laughing at my rhyme and making another.

"Actually, Daisy's being very nice to Johnny. Considering. But she can't trust him anymore. Plus, I think she's up for a real lifestyle change."

Natalie inspects her manicured nails and then raps them on the desk almost as if she's playing a tune. "What about you and Alexandre? You told me there were issues with the ex."

"Resolved," I say quickly. "You know what, Natalie? I really think we need to go through the credit titles again. We've been chit-chatting way too long – we should get back to work before the day's gone. I'm so thrilled for you about Miles. Keep him guessing – keep him on his toes."

She springs from my chair and picks up her tablet. "Oh, I will."

"I still can't get over those donations that came out of the blue." I'll need to find out what Alexandre has been up to.

We start our slow amble as we exit my office. "You don't mind that Miles isn't a six figure earner?" I ask, wondering if Natalie remembered the vow she made a year ago.

"He's a nice guy and that's what counts most. My daughters

like him."

"They've met him? Okay, I see this really *is* serious."

Then she whispers, "The truth is, Pearl, he's a magician in bed. He takes his time, he's so *into* me, you know – he makes me feel like I'm the most incredible woman who's ever walked the earth."

I nod knowingly. "Yup, you're hooked, alright."

Then we both burst out at once, "HookedUp!"

I add, "It amuses me no end, the name HookedUp Enterprises. It's like Star Trek, you know, as if we're on a space ship."

"We're on a journey alright. The journey of our life. They say 'life begins at forty' and you know what? I think they're right!"

A few hours later, just as I am grabbing my coat to leave the office, my landline rings.

Jeanine informs me, "The person wouldn't tell me who she was."

"A woman?"

"A *British* woman."

"Thanks Jeanine, put her through."

I hold the receiver with trepidation. "Hello?"

"Sorry to bother you at work, Pearl, but I had no choice."

It's HER.

"What do you want, Laura." No question mark.

"I realize I was rash when I told you my secret about your mobile." Mobile…ah yes, British for cell phone.

"So you couldn't spy on me anymore, you mean?"

"Just keeping tabs."

"Well, I'm no longer using my 'mobile' anyway."

"So I gathered. That's why I'm calling you at work."

"I know what you're up to, Laura. Alexandre's told me everything."

"Ah, yes. The hip replacement. And the rather sorry-looking teeth. Why is it that Americans have such perfect knashers and we sad Europeans get lumped with bad dental care all our lives? Well, not blowing my own trumpet, or anything, but mine were sorted out and are in mint condition. But, you know, in general. Especially the French. Not Sophie and Alexandre, though, their sparkling white teeth are pretty perfect, except for that oh so slightly crooked one he has, but that, of course, is part of his charm—"

I cut her short. "Why are you calling, Laura?"

"I feel lonely. Left out. Alexandre's not answering my calls and I want to know what he's decided."

I take a deep breath and tell her, "He doesn't love you, Laura."

"He loved me once and he can love me again. Once I've had his child then we can be happy again. I mean, let's face it Pearl, that's something you can't give him. He wants to be a father."

"He's going to be a father," I blurt out.

"Come again?"

"I'm pregnant, Laura. Alexandre and I are going to be parents." *Oh God, why did I say that?* Why did I let her know that? I feel instantly foolish – this woman is nuts. This information could drive her over the edge of reason.

There's silence and then she replies with a hiss, "Bollocks. You're just saying that to rile me up!"

I don't answer.

"Pearl? Are you there?"

I want to hang up on her, but also don't dare to.

"Pearl?" Her voice sounds tearful. *Laura crying?* That I cannot imagine.

"I'm still here," I answer.

"Did you do IVF?"

"No, Laura. He fucked my ARSE with an R off, and his sperm shot inside my womb and I got pregnant naturally." *Oh no, now what have I said?*

She slams the phone down on me.

My moment of triumphant glory is overtaken by an overwhelming feeling of stupidity. Uh, oh. I've really gone and done it now. My heart's racing. That little payback instant felt sooo good….but….

The telephone rings again. I grab it, morbidly curious as to what will happen next. I hope my outburst isn't going to land Alexandre's mother in jail.

"It's the British woman again," Jeanine lets me know.

"Thanks, Jeanine, we got cut off, please put her through." I sit down in my swivel chair.

"Okay," Laura begins, "I'm willing to negotiate."

Negotiate? "I'm listening."

"This relationship seems to be far, far more serious than I had imagined."

"What relationship?" I ask tentatively.

"Yours and Alex's, of course."

"We're in love, Laura." *Ooh, that felt good, too.*

"His dick has obviously got the better of him. But that's by the by. I'm not a home wrecker, whatever you may think of me.

155

How far gone are you?"

"Three months," I lie. "It's all happening, Laura. The doctors are delighted with the scans. I'm carrying a very healthy fetus – no chance of miscarriage now." I hope I haven't jinxed my pregnancy by saying that. I wince at my words.

She puffs, "I see. Well, that will change the course of events somewhat."

Somewhat?

"Look Pearl. I'm willing to do a deal. You can keep Alexandre and your baby. But I *also* want a baby. You know, James couldn't have children and before that…well, I was in a bloody wheelchair, thank you very much. Having a child has been a dream of mine and I want that dream to come true at any cost. Do you understand, Pearl? I am *not* giving up on my dream. We can do IVF. Alex won't even have to have sex with me. Just his sperm, that's all I want."

This woman is a real nut-job. If this were a movie, I'd be laughing by this point. "Why don't you go to a sperm bank, Laura?"

"Ugh, that's disgusting. Some smelly old sperm from someone I don't know?"

"Don't you have a handsome gay friend who could help you out?"

"I'm not a fag-hag. I don't go round with poofs, and besides, d'you think I want my baby to have homo genes in his DNA?"

"Well, what about a one-night stand with some gorgeous guy?" I suggest.

"I want brains as well as beauty. I want it *all* for my baby."

I propose an idea which I'm sure she'll shut down. I go ahead and suggest it anyway, "There are lots of clever, handsome men.

You can afford it – advertise – you could even do it on eBay. I'm sure Alexandre would pay for any costs involved. Or I can help out."

"You think I'd degrade myself like that, Pearl? Purr…lease."

"There must be a better way, Laura - a way that doesn't involve Alexandre doing something against his will."

"Pearl, I think you've forgotten something key here. I hold the cards. I have the power. I want Alexandre's sperm in that little test tube - and nobody else's - and if I don't get it I might just be inclined to make a very big scene!"

"Don't do that, Laura! You'll break his heart if you…you know….say anything."

"What about *me?* What about my bloody broken heart! I look at myself in the mirror and I see a fuck-off, babelicious blonde looking bloody good for her age – then I see you with your big forty year-old arse and wonder…what the fuck does he see in her?"

Big ass? I have to tread carefully here. I mustn't let this woman get to me. I force myself to remain calm and take another deep breath. *Breath in, breath out.* "We're both into dogs, Laura…things like that. We have a connection. A bond."

"Look, Pearl, I think I'm being bloody magnanimous as it is - I'm letting you keep Alexandre. All I'm asking for is his bloody semen!"

I'm speechless – I can't think of how to reply.

She carries on in her posh drawl, "You talk to him. Tell him that if he doesn't agree – in writing by the way – to come to the clinic with me, then I'll be perfectly happy to spill the beans about 'you know who', and what that 'you know who' did."

"Where is the 'you know what,' Laura?"

"The 'you know what' is in a safety deposit box in a fuck-off vault in one of London's most protected banks, so don't even think about fucking with me."

I try to sound composed. "I'm sure you wouldn't do anything rash, Laura."

"I always hated that silly cow anyway. To be honest, she's got it coming to her. What kind of a person would do what she did? Not the topping off part but abandoning her children."

I hate to say it, but Laura does have a point. I have never met Alexandre's mother but she doesn't sound like the most stable of people. Nor, the most loyal.

But I say, "We mustn't judge her. And whatever *we* might think, Alexandre loves her."

"Anyway, you need to have a chat with him and let him know where I stand. I'm thirty-three years old and I want that baby A.S.A.P. I've already started the hormone therapy and I want that French fuck's sperm in that test tube within the next few weeks."

"Laura, if you think he's a 'French fuck' why do you want his baby in the first place?"

"Because he happens to be the most intelligent person I know. He's a genius, Pearl. Do you appreciate how clever he is? His mind is like a quantum theory computer. He is also stunningly handsome with a perfect, well-proportioned body. With his brains and his beauty and my brains and my beauty we'll produce a wonder child."

She sounds like the baddie in one of those mad, science fiction movies. "And then what?" I ask.

"I get his sperm, wait until I have the actual baby - just in case. Might even have some extra frozen for the future just for good measure. I'll also want a nice trust set up for the child -

several million's worth – *several* million – and then he can have everything in that vault and we'll never speak of the subject again."

"What about the child? You'll want it to have a father, surely? Is Alexandre expected to play daddy?"

"I haven't thought that part through, yet. I have to ponder what's 'best for baby'. Now *you're* pregnant. Pearl, it really puts a spanner in the works."

"What about James?" I ask, half imagining him lying dead somewhere, poisoned by her.

"I was getting geared up to divorce him but he could come in handy. Good point, Pearl. I need to mull all that side of things over. I really had imagined myself back with Alex until you and your fat arse got in the way. I'm sure he'll get bored with you, eventually. We'll cross that bridge when we come to it."

I want to scream and shout at her but I also don't want to rock us both out of the very wobbly boat we're in – we could capsize and end up drowning, the pair of us.

"What if the IVF doesn't work, Laura? There's only a fifteen percent success rate, you know."

Silence.

Then she replies chirpily, "I feel very confident. Oh yes, and Alex will need to do his bit, too. A multivitamin. He'll need to stop drinking, no soy products, eat organic, no food from plastic containers. The positive thing about you being pregnant, Pearl, is that it's proof that his semen is working just fine. I mean, it must be extra powerful to have got you, a forty year-old pregnant. I'll give him a list about the do's and don'ts when we speak later. Well, bye then. Nice chatting. Tell Alex to call me A.S.A.P."

"I will," I answer, my blood boiling. I hang up. *What a basket case.* She really must have fallen hard on her head in that accident.

As soon as I get home, I search for Alexandre. He's in his study talking on the phone. Deadly serious. He shoots me a 'do-not-interrupt' glance. Normally, I'd slip away and come back later, but I hover. He's wearing a hand-tailored, charcoal gray suit and looks extremely dapper. I have to say, he really is one of the most handsome men I have ever seen in my life.

"No, I didn't say that. What I said was that we need to invest another twenty million. You know how these things are. If you want quality, you have to pay for it, and what we need is…what we need…look, what we mustn't skimp on is talent. If that's what his fee is, then that's simply what we have to pay. Green-light that, Jim, yes, we have to. She said what? That's bullshit. There's room out there for games that don't involve shooting people. You see, Jim, that's what I'm talking about. That's what I liked about it. It has an epic heart-tugging story, glorious environments, kind of a sweet light magic and dark magic and a simply stunning soundtrack."

I observe my fiancé as his face reveals a gamut of emotions between smiles, frowns and furious brow creasing – animated by this conversation which is obviously about the next big video game. I have gathered that their budgets are bigger than block-buster movies.

Alexandre loosens his tie. "That's right. What consumers want are handhelds that run Android so they can have a nice portable emulator. Okay, Jim. Speak to them and get back to me in the next few hours. Thanks."

"Sorry to bother you, baby." I'm lingering at the doorway.

"You never bother me, chérie; I'm always glad to see you. Come here and sit on my lap - just give me a couple more minutes – I need to write something down before I forget."

But I can't hold it in. His wheeling and dealing may be important but nothing as life-changing as being, or not being, a father. I blurt out, "Laura called me. We need to do something. She's on the warpath, still." *The sperm warpath.*

He closes his lids as if that will wipe her from his mind. "I keep hoping she'll give up and go away."

"Not a chance. But things are looking up a little," I say, hopefully, as I settle on his knee.

He puts his arms about my waist and breathes in the scent of my hair. "What d'you mean?"

"She's given up on wanting you, yourself, although she still wants part of you."

He shakes his head. "She's such a nutter. What did she say?"

"She wants you to go to the IVF clinic with her."

"Oh Christ."

"Well at least she's stopped harping on about marriage with you and living happily ever after."

He raises his eyebrows.

"I told her I was pregnant."

He furrows his temple. "Was that wise? She's so off the rails she's capable of anything. I really want her to keep away from you, Pearl – she could get consumed by jealousy."

"Strangely enough, I think it's had the opposite effect – it seems to have cooled her down. She's delighted your semen is so potent. She says she's not a home wrecker."

"She's a wrecker, period."

I nuzzle into his embrace and squeeze my arms about his broad chest. "Maybe you should—"

"No, Pearl."

"I've got *you*, that's all that counts."

"I am not giving into her. She is *not* having my child."

"She says if she doesn't get what she wants - your semen in a test tube, plus several million, she'll make a scene."

"She can have the money – I'll pay her off, but she's not getting her way."

"She's determined. Nobody else's sperm will do. She wants yours and yours alone – she thinks you're a genius, wants a wonder child."

"I can't believe how insane she's being. This is not the Laura I once knew."

"I know, it sounds like some twisted black comedy or something – it's so far-fetched, so larger than life, I keep pinching myself to make sure I'm not floating about in one of my nightmares again."

He takes off his jacket and throws it on his desk. "She's totally out to lunch, she's morphed into a fucking lunatic."

"She wants you to call her tonight. Oh yes, and she reminded me about the evidence being in the bank vault."

He loosens his tie some more as if the Laura news is making him feel strangled. "You didn't discuss that over the phone, did you? She could have been recording it."

I run my fingers through his dark hair. It feels soft and comforting in the midst of the tangle of mess we're in. "We sort of spoke in code. Your mother was just referred to as 'she' and the evidence, 'you know what'. Something tells me Laura's enjoying

162

the drama of it all. The way she was speaking made me feel that if it came to the crunch she wouldn't actually go through with her threat. I think she might just be playing power games."

"Too much of a risk to take, though. I'm too nervous about this to call her bluff."

"Still no word from James?"

"No, he still hasn't returned my calls."

I grimace. "You don't think she'd be capable of murder, do you?"

"No. But then again, this new persona of Laura's is a total shock to me. I don't know who she is anymore."

"You really think she suffered brain damage in the fall?"

"Either that, or some mind-altering medication she's on. Maybe she's taking something for the pain, who knows. But she's not being rational, anyway."

"What if you humored her? Pretended you agreed? But give her someone else's sperm. Get the teeth and hip parts back and she'll be pregnant with an anonymous donor, thinking it's you. You'll still have to pay her the 'settlement' but at least it won't be your child she's carrying."

"I'd have to sign legal documents, though, wouldn't I? And we'd have to be in cahoots with the doctors. Doctors are hard to bribe or they could lose their license to practice."

"Not necessarily. If you can get the exact same container they give you, or bring in your fake sample in a sanitized container and swap it over, who's to know?"

"Laura's too savvy. She will have probably thought of that – would probably want me to masturbate into the container in front of her."

"Maybe, but you could try."

"How long does sperm live?"

"A few hours, I think. You could pay someone who looks like you to come to the clinic with you. Get it fresh."

He rubs his eyes. "Listen to us. This conversation is crazy! This whole situation is fucking surreal."

"We have to come up with some plan, though."

"What about our last idea? The fake passport idea – paying an actress to go to the bank?"

"That's riskier. It's breaking the law. Whereas with this idea we'd get a slap on the wrist, not slung in jail."

"True."

"Could we trust her to keep to her side of the bargain, though?"

"The way she's been behaving? I doubt it."

A question has been on my lips for a long time. "Just out of curiosity, what *was* it about Laura that you loved? Apart from her physical beauty? Before, the accident, I mean."

"Funny you should ask that. I've been mulling that one over myself, recently. You know, I think I was...I don't know."

"What?"

"Very young. She was my first serious girlfriend. I'd always been with older women, friends of my sister's."

"Prostitutes?" I ask.

"Sex workers, yes. They were high class hookers, if you like. Not the sort that lurked in an alley somewhere. Not at all. These girls were more like consorts – dined out with politicians and extremely wealthy, older men. They were vetted, tested regularly. Always impeccably dressed, often very educated, too. They knew all sorts, about good food, fine wines, current affairs and could really hold an intelligent conversation – it was part of their job.

That was the kind of work Sophie did. Anyway, I had relation-ships primarily with them simply because they were friends of my sister's. I never paid for sex, obviously."

Obviously. They should have been paying *him*.

"Then I met Laura. She was a buddy really, like my best friend, at the time. Sophie has never really been a 'friend' because she was too busy playing my mother figure and I'd never stayed long in one school so I didn't have so many guy friends. Laura was my mate. But now I look back on it, I don't think I really loved her. I mean, I did, but nothing, nothing compared to how I feel for you. Physically, there wasn't that fusion, you know, and I never had that soul connection with her, not like I have with you, Pearl."

I thread my fingers through his. It's so good to feel close again. To know he's mine. What he's saying about loving me more than he loved Laura is like a cool breeze on a sweltering day.

"Thanks," I say.

"Sometimes my stomach wells up with jealousy when I think of Saul or Brad – Silly, I know, but I get furious knowing you've loved others before me."

My lips curl up. I love him being jealous – how childish is that? But I put his fears at bay and tell him, "Ditto, Alexandre. I never felt about them the way I do about you. But you don't know what love really is when you're with someone in the moment, especially when you're young. You're not aware how in love you are until you have someone else to compare it to. If I hadn't been with them, maybe I wouldn't appreciate *you*, now." I think of men I have been with before Alexandre and a nasty memory comes to mind. Which leads me to my next thought:

Jane Doe. We've been so consumed by the Laura drama that I had almost forgotten to ask Alexandre about the mystery money and the charity that he set up.

"By the way, Alexandre, I think there's something you have omitted to tell me."

He looks defensive. "I've bloody told you everything. I'm not holding back secrets about Laura, I swear."

I stroke his earlobe and say, "Tell me about the Jane Doe Foundation."

He nods his head with the faintest smile edging his lips. "Ah, yes. That."

I shoot him a sideways glance. "Yes. That. Where did the money come from?"

"From those fuckwits who nearly ruined your life."

"The footballers?"

"Yup, those fat fucks." His mouth puckers to show his disdain.

"How did you even find them? I mean, *I* don't even know who they are."

"And you never shall. I don't even want you to give them another thought, Pearl. They've had their comeuppance. Well, not exactly – they've been let off lightly, but I hit them where it probably hurts most – in their wallets, and reminded them that violent actions have their consequences."

I snuggle up against Alexandre's chest and snake my hand under his shirt. I feel his steady heart beat and feel at peace. "I don't understand. How did you get them to donate? Types like that rarely turn out to be saints."

"One of them seemed repentant. He donated quite a bit extra."

I pull my neck back and look him in the eye. "But nobody just goes round doling out that kind of money, even if it is to charity. How did you get them to *do* it?"

He cocks a dark eyebrow. "I made them an offer they couldn't refuse."

I titter nervously. "No, seriously"

"I am being serious." *Serioose.*

"Can I ask how?"

"You can ask, but I won't tell."

"*Don't ask me about my business.* Is that it?"

He gives me a wry, mischievous smile. "Exactly."

The fact that Alexandre has protected me in this roundabout fashion – ensuring money is given to abused girls who deserve safeguarding - warms my soul. God knows what unorthodox method he used, but I feel strangely proud. Perhaps he's right; I don't want to give these men another thought. Knowing that justice has been served is enough. What he has done for me is, in effect, every woman's fantasy. He's stuck up for me. Fought for my rights - for women's rights in general. Showed his solidarity. He has demonstrated the extent of his love with actions, not just words.

"That's the sexiest thing any man has ever done for me."

Funny how words can have an effect. I feel his groin swell against my butt. He's getting hard. Hard as a diamond. I push my ass into him and feel the thick ridge of his erection rub against me through the fabric of his pants in just my perfect spot. He clasps his large hands on my hips and draws me closer, rocking against me, his mouth resting tenderly on the nape of my hairline.

"You beautiful thing, Pearl," he whispers, kissing my neck. "Your skin is as soft as a dove's."

His warm breath makes me shudder; a tingle runs through me like the ring of a tiny, silver bell. Our clothes between us have me imagining - all the more - what will finally happen when he penetrates me again. Yes, I think - I'll feel like a virgin.

He guides my butt up and down his length, and the friction makes my nerve endings converge in a spool of longing, wanting and neediness. I edge my behind up higher, and his fingers walk their way under my silk shirt, up my belly to my breasts. He unhooks my lacey bra so my boobs are free, cups them, groaning a little as they fill his hands.

"So sexy, so full and sensitive, chérie." He flickers his fingertips on my tight nipples, pinching them gently as I continue my slow, steady rub along the seam of his fly opening, the bulge reassuringly, monumentally solid as it pleasures my clit. I can always rely on Alexandre; not once, even when he's been drinking, has he failed me. He's always ready, always turned on, even if all I do is give him a provocative look.

As my ass slaps up and down against him, I'm reminded of Laura's insult, 'fat arse' (with an R) and wonder if Alexandre sees me that way. I don't think so – he's forever telling me what a gorgeous behind I have. I lean forward so my clit is getting the full-on massage it craves, even though the finest, merino wool of his expensive suit fabric is between us. My lids start fluttering, my core tightens – I'm entering the seventh heaven zone, the zone where my mind blanks out, and colors and stars have me concentrating on nothing but my impending orgasm. Alexandre lifts my hair away from my neck and kisses me there again, tweaking the nubs of my sensitive nipples at the same time. I keep grinding against his solid form, turned on, even more, by his promises.

"You know how I'm going to fuck you on our wedding night,

don't you, baby? I'm going to stretch that little pearlette open and fuck you so deep and slow, fill you up, chérie, fill up your Tight. Little. Pussy. I'll have to fuck you hard. I'll have to ravage you a bit, though; I won't be able to resist. I want you coming all around my stiff cock. I love it when you cry out my name."

My hips buck backward as he tilts his groin even more firmly up against me. I close my eyes. The image of him deep inside me has me revved up, and one last push against my clit makes my core spasm and has me coming in a rush of relief. I still myself as rippling waves shimmy through my center. I can hear my quiet moans tremble through my body.

"Alexandre...oh God, you've done it again."

"That's right baby, your body needs this - it's healthy for you. I love the way you whimper when you come for me."

His fingers are still tweaking my nipples so the aftershocks linger on; my moans fading slowly as I come down from my climax.

I let myself bask in the glory of my orgasm and after a while, I climb off his lap and kneel on the floor, dipping my head in his crotch.

He lifts my face up and looks into my hungry eyes. "You don't need to do that, chérie."

"Oh, but I want to." His erection is tight up against his pants. I unbutton them, letting my fingers linger on the fine, smooth fabric, and free him from his entrapment. "Raise your butt up," I order, and he lifts himself an inch so that I can pull the tailored pants free. I roll them carefully down his thighs. I bury my head in his crotch and smell the unique Alexandre elixir mixed with a sweet whiff of lavender, and Marseille soap powder from his freshly laundered boxer briefs.

His fingers tangle in my hair and he flexes his hips forward and groans. "Fuck, you make me hard."

I don't take off his underwear – not yet anyway. I nibble my teeth gently along the solidity of his length, nipping him through the soft, combed cotton.

His hands clasp my head and I know he's hot for me. His cock flexes as if it's a separate entity; a creature that's alive. Alexandre leans back languidly in his leather chair and I look up at him from under my lashes. His stomach is taut and faintly tanned and I lick that smooth fine line of hair that reaches from his belly button down to his core.

My God, he's gorgeous. I mean, *gorgeous*. Is there any movie star who can compete with his looks? Any rock star? Anyone at all? Not for me, anyway. Cary Grant is dead, so are Paul Newman and James Dean. Alexandre isn't like other modern men. He is *beyond*. He has the kind of charisma Hollywood actors used to have. Mysterious. Brooding. Just a look from him could weaken a nun. Never in my life had I imagined I would be attracted to a man so much younger than myself, yet here I am relishing the anticipation as I am about to go down on him.

"If you'd had an outie that would have been a deal breaker," I tell him with a naughty smile.

"An outie? What's that?"

"An innie or an outie – the way your belly-button is. I'm not a fan of outies – yours is perfect."

"Lucky, then."

"Very lucky."

I pull his boxer briefs carefully over his massive erection and wonder how other men must feel if they catch a glimpse of Alexandre – even 'resting' he's extremely well endowed. Love is like snow, you never know how many inches you're going to get. And I've lucked out.

He edges his butt up a fraction and I roll the boxer briefs down, taking my time. Eye candy. Deeelicious. I'm savoring every second of this sweet treat I'm about to devour.

I lean up and nuzzle my head against his strong chest. His torso's not 'pumped' like some men who work out. No, his is an integral strength, the muscles taut and lean but not bulky. I breathe in his scent, stroking my nose along his pecs. His nipples are firm and flat – I lick one, flickering my tongue around, sucking on it hard until he groans quietly. His erection flexes and he bucks his hips up a touch, as if that part of his anatomy is saying, 'me too'.

Don't worry, I think – you next, you perfect specimen. I'm still on my knees and I dip my head further south, tracing my tongue down his taut stomach, then taking his crown gently between my lips, nipping the satiny crest with just my pursed lips, no teeth, pulling and tightening them around the smooth head of his proud penis. A whimper of pleasure escapes my throat and I take it all in now, as much as I possibly can, holding the root of his shaft with my tightened fist, controlling it so I don't gag with his size.

Alexandre growls quietly. "Fuck, Pearl. You're incredible."

His words spur me on. I feel the pulse of my clit – knowing I'm driving him wild is my aphrodisiac. This is all about him now. This is my gift. I hollow my cheeks to create suction and move my head up and down along his thick length. My golden hair is falling over his stomach and he brushes it away from my face so he can see me work on him, as he bites his lower lip with pleasure.

"Nobody has ever given me such a good…oh fuck, Pearl baby, you're the best...oh fuck...I love this so fucking much."

'Baby you're the best.' I think of *The Spy Who Loved Me.... Nobody does it better...Just keep it comin'...*

One hand of his is gripping the nape of my neck and the other clawing the chair. He's driving his hips upwards to meet my actions and he's moaning now, almost scowling. I flicker my tongue on the end of his crown and then suck hard back down. That's it - he bursts inside my mouth in a hot rush, emptying himself with a cry.

"Oh baby, can't get enough of you." His hands are on my breasts again, kneading them, cupping them. I suck harder, making sure I have all of his cum, every last drop.

His hard buttocks relax their tension and his climax is spent. A rumbling growl of contentment escapes his throat; low and satisfied. "Thank you, baby, for making me forget," he says. "And making me remember how insanely in love I am with you."

He then gives one last, unexpected thrust and another rush spurts into my mouth. I suck it all in, relishing him. I rim my tongue around the top to wash him clean, kiss him there, then lick my lips like a lioness savoring her prey, satisfied at a 'job' well done. Alexandre's sperm is mine, and mine alone. No other woman in the world is getting any.

His semen belongs to *me*, I think greedily – to swallow, to smear on my tits, to lavish between my thighs and all the way inside me.

That bitch, Laura, isn't getting one single drop.

11

Alexandre announced yesterday that we're going to Paris to visit his mother. I was worried about flying but I am past eight weeks, the most vulnerable period for clots or unforeseen problems and my gynecologist has given me the green light. I even rang the Indian doctor to double check and she confirmed it was okay, but to drink plenty of fluids and not sit in my seat without moving for too long a period. We'll be flying by private jet, anyway, so the stress factor will be almost nil. Call me a carbon footprint culprit, I am.

However, my guilt is alleviated as our plane will be full. We are taking a posse of people with us. Daisy and Amy, and some underprivileged twelve year-old girls from the Bronx, along with two of their teachers with whom Daisy has been working. They are planning a sightseeing trip; Alexandre is paying for everything; the accommodation and all expenses. Five days.

That's one of the things I love about him so much. He shares his wealth. He believes in waving magic wands for people – one kind gesture, one experience of a lifetime for a child could change their outlook on the world, forever. That's what he believes, and I agree. Yes, we could both be sitting in our private jet (did I say 'our'??) sipping champagne and feeling gloriously glamorous, but giving something back is the biggest buzz of all. It may be chaos, though, eight kids (nine, including Amy) screaming and squealing with excitement. The Eiffel Tower, Montmartre, Notre Dame, The Louvre, La Place Vendôme (where my beautiful pearl necklace came from), and all the other delights and secrets of that magnificent city; whatever we can squeeze into five days.

I never have been to Paris. When I was a child, we went to the South of France, traveling from Italy by train and then back to Rome again where we were based. I imagine that everybody should visit Paris at some time in their lives; I hope it will be as splendid as people say.

While I'm in Paris, Alexandre will go to London to visit the dreaded Laura. They've spoken a couple of times on the phone, arguing, mostly. He has been trying to dissuade her, meanwhile, also trying to come up with some kind of plan in his head. She's adamant – she wants him to go to London and produce his seed for her, no matter what. He even told her that he feared he had a recessive genetic disease or sickle cell anemia - anything to try and put her off - but she's not buying it.

I feel powerless; all I can do is watch the show unravel. Perhaps a double bill. I'm on tender hooks.

Anyway, Alexandre has managed to not commit himself to any promise. One thing I've learned about him is that he doesn't like lying and he is, ostensibly, honorable. Okay, he may not disclose everything, may keep things to himself but, basically, he's an honest person. He's not going to promise Laura something and double cross her; it simply isn't his style. All those times I had accused him in my head of being untruthful when, in fact, he wasn't at all. He has never actually lied to me. He may have kept information at bay, but he has never *lied*.

He hasn't told Laura anything concrete, has made no promises except that he'll see her face to face and 'work something out'. He has told *me*, however, that she isn't getting one droplet of his sperm and that I must stop worrying – it's his dilemma and he'll sort it out. I wish I were the type of woman who could sit back and relax, just worry about what shoes I should wear, or what wallpaper to choose. Alas, I can hardly think of anything else except the Laura drama.

I just can't believe anybody would stoop so low, especially someone as proud as she is. I still have this vision of her standing at her front door like some glorious ship's figurehead in her blue satin robe, pretending that she'd had afternoon sex with Alexandre. Like a fool, I was gullible enough to believe her. The other day, I asked Sophie about the phone call (when Laura chatted away to her in perfect French when I was sitting right there in her living room). Sophie laughed and said that Laura must have been talking to the speaking clock. '*At the third stroke the time will be…*' Or perhaps, she said, she programmed a call to come through to herself from her cell phone. Whatever, Sophie said they hadn't spoken.

There is no doubt that Laura is a clever, scheming woman and, as she said herself, like a Rottweiler with a bone. I really don't want my fingers chewed off, but at the same time, how dare she get away with any of it? It just wouldn't be fair. Finally, at age forty, I have found love and have the chance to start a family and

Laura comes along with her bacteria-laden, wooden spoon to stir it all up. If Alexandre doesn't manage to get rid of her, I will. I need to think of Plan B.

I wonder if her nature wasn't always like that, and Alexandre was too young, too sweet to see her true colors. I find it hard to believe that she has become this way from the accident or from medication. Her conniving demeanor suits her a little too well – she looks too comfortable in her own skin.

Meanwhile, James is still missing in action. Laura has told Alexandre 'he's taking a holiday'. I know I seem like some foolish amateur super-sleuth (not so super) but Laura was convinced that Alexandre would get back together with her – perhaps James was in the way? If she's capable of blackmail…what else could she do?

My suitcase is packed. What to wear? I have visions of sophisticated Parisian women tottering about in Christian Louboutins with chic haircuts, but Alexandre tells me that I may be disappointed, that Parisians are no more glamorous than anybody else.

There are so many paintings I want to see in 'the flesh'; the *Mona Lisa, Venus de Milo*, just for starters. So many pastries I need to sample, so many…of everything, I'm feeling giddy with nerves.

Alexandre and I are set up at the George V, one of Paris's most opulent hotels. It describes itself as 'located just steps from the Champs-Elysées, with private terraces that command all of Paris, lovingly restored 18th-century tapestries, and a defining spirit of

elegance and charm, Four Seasons Hotel George V, Paris rede-
fines luxury in the City of Light.'

Every word is true. He couldn't have picked a more stunning
place.

So far, I am wandering around with flutters in my stomach,
not so different from the first time I set eyes on Alexandre. The
hotel, in itself, is a feast for the senses, let alone the rest of Paris.
We are staying in the Presidential Suite – I dare not even imagine
the cost, but Alexandre has insisted that I experience Paris in all
its glory.

He didn't care to stay with his mother, as he wants us to be
completely free and not feel obliged to hang out with them if we
don't want to. I have mixed emotions about meeting her; I can't
shake off the fact that she is a *murderess*. I am partly in awe that
she had the guts to go through with it, but also horrified. Surely,
there could have been another way? Why couldn't she have
escaped in the dead of night and hidden in a small village in
South America somewhere? But murder? I look forward to
meeting her, with both trepidation and wonder.

Daisy insisted on staying with the group. Alexandre has rented an apartment for them, replete with kitchen and plenty of
room for everyone to run about and make a mess. The girls have
all been rendered speechless and are less wild than I had imagined; a lot of them never having left New York, let alone visit
another country. One of them asked if French Fries came from
France – a good question and it made me laugh. Although we'll
be spending time with them, I am primarily here to be with
Alexandre and meet his family, except for when he goes to
London.

This evening, Alexandre and I will be alone for a romantic

dinner. As we walk into the foyer, a smell of flowers invades my nostrils – the floral arrangement of purple orchids is breathtaking. Bunches of blue hydrangeas, orchids and delphiniums are balanced on the edge of tall vases. Red dahlias are used sparingly for contrast. Indigo-blue, purple, mauve – all theses matching tones complement each other in a harmonious dance of color. I'm in a daze.

"You know why I always pick this place?" Alexandre asks me without waiting for an answer. "Because of the famous flower arrangements here, designed by the florist extraordinaire, Jeff Leatham. I can always be guaranteed to walk into another world when I arrive at the George V. After a tense meeting, it's what I always crave."

"So you never stay at your mother's or with Sophie?"

He hands over his credit card to the concierge. "Not often. I like to be free to do my own thing. Not be beholden to anyone. Besides, here it's all perfect. If I need to borrow an umbrella it's there. The towels are fluffy and plentiful, I can order room service when I want. The suite comes with my own private gym. The spa is relaxing, the massages exquisite – you get the picture."

"You've become a spoiled business man with a penchant for luxury."

"Yes, I'm guilty. Sue me." He gives me a sly wink.

"Bonsoir, monsieur." The concierge rattles away to Alexandre in French while I survey the beautiful surroundings. Our bags have already been whisked away from us, and we're free to meander.

We wander through the lobby to an inner courtyard open to the elements, and I see that these same, stunning orchids in the floral displays have been suspended in the air by seemingly invisible threads, covering the expanse as if they are floating in the air. Instead of a carpet of color, it is like a cloud of color and reminds me of Alexandre's lavender fields at his house in Provence.

When we arrive at our suite, our bags have been delivered ahead of us. It is stunning. The walls are decorated in China blue and white brocade. The place is the size of a generous apartment with two bedrooms, a living room, a dining room, a private gym and three bathrooms. The rooms boast antique, Louis XIV furniture, crystal chandeliers, huge sofas, a dining room table and chairs, and even a marble fireplace overhung with a vast Italian gilt mirror. The master bedroom has sumptuous king-size bed which is majestically backed with swathes of the same blue fabric. The oversized, marble bathroom includes a steam room, sauna, bidet and a private walk-in dressing room, plus a guest powder room, no less. We could have fit Daisy's entire entourage in here but we have it all to ourselves. Really, it seems a shame that we have to leave this hotel for even five minutes. We are in *Paris* - that, in itself is enough of a treat - a broom closet would have been enough – but this? This is sinful.

Alexandre is eying me up with amusement. "Don't tell me you're feeling guilty?" He knows me so well – funny how he can read my thoughts just by my expression.

"Not guilty, just…well, this is overwhelming. Just coming for a cocktail to the George V would be enough, but this is—"

"You're not allowed cocktails, chérie."

"Don't I *know* it! Not allowed anything I yearn for."

"Only three more weeks, baby, till your trimester is up, and then you can have what you want most."

The Weapon of Mass Destruction or, as I now see it, the *Tool of*

Creation.

He steps closer and lays his arms about my shoulders, drawing me into him, inhaling me as if I were one of the sweet-smelling floral arrangements.

"You know how much I think about fucking you?" His eyes light up, then narrow into lascivious slits.

"Sometimes you frighten me," I say, the way Little Red Riding Hood might have said to the Big Bad Wolf, while licking his chops.

"I'll go slow, but boy, am I going to do things to you the moment I can."

"You could now," I suggest, gripping the collar of his shirt and pulling him towards me.

"I wouldn't trust myself. Anyway, waiting makes the prize all the sweeter, chérie. I'm a patient man."

His face meets mine and he kisses the corner of my mouth, letting his lips trail even softer kisses along my jaw-line. I tilt my head up and he runs his lips down my neck making little nips as he pulls me tightly to him, as if he never wants to let me go. I feel his erection pressed up against my belly and I part my mouth, my eyes closed.

"You smell so good," he breathes. One of his hands grips my waist and the other caresses my stomach, sketching his fingertips about the curves. "Nice, I can feel that there's life inside of you."

"It's too early to feel a heartbeat though, isn't it?"

"Not a heartbeat, but I feel a little belly growing. Very sexy. There's nothing more erotic than a pregnant woman. Well, a pregnant woman carrying *my* child, anyway."

My jaw suddenly clenches; his words make me remember something extremely unpleasant. "When are you going to London?"

He winces. "I don't want to think about Laura, right now. I just want to enjoy this evening with you and savor every second with the woman I'm in love with."

He parts my lips with his tongue and begins a demanding but slow kiss, probing his tongue inside my mouth and then clasping his teeth gently about my lower lip. A deep growl stirs somewhere deep inside him. He lets go and murmurs, "Sorry, that was a bit rough - you bring out the beast in me, Pearl."

"I bring out the *best* in you," I whisper against his perfect mouth, and then return his kiss, clinching my hands about the back of his neck and pulling his head to mine so there is no space between us. Our tongues begin their erotic tango of tease and pull, tantalizing and coaxing, hot and sensual. I can feel my nipples harden, my stomach pool with desire. I stroke my tongue along his and he moans into my mouth. "I'd do anything for you, chérie. I'd kill for you - I'd do anything to protect you, my precious Pearl."

"Me too," I reply. "I'd do anything. And I swear, I'll never run from you again, no matter what."

"Dance with me."

"I didn't know you liked dancing."

"There are a few things about me you've yet to find out," he tells me in a soft, enigmatic voice. He takes out his iPod and puts on a song a slow, sexy salsa beat, sung in French.

"What's this?"

"*Mon Ami* by Kim. Listen to the lyrics – the words are perfect for us, chérie – they tell our story."

He places his hands around the small of my back and begins to languidly move his hips in time with the music. He presses his thigh in between my legs and keeps up a sweet pressure as he rocks his groin with the rhythm of the beat, leading me about the room in slow circles. He's a great dancer. I relax into him, letting him guide me. My French isn't perfect but I get the gist what Kim is singing about. Mon Ami – my friend. I listen to the words, catching snippets of bits I understand….*nobody can separate us….I'd do anything for us…I would do anything for you… …I'll be there for you…you need me…you can count on me…only you can enter my secret garden…I want to share everything with you…the good and the bad.*

True, this song was written for us.

"What else are you hiding from me?" I whisper into his hair.

"I'm a black-belt in Taekwondo."

Ripples of excitement shimmer through me. There is nothing sexier that a trained killer who knows how to control himself. "That figures. I always wondered where those thigh muscles came from," I say, pressing myself even harder against his leg. Can you break blocks in two?"

"I can break a lot of things in two, chérie," he says, turning me with the rhythm. "I *can* but I usually don't."

"Just so long as you don't break my heart in two."

His lips curve upwards and he turns me again, leaning me back a little. I arch, relishing the sensation as he locks his mouth on my throat, kissing me there, then trailing his lips across my shoulders. I'm wearing a thin, cotton tank top and goose-pimples sprinkle themselves all over my sensitive body. He pulls me close again and nips my earlobe seductively.

"What other secrets have you been hiding from me?" I whisper.

"That I joined la *Légion Etrangère*."

The French Foreign Legion – some of the toughest men in the world. A fighting force designed to make use of prisoners and convicts, offering them a better life, people with no families and nowhere to go – men with criminal records. Nice.

"I thought only madmen joined the French Foreign Legion," I tease.

He sways his hips to the rhythm of the music, cupping my butt and murmurs, "We came from over a hundred and forty different countries. True, some of the men had very dubious pasts and criminal records, but they were some of the most loyal, trustworthy people in the world. They don't let axe murderers sign up any more, though. These days, they do screen recruits but yes, there are some pretty tough characters who join. It offers men a second chance. When you join up you get a new name, a new identity – you become a blank canvas."

"A killing machine," I say.

He laughs and then nibbles my ear. I get that brain-numbing feeling again, but I want to know more about this dark horse who is my husband to-be, so I don't let it distract me, which is obviously his intention. *Geez, how many more secrets does Alexandre Chevalier have?*

"So, how long were you in the French Foreign Legion?"

"You sign up for five years. I was fifteen but I forged my I.D. and managed to fool the recruiting officer. I was there for just under eighteen months when my mother found out where I was and reported them for recruiting someone underage. In the end, I got sent home."

"They didn't realize?"

"I looked older than my years. Maybe they did have an inkling but turned a blind eye, until my mother got on their case. I did well there. I was a force to be reckoned with at that age – I was pretty wild. They wanted me to come back when I was eighteen but I had other interests by that point."

"How come you never told me all this about your past?"

"I'm a businessman now – I left that part of me behind."

I have a feeling it must have been gruesome so that's why he didn't want to tell me - trying to forget. I want to ask him how many men's lives he's taken, but I stop myself. Do I really want to know? Killing obviously runs in his family's blood; makes up his DNA.

I tighten my hold on him, instead, "A businessman, huh? You're my own, private Michael Corleone."

He sniggers. "Is he your secret hero?"

"Al Pacino when he was young playing him. Yes."

"Very…um…what can I say? Quite a ruthless figure."

"He had to be. He had no choice."

"External forces."

"Yes," I agree. "External forces."

"Well, we both know about that, don't we?"

"We do," I reply, nestling my head against the crook of his neck. He smells so good and he is mine. All mine.

The song has ended. My heart's racing from the measured sensuality of our dance; we're united by the lyrics, understanding each other's dark passengers who travel beside each of us – our shadows, our alter egos. I like bad boys, obviously. Anthony was right. Nobody else had been dark enough for me…until I met Alexandre. Perhaps, in another era, in other circumstance, I could have been Bonnie to his Clyde. A fantasy, but one that I can almost taste.

"Dinner?" he asks.

"Yeah, I'm feeling a little hungry." I know he's taking me

downstairs to *Le Cinq* – famous for its delicious cuisine.

"Me too – but I think I'll have a little snack first." His green eyes glimmer with irony.

He lifts up my top, unhooks my bra, pushing it away from my breasts very slowly and deliberately, then begins to suck my nipples, one by one. Our dance has me already turned on, as it is, but this…? My eyelids are doing their fluttering thing which means I'm entering the zone…oh my…. He holds my body steady as he feeds on me like a vampire - pressing that strong, Taekwondo thigh tight between my legs. I'm on fire. The dance was a prelude…making me desirous for more. Lately, I keep wanting more…oh wow…his sucking feels incredible. His soft hair is tickling my skin, my nipples might as well be my vagina, itself. I feel so turned on. This is numbing my brain…turning me into a sex zombie…oh my God…oh wow… he's feeding on me and it feels…out of this freakin' world. The next thing I'm aware of, in my semi state of unconsciousness, is a rippling orgasm pushing its way through my hot, moist kernel crashing in a giant wave. I cling to him and moan out his name.

"Alexandre….oh Jesus….aaah."

He stops suckling and just flickers his tongue against my nipple as I float down slowly from my pedestal amidst the clouds.

Déjà-vu all over again.

12

The next morning, Alexandre decides that the best way for me to get a feel of Paris is for us to just amble about and avoid the teeming tourist spots. He tells me that Paris is a *feeling*, not just a city. Interesting.

He's already dressed in jeans and a black T-shirt and I'm lounging in bed, propped up with a sinful amount of down pillows like a princess in a vast, sumptuous throne. We're enjoying a huge spread of breakfast, devouring mouth-watering *patisseries* – breakfast in bed. Half of me doesn't want to leave our suite, ever. I've had a long lie-in this morning and feel well rested.

This pregnancy is definitely making me tired. Luckily, I have only had a little morning sickness but the idea of rushing about the city, cramming in every sight is exhausting me just thinking about it.

"Don't worry, chérie, the best of Paris isn't very big. We don't have to go anywhere in particular. And if you get tired, we'll hail a cab."

I take a long sip of freshly squeezed orange juice. "I'll be fine; I'm not some fragile egg that will break."

"I don't want to take any chances. Daisy and her entourage have already set off – they'll be chomping at the bit."

"She called?" I still don't use a cell phone so Alexandre is taking all my calls. I feel as if I have some extremely handsome PA.

"I told her you were mine today and that I didn't want to share you."

"Oh."

"She insists, anyway, that we have our romantic break together, that you get plenty of shut-eye and she won't hear of coming along and disturbing the peace with nine unruly children."

"They were being so jaw-droppingly quiet yesterday, though. They were going about open–mouthed in total awe."

"Not anymore – they're rampaging through the streets of Paris. Last night, they took a boat trip on the Seine and today it's the Eiffel Tower followed by the Louvre."

I sink back again into the plumped-up pillows, secretly not wanting to go anywhere. "And what about us?"

"I'm tempted to keep you here as my hostage."

"I might be all too willing and not very hostage-like."

He pulls back the drapes and gazes out of the window. "It's sunny out. A rare treat in Paris in winter. We can meander through the Rive Gauche along the river, or just pass by La Place de La Concorde and through Le Jardin des Tuileries. Then I thought we could have lunch with my mother."

My stomach flips. I'd momentarily forgotten about his mother – *the murderess*. Maybe she'll hate me, the way Sophie did at the beginning. I say nothing and smile. "How lovely."

"Don't be nervous, chérie, she won't bite."

"You can tell I'm nervous?"

"Yes, Pearl. I usually know what you're feeling; you're not very good at hiding your emotions." His crooked smile edges across his face and his eyes crinkle with mirth.

"I amuse you, Monsieur Chevalier?"

"Yes, you do. You make me laugh. The first time I met you, you told me that you were into classic TV shows like *I Love Lucy* and *Bewitched*. I knew, right then, that you had a silly, self-depreciating sense of humor and that you were someone who didn't take herself too seriously. I thought that was very brave of you to lay your cards on the table, like that, when it was obvious you liked me."

"I was trying to play it cool. I felt like a total idiot afterwards, I can tell you. Thought I'd blown my chances."

He comes and sits at the edge of the bed. He's been up and dressed for hours. I'm still naked, wearing nothing but Chanel N° 5, bathing in the luxurious zillion-count sheets.

He strokes my face with the back of his fingers. "You're not afraid to show your girlish side – that's unusual. You'll make a great mother, Pearl."

"You think so?"

"I know so."

"What? Because I act like a little girl, myself? Connect so well to my inner child?" I joke.

"Don't laugh. People spend years of therapy trying to achieve that."

I sigh. "Therapy…that's something I've never even dared try. I really should have seen someone after my nightmares about the rape but…I guess I was too chicken. I use swimming to let it all out, instead."

He pouts and blows his mouth the way the French do when they're discussing politics or something important (food, sometimes), and says, "We're all fucked up, one way or another. At least you and I are in this together. We make a good dysfunctional team."

I giggle. "You're right, we've met our match, the pair of us." My eyes stray from his intense gaze to the classic paintings in the room and the elaborate décor and I say, almost in a trance, "You know, some people assume you have everything all neatly worked out as you get older. It's true that you become a bit wiser, yet I'm still the same person inside as when I was seven years old. Certain things never change. You can put on make-up and heels. You can have a kick-ass job, but if you're a sensitive soul you're still a child inside, no matter how hard you try to hide it."

I think back to our meeting in the coffee shop and add, "You saw my girlish side but you were meant to find me sophisticated and *glamorous*, Alexandre, and the height of…. *je ne sais quoi*. I was wearing a suit!"

"The suit didn't fool me – which, by the way - I wanted to rip off the second I saw you and get my hands on that sexy ass underneath." He puts his warm hand under the bed clothes and gives me a little pinch on my butt.

"You don't think my ass is too big?"

"Why do women always ask that question?"

"Ah, caught you! Avoidance. You don't want to answer. So you *do* think I have a big butt."

He laughs. "There should be a Barbie doll with a wind up key that says," (imitating a robotic, high-pitched squeak), " 'Do you think my butt looks big in these jeans?' Your ass is perfect, Pearl.

189

And you *know* it."

I want to say, *Laura doesn't think so,* but I stop myself. I don't want thoughts of that witch to spoil my reverie in Paris.

"What else did you think of me when we met?" I ask, waving my fishing hook about.

"In English, when you're describing something or someone really special you have that expression, 'gem'. Like, when I bought my apartment, the real estate agent described it as a 'real gem'. Well, in France we say a 'rare pearl.' So when I met you and you told me that your name was Pearl, it confirmed everything."

"What did it confirm?"

"That I wanted you. I decided, then and there, that I must have you." He winks at me and runs his finger along my neck.

"You were subtle about it, though. Pretty slow."

"Buying a woman a string of Art Deco pearls after you've only been on one date together is subtle?"

"No, you're right – that was pretty intense but…well…you didn't jump my bones straight away – you wouldn't even come in for a night cap – a knight cap," I say (pun on the word knight - his last name, Chevalier, ha ha ha).

"The 'wham bam, thank you ma'am' method isn't my style, Pearl. I knew you needed time. Needed to be wooed gently. I had a sense that you were damaged and vulnerable on the inside but fancied yourself as some tough-nut New Yorker. I wasn't mistaken."

"I *am* a tough-nut New Yorker! You should see me doing deals – I can be mean."

He presses his lips to my nose. "You can pretend to be mean but you don't have a mean bone in your body."

"I can be a bitch, trust me."

He laughs. "You and Sophie have a lot in common, funnily enough."

"Will Sophie be at lunch today?"

"If she is, she'll only be there to see us. As I said, she doesn't visit my mother so often."

"I guess I'd better get out of bed. What should I wear?"

"Sneakers, as we'll be walking. Jeans. You really don't need to make an effort."

"Are you sure? Your mother's Parisian."

"Actually, she's not. She's originally from the Alsace region in the east."

"German stock."

"Yes, well, many Germans like to think of that region as theirs, still. After all, that part of the world did once belong to them."

"So that's where you get your height from? And your penchant for be organized and making lists," I tease.

His lips curve slightly. "Amongst other things."

"What other things?"

"Ah, that would be telling. You'll have the rest of your life to find out."

"What? You have *more* secrets? I thought you'd told me everything!"

"It would be a bit dull if you knew *everything* about me, wouldn't it?"

"Something tells me, Alexandre Chevalier, that life with you will never be dull."

The sky is mostly blue and clear but the air crisp. I pull up the collar of my coat and link my arm tightly with Alexandre's. I don't say much as everywhere I turn there is some spectacular building saying 'look at me, how proud and stunning I am' and I amble along in a daze. Paris does not disappoint but it's hard to put it into words – Alexandre is right, it's a feeling. A feeling of majesty, grandeur and pride.

We come across the *Grand Palais*, a magnificent *Belle Epoque* landmark and museum with Greek-style columns and a glimmering, glass domed roof supported by heavy cast iron beneath. It looms ahead of us. The *Petit Palais* is nearby, arranged around a courtyard and garden – manicured and laid out symmetrically. I see that Paris is highly structured, nothing left to chance, nothing abandoned, at least, not here, where everything is neat and tended. The buildings face a beautiful arched bridge that crosses the Seine, the artery of Paris.

"That's my bridge," Alexandre tells me with a wink.

"Because it's so beautiful?"

"No, because it's named after me," he jokes. "It's called Alexandre III."

We cross the road and saunter towards it. At either end of the bridge are high stone columns topped with gilded, winged horses overlooking the river as if they are guarding the bridge. The whole way along the sides of the bridge, itself, are cherubs and ornate Art Deco lamps with globes of hand blown glass. Everything is in such tip-top condition, it feels like going back in time a hundred years ago. No filth or soot coats the surrounding buildings or bridge, despite the traffic. No, everything gleams and twinkles as if invisible hands were polishing the stone edifices and as if the horse statues had been gilded with gold-leaf, just last week. Alexandre tells me that it was all restored a few years ago, that the gold is real. I marvel, wondering if this would all still be in one piece if it were New York City. The Parisians must have real respect for their treasures, although he tells me the outskirts of the city are a different story with graffiti everywhere and tower blocks.

We make our way to the middle of the bridge. Behind, in the distance, is the Eiffel Tower and ahead the Seine meanders its way under more elegant bridges. There are some moored boats and barges below. The river swirls in little eddies and I instinctively clutch my belly knowing that there is life inside me; blood and fluids ebbing and flowing through my body just like the river, giving life to this newcomer – our baby. I lean over the bridge and stare into the water below, wondering what our child will be like, and grateful that I have Alexandre back in my life - that I won't be venturing into parenthood alone.

He notices my hand spread across my stomach and asks me, "Was everything okay with your last check-up?"

"It all looked great; the ultrasound shows a tiny beating heart. Just over two more weeks until the trimester is done and then I'll feel completely safe."

He lays his large hand on top of mine. "You'll be fine – it's meant to be."

Paris is one big superlative. Everywhere are tree-lined avenues and stunning historic buildings. I can see that it would take years to do this city justice. We meander slowly back, past the *Petit Palais* towards the *Place de la Concorde*. What I had imagined to be a quaint square is massive, boasting a towering obelisk in the middle, flanked by two grandiose fountains and more historic buildings at one end.

A frisson of excitement runs up my spine. The awesome beauty and wonder of the architecture against the icy blue of the sky, and the way the square is ideally situated so that you see the most magnificent monuments of the city, including the Arc de Triomphe, the Champs Elysees, the Alexandre III Bridge, the Grand Palais, the Assemblée Nationale, the Tuilleries Gardens, and the Eiffel Tower, all at once, is a testament to how clever the design is. Looking at my little map, my eyes scan all around to find my bearings, even though I don't need a map, having Alexandre by my side. I'm your archetypal American tourist with my sneakers and sensible clothes, clutching a map. Just to add to the look, I whip out my camera and take a few snaps. Alexandre stands there, amused and happy that his city is obviously giving me goose bumps and spreading such a huge grin across my face.

A skinny man in glasses rushes up beside us - we look like sitting ducks; the quintessential sightseers, at least I do. He shuffles up next to me and gushes forth in a heavy accent at breakneck speed without stopping for breath:

"It is in this place that was signed on sixth of February 1778 the Treaty of Friendships and Exchanges between King Louis Sixteenth and the thirteen States Independents of America. Benjamin Franklin counted among the signatories representing the United States… Today at the place even where the King Louis Sixteenth was guillotined, is an obelisk offered by the Egyptians. Where many people came to see falling down the heads formerly, come much there today to admire the view of the Champs-Elysées…"

We both laugh when he says, 'Falling down of heads,' and then Alexandre blurts out something in French. The poor man is mortified and scurries off to see if he can nab some other, more bona fide tourists.

"Poor thing wanted to be our guide for the day, I guess," I say. "I forgot that it was you guys who invented the guillotine. Nice touch. So who got beheaded here in this square? I didn't quite catch what that man said."

Alexandre cocks a dark-winged eyebrow at me. "Everybody and his cousin, basically. Marie Antoinette, Louis XVI, Robespierre. They called it la 'Place de la Révolution' in those days. Just in one summer alone, I think it was in 1794, over a thousand people were beheaded here in this square, not to mention the bloodshed going on all over the rest of the country."

"All because of what Marie Antoinette said, 'Let them eat cake' when the people complained there was no bread?"

"Supposedly, she never said that, but that's right – the people were starving and fed up with the unfair tax system and lavish lives of the royalty and aristocracy. Everyone always imagines it was only the peasants that started the Revolution but it was several groups; the intellectuals, the bourgeoisie – even poorer members of the clergy."

I fix my gaze at one of the beautiful stone fountains with mythical bronze figures encircling the basin. In the water below, in the bigger basin, are more characters; their torsos dark bronze, almost black; their mermen and mermaid bottom-halves a beautiful green verdigris, and the fish they hold gilded with gold leaf. Water gushes from the fishes' mouths. Incredible.

Alexandre continues with his history lesson, which is almost drowned out by the sound of gurgling water. "But before all that, things were just as gruesome. Nobility were sometimes entertained by watching convicted criminals being dismembered alive. La Place de la Révolution was payback time when the people punished the nobility for their crimes - not the other way around, as it had always been before."

"My God, France has so much crazy history – enough to make you dizzy," I say as I stare up at yet another sight - the Egyptian obelisk decorated with hieroglyphics - a giant red granite column pointing erect like a rocket to the sky. I smile to myself and think of Alexandre's Weapon of Mass Destruction.

"What are you smirking about?" he asks.

"Nothing, just thinking about what you've been saying."

He's oblivious to my naughty musings and continues with his spiel. "Funnily enough, you lot contributed in some ways to the French Revolution. French troops who served as anti-British mercenaries in America during the American Revolution helped spread revolutionary ideals to the French people."

I laugh. "So you blame us?"

"Didn't you know? The French blame the Americans for everything. I blame you, Pearl."

"For what?"

"For causing a revolution in my heart."

"To have a sexy Frenchman telling me things like that in Paris, itself, is almost sinful."

"I can shut up if you like." He winks at me and a little tremor capsizes my insides. I think of my baby and wonder if he (or she) can feel what I feel; the thrill of absolute love.

I squeeze his hand, glove on glove. "Don't you dare. I want to hear sweet talk for the rest of my life."

Alexandre suddenly envelops his arms about my hips and lifts me into the air, the way my father sometimes did when I was a child. I wrap my legs about him and we kiss. When he sets me down he says, "It feels good, doesn't it, baby, knowing we're getting married? Knowing we share each other's secrets? I've carried such a burden all these years. What my mother did, my abusive past. Now Laura. Thank God it's all out in the open, finally."

I reply, "I know. What a relief."

As unexpected as the lift was, Alexandre's cell rings. It makes us both jump. He fishes it out of his coat pocket, looks at it and connects the call. "Hi Daisy, where are you all? We're kind of slowly making our way to Notre Dame – very slowly, walking and talking about charming things like decapitated rolling heads and…" He pauses to listen. "You've done all that already? Jesus! Alright, we'll meet for ice cream. We probably won't have one as we're on our way to lunch – well Pearl should, ice-cream is good for her but…perfect. See you there in an hour and a half." He looks at me. "I know it's winter but this ice cream place is very famous." Just as he's putting his phone back in his pocket, it rings again. "Daisy?" But his smile quickly vanishes - a dusky cloud sweeps across his face.

"Who is it?" I mouth, fearing I already know the answer.

Alexandre's lips twitch with a mixture of sadness and anger. "Look, Laura, just calm down." He says nothing, just rolls his eyes. I can hear her screaming through the line, although what she's saying isn't clear. "I can't alright, I have commitments," he says through gritted teeth, his jaw clenched.

I look up at him expectantly, terrified Laura's going to steal him from me – steal our happiness away like the thief she is.

"I told you, I can't fucking well come right now. I have a meeting, I have—" he bites his lip, closes his lids and lets out a menaced groan. She has obviously slammed the receiver down on him. When he opens his eyes again, the green of his irises shine like wet moss. He shoots me an apologetic glance and says, "If I don't go now, she's going to do something crazy. She's going nuts."

"What about lunch with your mother?"

"You'll have to go on ahead without me."

"No way, Alexandre. No. I want to meet your mom with you there."

"Okay, I understand. Well, we'll just have to postpone it, then, and go when I return."

"When will you be back?"

He rakes his hands furiously through his hair. "As soon as I fucking can. Jesus, this bitch is ruining our lives - I could fucking kill her!"

"You mean, you're going to just leave, right now?"

"I have no choice. You could come with me if you like."

"Somehow, I think that might make things worse."

"You're right. If I can get back late tonight, I will. If not, I'll be back tomorrow by midday. I need to sort this shit out, once and for all."

"What are you going to say? Tell her you'll go ahead with the IVF?"

He shakes his head solemnly. "I just don't know."

"Are you going to the airport, right now?"

"That, or the train, which actually might be faster; it's so quick these days - just over two hours. I need to go back to the hotel to get my passport first, just in case I do end up flying. You can get some rest."

"If you're not going to be hanging out at the hotel with me, there's no point. I'll carry on with my walk and meet Daisy, as arranged."

"You're sure?"

"I'm a big girl. This is Paris not South Central LA."

"Well, if you're sure. You can't go wrong and you've got your map." He points left. "Go through the park, Le Jardin des Tuileries – you'll hit the Louvre – then head across one of the bridges to Isle St-Louis. The ice cream place is famous, it's called Berthillon Glacier. The little island next to it, Ile de la Cité, is right where Notre Dame is. Here, take this." He stuffs a massive wad of Euro notes in my hand and a credit card. "My code is 1492 – Fourteen ninety-two, Columbus sailed the ocean blue. You can withdraw as much cash as you need or punch in that code when you buy things. Treat yourself to whatever you want; go on a spree."

"Don't be silly, Alexandre, I have money."

He widens his eyes as if to say, 'don't argue' and holds me tight against his chest. "I love you, Pearl. Have fun today. Don't exhaust yourself. Just jump in a cab if you get tired. I'll call you at the hotel later."

"I don't have a cell phone, remember."

"I know. But you can call me any time from the hotel and I think you should stay in tonight anyway, and take it easy."

"I will, I'll order room service. I mean, hello, how much punishment is it to slob out in one of the most beautiful hotels in the world?"

"Get Daisy and Amy over – they can spend the night; we might as well make use of that big suite."

"Good idea." I look square into his eyes which are flickering with fear. I have never seen him look that way. Ever. "I love you, Alexandre. Good luck with 'you know who.' I'll support whatever you decide."

"Thanks. I needed to hear that. Although, what that decision will be, I haven't the faintest fucking idea." He gives me a weak smile then hugs me again. We kiss but the kiss isn't romantic. How can it be with Laura as good as standing, right there, between us? He turns on his heel to go and we both look back several times, hardly bearing to let go of each other, even for one second, let alone the whole night.

13

Laura is infiltrating my mind, polluting the beauty I see about me like toxic waste in a meadow. Ten minutes ago, the world was awash with perfection but sank instantly with one jarring phone call.

The Tuileries Gardens are bleak in winter yet breathtakingly beautiful, but I walk along with misty eyes, wishing that Alexandre hadn't been snatched away from me and wondering how in the world he's going to extricate himself from Laura's tangled web. Is it possible that he can convince her to drop this madness? I doubt it. I can't see a way out of this. One thing I have learned about him is his fierce loyalty to his loved ones – he won't let his mother down, of that I'm sure. He feels responsible – had he not gotten involved, those stupid, hip bits and teeth remnants would still be hidden in her attic. It's true; in a sense it is his fault that Laura got her bony hands on it all. But poor man, how could he have envisioned what could have ensued? How could *anybody* have imagined? Not even the script writers for *CSI* could come up with such an insane scenario.

The only good thing about having my eyes on the ground, as I scurry along through the park (to avoid people's stares – I'm crying shamelessly now) – is that I miss stepping in some dog poop right in my path. Yes, I'd heard Paris was famous for that. Just like Laura, it is unexpected; a blight on perfection. The gardens have an air of formality with flower beds set out in a pattern; gravel paths lined with rows of trees, so the dog shit seems incongruous here where everything is in such order. A mess left to be picked up by some innocent bystander, or for someone to tread in and have smeared all over their shoe. I think of Laura again – it is as if the dog shit is a symbol of everything that has gone wrong.

I sit down on a stone bench to pull myself together and get my breath back. Not from the walk, but the torrent of emotions churning around my body, draining me of oxygen. I want my baby to feel serene and peaceful inside me, not all riled up and bubbling with rage. Surely they can feel everything?

I raise my head up to the sky as a cloud lifts with the breeze and the blue is once again revealed. A warm sun is welcome with the biting chill and I let it caress my cold cheeks. That feels so good. I think of our baby, again, and take my iPod out of my Birkin and go through my playlist until I find what I'm looking for – *Here Comes the Sun* by George Harrison. I mustn't dwell on Laura. Just a couple of months ago, I thought I had lost Alexandre for good but our bond is stronger than ever. I have *him* and his baby and that's what counts, no matter what happens with this IVF threat. Alexandre loves me, not Laura. *That* is what I am holding onto right now. And I need to trust him to make the right decision.

"This song's for you, little baby," I tell my belly, smoothing my gloved hand over myself. And it's true; the being inside me *is* the sun. Maybe even the 'son.' I don't care if it's a boy or a girl, I am just grateful, and pray that I'll make it to the first trimester, and there won't be any complications with the birth and that he, or she, will be healthy.

The song has lifted my spirits and I continue walking. I'm feeling positive and hopeful. If Alexandre can manage all the thousands of people who work for him in his multi-billion dollar empire, surely he can handle Laura. I have faith. It *will* work out.

As I wander through the park, I have the sensation that I'm meandering through an open-air museum, and I'm glad for the distraction. There are classical marble sculptures dotted every-where – characters from Greek myths and some modern ones, too. A few people are sitting on metal garden chairs placed along the paths or about the octagonal pond. It seems that it is forbid-den to sit on the grass in this park, even in summer. I watch water spurt out of the pond's fountain but my gaze gets distract-ed by a huge Ferris wheel in the distance with the Louvre in the background.

As I approach, I soak up the pure majesty of the Louvre set like a horseshoe in an expansive courtyard – the space in front giving the facade the added grandeur it merits. The modern glass pyramid (that caused such a stir when it was first erected) seems like a rebellious teenager in contrast to the classical Renaissance of the Louvre - probably the most famous museum in the world, once a royal palace. The vast glass and metal pyramid is sur-rounded by three smaller ones. Being able to see through the pyramid is interesting because it doesn't block out the honey-colored stone of the old Louvre behind. But if I tilt my head, the reflection of clouds gives it a different feel. Do I like the Pyramid? I'm still not sure. There's no doubt in my mind that it's interesting and probably something that needs a lot of mulling over. I could stand here and pontificate all day long.

But I can't, and there's no chance of a visit or I'll be late meeting Daisy. So I continue on my merry way, still humming *Here Comes the Sun* and blanking out my thoughts from any word beginning with L.

I come across a little pedestrian bridge with wooden decking which I realize is the famous *Pont des Arts*. All over the sides are little padlocks clipped to the railings – 'lovelocks' with names of lovers written or engraved on each one. One even says 'Bonnie and Clyde.' Another rusted one, has a pink lipstick mark with scratched-on hearts and the initials B and P at each end. Everlasting, locked love, left in Paris. I wonder how many of these couples are still together. As I am reading some of the messages, a man in a black wool hat tells me, "Zee Pont des Arts used to be one of my favorite bridges, now I can't stand to see it. I bet zaire is some jerk selling padlocks near ze bridge, with little hearts on them. He should be shot."

I turn around, surprised that he's talking to me in English. How does he know I'm not French? Do I look so obviously like a tourist? But then I realize I still have the map in my hand. "Oh, you don't like the padlocks?" I ask. "You don't think it's romantic?"

"Ze Pont des Arts used to be a beautiful, delicate bridge, now it looks like it's covered wiz some kind of metallic disease in zis mindless graffiti rusting on ze padlocks. Zis and ze dog crap everywhere." He gesticulates with his arms in the air and blows out air through his lips.

"Yes, I noticed the dog poop," I reply, and Laura shoots into my mind again. "Well bye, have a nice day. Au revoir," I say, and scurry off in the direction of Notre Dame.

I swing my Reverso watch around to Parisian time and see that I won't have a chance to go inside Notre Dame, itself, or I'll be late for Daisy and her gang. The cathedral looks majestic in its Gothic glory, commanding the ancient Île de la Cité with its flying buttresses and extraordinary gargoyles. It's both a chilling and comforting thought to know that heads once rolled in Paris, yet this great stone building still remains through all that turmoil – more real to us than what was once flesh and blood – people that are now no more than words in a history book.

I know I'll need time to explore Notre Dame to do it justice. I shouldn't be worried – I am marrying a *Frenchman*, for Pete's sake - Paris isn't going anywhere fast, so I shouldn't feel I need to do a whirlwind sightseeing trip all in one day. *Chill out, Pearl.* Take your time.

I pass a man playing Edith Piaff's *Non, Je Ne Regrette Rien* on an accordion, and I think back to the conversation I had with Alexandre in LA about regrets, life and external forces. The evidence he didn't destroy – that's sure to be one of his regrets.

The smell of something deliciously sweet wafts before me, and when I turn the corner, there is a wheeled cart with a knobbly-faced old man selling honeyed almonds. I buy a little bag – the last thing I want is ice-cream right now; it's simply too cold. Honeyed almonds are far more tempting.

When I arrive at the ice cream parlor, I see the posse of exhausted twelve year-olds licking their cones with great concentration. Daisy is in a heated discussion with Mary, one of the teachers, and Amy is looking up adoringly at the eldest child in the group; a girl named Vanessa.

"Daisy!" I shout. Amy rushes over and flings her little arms about my legs.

"Auntie Pearl!" I have been promoted to 'auntie' since Christmas.

"Hi guys, hi Mary, hi Susan – hey girls have you been having fun?" I ask the small crowd. They all start shouting at once, squealing about their adventures and discussing which of the outings has been their favorite, so far.

We chat about how beautiful Paris is, and they relay their activities which have been non-stop since dawn. A bus ride, the Eiffel Tower, Notre Dame – I'm exhausted just listening to it.

Then Daisy mouths to me silently, "Take me away from this, Pearl, I'm wiped out!"

I laugh and whisper, "Do you want to come and hang out in the lap of luxury?"

"Yes, I bloody well do! But just us, not the whole lot 'cause they're too wild and excitable." She turns to Susan and says, "Would you mind if Amy and I go off with Pearl for the rest of the day?"

Susan, a lanky woman with glasses and a Trilby hat (who reminds me of Diane Keaton in *Annie Hall*) replies, "Throwing in the towel already, you lightweight?"

"Yes I am, because I know what's next and I think Amy's a little young for it."

"What have you all got planned?" I ask.

"A bicycle tour around the city with a company called Fat Tire."

"*Tire* being the operative word," I joke.

"We saw them this morning by the Eiffel Tower, it looked really fun," Susan tells me. "Perfect for the girls."

"Wow, you lot are going to know Paris like the back of your hands by the end of this trip. It puts me to shame."

"Shall we get going, then?" Daisy asks eagerly. "Come on Amy, we're going with Pearl back to her hotel."

"Mommy, I want to stay."

Daisy hesitates but then tells her, "No, sweetie, you're still too young. But you'll be back with the big girls tomorrow, all day."

"I hate my age," Amy grumbles to her mother with a pout. "It sucks being five."

"Rubbish. Five is the best age ever. Now come on, or we'll be late for lunch."

Mary, the other teacher on this trip, bustles up to me and says, "Thank you Pearl, you have no idea what this means to the girls - and to us, too. This is an experience of a lifetime." She is the antithesis to Susan and they look like a comic duo. Mary is so round and podgy, all you want to do is squeeze her; next to Susan's towering skinny frame, they could be a female version of Laurel and Hardy.

I smile and reply, "It's not me, but my fiancé. It was his idea. He's the one who organized everything."

"He's so incredibly generous! I mean, our apartment is divine. The spending money he gave us is way too much...I feel...I mean...I don't know how to *repay* that level of kindness, I don't—"

"Just knowing how much fun you're having in France will be payment enough, believe me. He's the kind of person who gets a real kick out of helping people and seeing he can make a small difference."

"I mean, these kids haven't even been out of the Bronx and now one of them is saying she wants to be a pilot, to fly a private jet, one day."

"You see, that's what seeing another slice of life can do," I tell her.

I can tell that Vanessa is Amy's crush. She's an elegant black girl with soulful, sparkling eyes. She bounds up to us and exclaims, "And I'm going to live here in Paris when I grow up, and learn to speak French."

Amy tugs on her mom's coat and asks, "Where are we going for lunch?"

"To the Marais. I'm treating you and Pearl."

"What's the Marais?"

"It's a neighborhood, darling. *Marais* means swamp in French – that's what it was hundreds of years ago. Now it has itty bitty winding streets and lots of galleries, beautiful medieval buildings and amazing boutiques. I'll buy you a present, if you're a good girl."

"I'm always good." Amy looks up at me with her large brown eyes as if to gain an ally and I laugh.

"I'll buy you a gift, too," I whisper, "and maybe you can choose something for each and every one of the girls."

"Cool!"

"See you guys later," Daisy says, linking arms with me and Amy, and pulling us off in the direction of Le Marais.

I wave the group goodbye and I feel relieved that I have a distraction from straying thoughts of Laura and the damage that she's sure to be planning. Let's hope Alexandre can stop her.

How, I don't know, but I'm sure he'll come up with something.

14

Alexandre forced himself to relax against the soft leather of the back seat of the Daimler; anything to ease the tension gathering like sailor's knots in his shoulders. He had Laura on his mind; He was now being driven to her house in Chelsea - she was expecting him.

He and Sophie always used this chauffeur when they came to London; it was so much easier than messing about with diesel-belching taxis with chatty Cockney drivers who wanted to talk about the weather. Not that he was knocking them, no – they were the most knowledgeable taxi drivers of probably any city in the world. They had to pass an exam called The Knowledge, could take you to any tiny corner of London by memory – but still, having a private chauffeur was one of the perks of having money to burn. And it was one of his secret pleasures.

It still felt at odds, that…being so bloody wealthy, yet it was something Alexandre never took for granted. It seemed only yesterday when he was rummaging through his jeans' pockets or picking coins off the floor to scrape up enough money to buy a sandwich or a cup of coffee. Being poor stank, but being rich and not appreciating what you had was worse. That's why he needed to justify that private jet – it made him feel too guilty to swan about the globe in jets without good reason. He felt it was only fair to spread the wealth a bit and share his good fortune. He hoped those Bronx girls were having fun and didn't see it as 'charity,' though. He hated that, being the magnanimous 'do-gooder'. No, it was simply a question of dividing things out, like buying a round of drinks at the pub – a British tradition that he liked. If you had the money, it was your 'round' and if you didn't have enough from your paycheck that week, never mind – you'd do it another day – your mate would pay instead.

Your mate. The pub. That's where he'd met Laura. She was there with a group of friends and they'd started up a conversation. Strange that – as beautiful as Laura was, Alexandre never did have that 'love at first sight' thing with her, the way he did with Pearl. It was more a case of feeling lonely in a new city, a need for companionship. They got talking and then soon started going out to movies together, or art exhibitions. It was a nice change from hanging out with Sophie all the time, and Sophie was in Paris, anyway. He didn't like male company so much, either – it reminded him of *La Légion* and all its madness. When he arrived in London all those years ago, he felt lonely, screwed-up; he needed a friend, wanted some female company, and Laura was right there.

La Légion…a part of his life he'd rather forget. He'd joined up at fifteen, an underage romantic idealist. Death seemed glamorous at the time – even welcome. The French Foreign

Legion was infamous for having one of the highest fatality rates of any modern military. He wanted to be one of the 'chosen ones' - feel that he could stand amongst the world's hardest and not even blink.

There were three types of people who joined La Legion. The men who needed to be there, because they had nothing else, the fly-by-night dreamers, and the complete, fucking lunatics.

He never had been sure which category he fit into best – perhaps a mixture of all three.

Alexandre remembered the eerie words of one guy, an Australian, who said, 'I'll get a second chance at achieving something real, anything, even if it's just a shallow grave.'

Alexandre had seen enough shallow graves for a lifetime; bodies blown to smithereens. La Légion was tougher than any army, any professional fighting force. It was no fucking picnic. If he'd stayed, he would probably be dead by now.

He remembered the march of La Légion; *Le Boudin*. Eighty-eight steps a minute. 88, the magic number, the number of pearls on the Art Deco necklace he gave Pearl. He seemed to be wedded to that lucky number. Eighty-eight.

He now gazed out of the car window, humming the first verse of the marching song to himself:

Nous sommes des dégourdis,
Nous sommes des lascars
Des types pas ordinaires.
Nous avons souvent notre cafard,
Nous sommes des légionnaires.

Translated into English was:

We are crafty.

We are rogues.

We are no ordinary guys.

We've often got our black moods,

For we are Legionnaires.

Their motto was - *Legio Patria Nostra* - The Legion is our home. Thank God he had a real home, now, with Pearl. He had been searching all this time and knew he'd finally found what he was looking for.

An unwelcome image of Laura being pregnant flashed before him. He groaned and felt tension clamp at his jaw. He cursed the day she opened her bee-sting lips and asked him the time. He should have just kept her as a friend, not started fucking her. The truth was, that she was pretty unsexy in bed, anyway; all angles and bones - never letting go – too uptight, too neurotic. He felt bad judging someone like that but fuck, he felt no remorse now, in ripping Laura's personality to pieces – she was proving to be a bitch of the first order. But the worst thing was that she didn't even seem to be aware of what a monster she was being. As if all her demands were 'by the by' – the sort of, 'oh by the way, I need a baby and it has to be yours.' As if her actions wouldn't have consequences for all involved. Had she thought of the child, itself? He doubted it. Doubted Laura would have thought far outside the little box that was her own selfish head.

He'd told Pearl that Laura had become 'doolally' because of the accident, but he was now aware that that wasn't quite true. She had always been self-absorbed - it just didn't seem to matter when he was younger. Telling Pearl that – excusing Laura's behavior - somehow justified having been with Laura in the first place. Modeling hadn't helped her, one bit. Take an egotistical person and shove them into the modeling world, and all it does is magnify the problem. And all that money she'd grown accustomed to with James. She'd become a spoiled brat, used to getting her way.

What a fuck-up! He still didn't know what he was going to say to her. He'd come up with a solution – he'd have to. As much as he had goals and wrote lists, he always played things by instinct. It drove Sophie nuts. Sometimes, he'd go in the opposite direction than planned just before an important business meeting. If he instinctively trusted someone… or the reverse; had a suspicion that someone would double-cross him, a gut feeling, then he might change his course altogether. It had made him a rich man and he wasn't going to change tactics now.

He'd play it by ear. Read Laura by looking into her eyes. Maybe it was all about money and she could be bought off.

He couldn't imagine her as a mother, anyway – surely it was some crazy fantasy of hers? The idea seemed preposterous - the woman could hardly boil an egg. Changing diapers? Forget it – she'd want a 24/7 nanny. Two nannies, in fact, a team of cleaners and God knows what else. He'd talk her out of it. Woo her with cash. Anybody could be bought at a price. Anybody.

Except Pearl, funnily enough. She was the one person he knew who really wasn't motivated by money. He believed that if he lost his whole portfolio, overnight, she wouldn't give a damn. Maybe, she'd even feel relieved.

Oh yes, you could add Elodie to the list. She was even embarrassed by being wealthy; a reaction, no doubt, against her mother – well, Sophie was her step-mother, but it amounted to the same thing. Poor Elodie – such a loner; he wondered if she had ever gone on a real date with a boy. Probably not. She was a nerd, like him, and preferred to stay in and play video games.

Alexandre looked out of the window at Trafalgar Square, home to the landmark, Nelson's Column, proud as ever, guarded by the four, famous lion statues and ridiculous amounts of pigeons. It was erected to celebrate the Battle of Trafalgar, a British naval victory during the Napoleonic wars over France.

It was a pain in the neck being French sometimes; especially in England; he wondered if the two countries would have a love/hate relationship forever. The French had a reputation for being cocky and arrogant and he suspected people saw him that way. Alexandre was fond of London; it was a beautiful city, so he'd asked his driver to take him the scenic route. If it weren't for his impending meeting with Laura he would be enjoying the ride.

His mind shifted to Pearl. His rare pearl. His gem. He missed her already, and it had only been a few hours. It felt great opening up to her the way he had the day before. But it had unlocked so many emotions, and not in a good way. He had never realized the anger he'd silently, and unwittingly, harbored for his mother. It was true – she had abandoned him, her own son at so young an age. But still, he couldn't let her down now, and wouldn't. It was strange the way children could sometimes feel responsibility for their parents. It was common with children of alcoholics, too. His mom had never been a drinker but she had an addictive personality. His father had been her drug and now she relied on Alexandre for emotional support. Not the healthiest of relationships, yet he felt responsible for her happiness, somehow.

Large raindrops, like tears, slid down the glass of the windows as the car crawled along in the traffic. The streets were slick with wet, as usual. When did it not rain in London? The double-decker buses were stopping and starting as people piled in and out of them. It wasn't long ago that Alexandre had been hopping on and off buses; a taxi was a rare treat in those days. He couldn't believe how lucky he'd been with HookedUp - an American Dream if ever there was one – even if he wasn't American.

The Daimler was now cruising through Admiral Arch and along The Mall towards Buckingham Palace where the road was paved in red. He'd like to take Pearl there one day – so many plans, so many things for them to do together. And now there was a baby on the way; it would be fun to watch the Changing of the Guard – children loved that.

Everything was perfect, except for this fucking Laura fiasco.

His buzzing cell jolted him from his rumination and he fished it out of his coat pocket.

"Oui, hallo?" For a moment there, he was in Parisian mode.

The voice was excitable and he recognized it immediately – Anthony.

"Oh Alexandre, I am going crazy with this no cell phone ban thing. I never get to speak to my sister, anymore!"

"She's worried about radiation vibes damaging the fetus."

"So like our hippie parents. Must be the genes. But, of course she's worried, I can totally understand - she's carrying what is going to be the most beautiful baby in the world inside that little stomach of hers. No wonder. I mean, pur-lease. Is she there, by the way?"

"No, she's in Paris and I'm in London."

"Oh my God! No! Alexandre what has she done now – please don't tell me she's leapt out of another bathroom window? What have *you* done? I can't stand the agony of it! Please tell me you two guys are not on some stupid separation thing again."

Alexandre chuckled. "No, not at all. I'm just here on business. Briefly. Pearl's at the hotel. At the George V if you want to call her there this evening. In the Presidential Suite."

"Well, excuse *me* your royal highness, Mr. President."

Alexandre's lips tipped upwards. Anthony always brought a smile to his face, especially recently, since he had changed his tune with Pearl and was being so sweet to her.

Anthony blabbered on, "I'm glad I got you, anyway, because I want to be reassured that your wedding is going ahead as planned and that my sister is not behaving like Lucille Ball or Rachel Green from *Friends*. Is she acting like a grown-up or is she-"

"She's being extremely grown-up," Alexandre interrupted. "Don't worry, everything's going very smoothly with us." *If it weren't for goddam Laura, that would be true.* Alexandre added, "In fact, we're crazy in love with each other, more than ever, so don't worry, Anthony."

Anthony sighed in a sort of sing-song. "Aah, so cute. Well, I'll call her later at the hotel, then. Good luck with your business, Michael."

Did he just say Michael? "Excuse me?"

"I said good luck, Mr. Corleone, with your business meeting."

Alexandre chuckled. "Thanks. I need it."

"Make, whoever it is, an offer they can't refuse."

Anthony's comment made Alexandre freeze for a second. *Make Laura an offer she couldn't refuse?* Tempting.

Very bloody tempting.

The car drew up at James's and Laura's house.

James…where the fuck was he? He hadn't returned one single call.

Alexandre rarely felt nervous but a foreboding feeling suddenly clenched his gut. Laura could be dealt with; why he felt so jumpy, he couldn't explain.

His long fingers gripped the brass doorknocker and he rapped at her black front door. He'd heard, once, that lions for doorknockers were a good idea; it kept the burglars at bay – a subliminal message – 'don't fuck with me'. Laura did have a way of alienating people. She never had been much of a girls' girl. Not like Pearl, who everyone warmed to, straight away.

He waited. No reply. Rain suddenly shot down like cold needles and he'd left his umbrella in the car and told his driver to come back later. He knocked again. Nothing. Where was Mrs. Blake? Fuck Laura. Making him wait like some lackey. Typical. He remembered that he still had his key to the garage; he'd forgotten to give it back.

He set off around to the back towards the mews. He unlocked the side door to the garage. It was empty and seemed sad without his DB5, as if crying out for companionship. If it was true what Laura said about James losing all his money, they'd be selling up soon. Who knew? Maybe the bank already owned the house.

The door to the garden was unlocked.

The grass was long and hadn't been mowed for a while; a sure sign that things with James and Laura had gone downhill. They'd always had a gardener. That meant she'd really want to take Alexandre to the cleaners, big time. That was, if he was able get this crazy baby idea out of her head, and pay her off instead.

He opened the kitchen door and thought how easy it would have been for somebody to break in. It was eerily quiet.

He shouted out. "Laura? Hello? Is anyone home?"

Nothing. Almost silent. Except the tick, tock of an old grand-father clock.

"Hell…o…ooo? Anyone in? Mrs. Blake?"

Just then, Alexandre heard a noise and nearly jumped out of his skin.

15

"To err is human, to loaf is Parisian," Daisy tells me with a rebellious look in her eye. We're lounging on my king-size bed in the Presidential Suite of the George V. Amy is sprawled out on the floor, busy with one of her coloring books. We ladies are drinking champagne (I am allowing myself two sips) and reclining like Marie Antoinette in the lap of luxury.

"To err is human, to loaf is Parisian," I repeat with amusement. "Who said that?"

Daisy sips her champagne. "Victor Hugo."

"The one who wrote *The Hunchback of Notre Dame?*"

"That's the one. What did you think of Notre Dame, Pearl?"

"I didn't have time to go in, just stood there mesmerized by its grandeur, gazing at those crazy gargoyles."

"Well, I have to say, I know it's wicked, and I'm only telling you this, because I know you'll keep it a secret, but I preferred just hanging out with you this afternoon. There's only so much sight-seeing you can do in one day. So glad I escaped." She takes another swig of champagne. "Let's have a butcher's then?" she asks, grabbing one of my shopping bags.

"What did you say?"

"Let's have a look inside that bag."

"No, what was that word you used?"

"Butchers. Butcher's hook. A look. Let's have a butchers. It's Cockney rhyming slang."

"What else can you say?"

"I can hail a sherbet."

"What's that?"

"A sherbet is a cab."

"How does that make sense?"

"Sherbert dab. Cab. Are you going to use the dog, then and call Alexandre?"

"The dog?"

"You're so slow, Pearl. Dog and bone. Phone."

"So you use the first word, but not the second?"

"Exactly, or it's too obvious. It was invented, or evolved, rather, to confuse people. Like a private language so nobody knew what they were talking about."

"So Cockneys are Londoners?"

"All Cockneys are Londoners but not all Londoners are Cockneys. I mean, I'm a Londoner but I'm hardly Cockney. I speak the Queen's English."

"So what makes someone a true Cockney, apart from their accent?"

"You have to be have been born within the sound of the Bow Bells; a church called St. Mary-le-Bow in the East End of

London. So pick up the dog, then, Pearl. The dog and bone – pick up the phone. You've been itching to call him all day."

"You're right, I have."

This is so awkward. I'm dying to divulge all to Daisy but of course, I can't. If I tell her about Laura's blackmail she'll want to know the whole story, and I'm sworn to secrecy. She knows Alexandre is in London but I've told her he's on business and just had to drop by Laura's to pick something up. Even that got her suspicious. I realize that it wasn't the best plan, after all, to have her over this evening, although I love hanging out with her. I lean over take a deep breath and grab the receiver of the hotel phone. I dial Alexandre's cell. It rings and rings until his voicemail picks up.

"Why isn't he answering?" I grumble under my breath. I leave a message. "Hey honey, just calling from the hotel. We had a lovely long day having lunch in the Marais, hanging out and shopping. Call me, I'm worried about you." I slowly hang up and look at Daisy. "Just…you know, he had an important business meeting with some new clients."

I hate lying to Daisy. She arches her eyebrows and I feel instantly guilty, as if she can read my mind. I need to ply her with more champagne. All I can think about is what Laura is going to say and do, and what Alexandre's reaction will be. I pour us both another glass.

"Isn't this delicious?" I say, taking a long sip. "I love pink champagne. So girly."

"Yeah, men aren't into it, so much, are they? It *is* a very girly thing. Hey, Pearl, put the dress on you bought."

A little voice pipes up from the carpet. "Yes Auntie Pearl, put that pretty dress on."

"Oh, by the way," and Daisy lowers her voice to an almost inaudible whisper, "Zac has been pushing me to move to Kauai. He says he's falling for me."

"But he hardly knows you."

She's twiddling her red curls between her fingers. When Daisy does that it means she's excited. "I think he's very keen."

I widen my eyes. "Are you going to go for it?"

"I've been checking out schools on the internet, and apartments."

"No?"

"I think I really might go for it."

"Well, the good thing is, if it's all a disaster, my father is there as a safety net."

"I don't know how safe your dad is, Pearl." Daisy cackles. She's pretty tipsy now. Good, it'll keep her off Alexandre's tail.

"What d'you mean?"

"It never rains, it pours."

"He made a move on you, too? What is with my father cherry picking my friends?"

"Not a *move*, exactly, but he did his fair share of flirting. He's bloody handsome, your dad. Very sexy for an older man."

"He's not that old, he's only fifty-eight."

"Exactly. His body! Bloody Norah!"

"You are *attracted* to my father?" I suddenly realize I'm talking too loud. Some smart little somebody might prick up her little pixie ears.

"Talk about *sexy*," hisses Daisy in another hoarse whisper. "Wouldn't mind giving him one on a cold, rainy night."

"Daisy!"

"Just feeling a little horny, that's all. I'm ready for a shag. Not that Johnny and I did it that much but when it's taken away from you, you miss it."

"Why are you two whispering?" Amy squeaks. "You told me it was rude to whisper, Mommy."

Daisy bursts out laughing. "So I did. So I did. You are absolutely right, Amy. I must not whisper!" She's slurring her words now and I know that they'll have to spend the night. Fine. This suite has an extra bedroom with en-suite bathroom.

She stretches her legs out on the bed and plumps up a couple of massive cushions behind her head. She lets out a sigh. "This is the life. You've really lucked out, Pearl. What a blast to be chilling out in hotels like this for the rest of your life. You'll never, ever, have to worry about paying a bill, ever again. Never have to do the washing up. Can drink pink champagne every bloody day of the week. What a laugh!"

The hotel phone rings. Thank God. It'll be Alexandre. I grab it eagerly.

"Alexandre?"

"Hello, Pearl?"

It's not Alexandre. It's Elodie.

"Hi Elodie. What's up?" Poor thing can probably detect disappointment in my voice.

"Why didn't you come to lunch today with my grandmother?"

"Alexandre couldn't make it and I didn't want to go alone."

"I was there."

"Oh, I'm sorry I missed you."

"I have so much news. I've applied to go to art school in London and I want to tell you about my maid of honor dress. I went to see Zang Toi for a fitting."

"Great! That's so exciting about art school, Elodie. And I can't wait to see you in the gown. What's it like?" *Ding, dong, it's my wedding, any second now.* Talk about fittings; I'll need my gown let out a little.

"It's so beautiful, oh mon Dieu. It's a Paris Pink, silk mousseline de soie fitted gown with a low draped back, caught with silk roses."

"Wow, it sounds amazing."

"Is the wedding still St. Valentine's Day?"

"Yes, Elodie. It is." I say this with confidence but I'm panicking inside. In fact, I have been so caught up in the Laura drama that I haven't been organizing my own freaking wedding. A good wake up call. I need to get moving. "Would you like to come over to the George V and hang out with us? Daisy and Amy are here."

"I can't, I have a rendezvous."

Elodie on a date! "That's great, Elodie, who's the lucky guy?"

"Nobody. Just a video game online with a bunch of people."

"Oh."

"Well, bye Pearl. Kisses to my uncle."

"Bye." I hang up.

Daisy squeals, "Oh my God! Your wedding! It's the fourteenth? Really? Still in Lapland?"

"Yes, I need to speak to the wedding planner again, but…yes. But hardly any guests. I woke up the other day and suddenly got a headache thinking about hundreds of people who, in reality, probably don't give a damn about us and would just be coming for the party. So we have a private jet booked and it's going to be just family and close friends."

"Am I a close friend? Am I invited?"

"And me!" Amy looks up from her coloring book.

224

"Of course you are, you silly fools. My dad, Anthony and Bruce – if he'll agree to fly. Natalie and her boyfriend-"

"She has a *boyfriend?*"

"A gorgeous hunk; a cross between young versions of Wesley Snipes and Denzel Washington, apparently. A firefighter."

"Very nice."

"I know."

"Who else is coming? Let's see…well, it's all a bit short notice so…oh yes, some old school friends, and then Alexandre's family, his new video game business partner, plus a couple of his old buddies."

"Not Laura, I hope."

"No. Certainly not." I wince. For a few minutes, thinking about my wedding, the dreaded Laura had slipped my mind.

"So I don't understand - *why*, again, is Alexandre going to her house?"

"He, um, he's dropping some books by."

"All those Folio novels she left in Provence?"

"Exactly," I lie. "Another glass?" Quick, I need to top her up before her brain starts working overtime again.

"What about food?"

"Are you hungry already? Shall we order room service?"

Daisy gulps down some more bubbly. "No, I mean wedding food."

"Well, it's Lapland – Finland, so they'll be a mixture of Scandinavian dishes and−"

"Will Santa Claus be at your wedding?" Amy stands up, rushes over, and leaps onto the bed.

"I think he'll be taking a well earned vacation, honey," I reply. "He worked so hard at Christmas; maybe he's by a beach somewhere drinking a cocktail."

Amy's mouth turns into the letter O. "Santa Claus drinks *cocktails?*" Whoops, I wish I hadn't said that.

"Non-alcoholic cocktails." A vision of Santa Claus on the beach flashes through my mind and it's wrong – very wrong. Poor Amy, what have I said? I quickly add. "Actually, no, Santa Claus never goes to the beach; he lives where it's snowy and cold and never leaves because he has to look after his reindeer."

Amy looks relieved. "Are you going to borrow Santa's reindeers for your wedding?"

"Actually, yes – he's lending them to me. Isn't that kind of him? And his sleigh."

"You spoke to *Santa*, himself?"

"Well, no. I don't think many people get to speak to Santa himself. Just his helpers." I suddenly feel terrible. I am outright lying. Is this what grown-ups do? Teach children how to lie – then we tell them how they must be honest with us. No wonder we confuse them – deceit starts early. I am about to bring a baby into the world and teach him or her, not only how to lie, but do it without flinching.

"What's your cake going to be like, Auntie Pearl?"

I gaze at her sweet, heart-shaped face full of innocence and wonder, and my stomach does a little flip. "Well, the traditional French wedding cake is made of chocolate profiteroles piled up into a big cone, like a tower."

Her eyes become pools of chocolaty desire. "Cool."

"And maybe we can have *two* wedding cakes, what do you think? One profiterole one, and a beautiful white one? White like my gown and with pink roses to match Elodie's gown…and you know what?"

"What?" slurs Daisy.

"I can't believe I didn't think of this earlier! Amy should be a bridesmaid. She can match Elodie. I'll speak to Zang Toi, I'm sure he can come up with something incredible for Amy."

"So glad you didn't rope me into being the maid of honor," Daisy murmurs, now half conked out, sprawled like a starfish across the bed.

"Well I did ask you but you didn't want to do it."

"I think a grown woman always looks awkward being a maid of honor. In England, we don't do the maid of honor thing, we have little girl bridesmaids."

"That's what made me suddenly think of Amy – she'd be adorable all in pink. I'll email Zang, right now, and tell him we have a beautiful little bridesmaid to dress."

Amy starts bouncing up and down on the bed, and for a moment, I'm envious. I remember doing that – the feeling of freedom and abandon, flying high underneath my light feet. Oh, to be five once more. "What will my dress be like?" she wants to know.

"I don't know, I'll ask him."

I grab my iPad and send Zang an e-mail which will go directly to his BlackBerry. "He's usually very fast at responding," I tell my eager audience. "So professional."

Then I pick up the hotel phone and call Alexandre again. No reply, just the goddam voicemail. He would have had plenty of time, by now, to sort stuff out with Laura – why isn't he picking up? I leave another message. Five minutes later, a message bleeps in from Zang:

How about a Paris Pink, silk taffeta baby doll, bordered

with pleated tulle & organza & grosgrain ruffles and grosgrain ribbon sash?

Wreath (Hair) and tiny basket of baby ivy and pink roses.

I repeat the message to Amy and Daisy. Amy squeals with delight and gets back to her bed jumping. Daisy rocks about, oblivious in her drunken stupor. I call Alexandre again. Nothing. I mumble to myself…

What the hell is going on?

16

Alexandre and James stood there glaring at each other. Then they both, simultaneously, looked down at Laura. There she was at the bottom of the staircase, a pool of blood about her head. The stairs were wooden, all except for the bottom step, which was made of old granite.

"She must have careened down the stairs like a sled," Alexandre suggested. "Her feet forward and her body slanted backwards, bashing it on the bottom step."

James didn't reply. He bent down for the third time to feel her pulse, but there was no doubt that she was dead. Laura was wearing a crimson, silk satin robe with a sexy negligee underneath. One pretty heeled slipper - the Fredericks of Hollywood kind - was on one foot; the other had obviously skidded across the floor with the fall. She looked all dressed up with a sly touch of rouge on her cheeks and mascara enhancing her almond-shaped, blue eyes, which were wide open in shock, staring up at the ceiling like shiny marbles. She knew Alexandre was coming over; was this her one last effort to seduce him, he wondered?

He surveyed the gruesome scene. It was hard to see where the silk ended and where the blood began; except the blood resembled gloss paint. He'd seen death before, on many occasions, but not like this. Laura's exit had been a glamorous one. Stairs again, thought Alexandre – was that Laura's fate, all along? Maybe she had been destined to die, that time. Maybe that was just a dress rehearsal for this.

"You fucking cunt," spat James. "You sneaky fucking bastard." He laid his palm across her heart. "You killed my wife!"

Alexandre raised his hands in the air as if making a surrendering gesture. "James, no! What are you saying? That's crazy. I *just* got here, at the same time you were coming through the front door. I swear. This is just as much a surprise for me as it is for you."

James looked up at Alexandre; a sneer set on his angular face. His blond hair was a little longer than usual, and he looked less like a banker and more like a regular guy that mowed the lawn on Sundays. Except, he knew that James wasn't the lawn-mowing type. He was wearing corduroy pants and a dark green cashmere sweater. Usually, he wore expensive suits. Not today. But he still had that upper class air about him: his clipped accent, his Eton education – a man who had been used to money and privileges his entire life.

"What I don't understand, is why. *Why*, Alexandre? Did you try to kill her last time, too? When she had that supposed 'accident' and she ended up in a bloody wheelchair? I mean, it's obvious she fell down the stairs. One push, that's all it must have taken. You fucking bastard."

A surge of fury gathered in the pit of Alexandre's stomach. He thought of the evidence in the safety deposit box. Laura dead was all he fucking needed right now. "Okay, James…this is just great. You accusing me of murder? How about I accuse *you*? Where the fuck have you been for the last couple of months? Eh? Suddenly appearing like this. Maybe you *knew* that I was coming over. Laura knew. I called her. Maybe it was really bloody convenient for you to bump her off and then blame me."

"I'm going to call the police," James spluttered, his eyes wet with emotion.

Blood was pounding in Alexandre's ears. He didn't know what to do. The evidence. Laura's note stowed with her lawyer revealing everything if she ever had an accident. What a fucking mess.

James pushed a few strands of Laura's hair from her face. "Laura wouldn't just fall down her own stairs in her own house now, would she?"

"It is possible, she had those heeled slippers on."

"How the fuck did you get in, anyway?"

"Through the back, from the garden," Alexandre replied. "I still have your garage keys."

"That's right - your Aston Martin." James shook his head. "I forgot."

Oh Christ. Now Alexandre would have to admit that no, his Aston Martin wasn't there anymore. He had no excuse, whatsoever for coming through the back. He looked really guilty now. Oh fuck. He'd have to tell the truth; James would soon find out. "Actually, I moved my car a while ago. I knocked on the front door but there was no answer, and Laura didn't pick up the phone. She was expecting me. So I came through the back."

"Nice excuse, Alex. Tell that to Scotland bloody Yard." James took out his cell and dialed 999. Alexandre watched him steadily. His heart was pounding like an out of beat drum but trying to stop James would be suicide. Fuck. This was it now. He saw his life flash before him. He'd heard that happened to people when they drowned; and now both the beautiful and hideous, like snapshots, flew through his mind. His father jabbing him in the butt with a broken bottle. His sister's screams. Riding on the back of a bicycle with his dad, he was smiling and happy – they were going on a picnic in the sun. An IED exploding and blowing off his best friend's head, only missing Alexandre because he'd gone to take a leak around the corner. Pearl's face when he last kissed her when they were dancing. Pearl having an orgasm, her body juddering in ecstasy…

James's voice sounded distant, even though he was right next to him. James was giving them his address. "Yes, that's right, some type of accident but she's definitely dead. I'm here with her ex-boyfriend. Yes, I'm her husband."

Oh God, that sounded just peachy – the ex. The ex who just happened to be the object of Laura's crazy desires. James disconnected the call. Alexandre knelt down beside Laura. Why did he feel so little compassion? She was dead, after all. Flesh and blood. He'd loved her once. Tears prickled his eyes but they weren't for Laura, they were for Pearl. And him. What the fuck was going to happen now? He wanted to get out of there and run, but that would make him look as guilty as sin.

He got up from his haunches and leaned against the wall to steady himself. "Where have you been, James? I've been calling and leaving messages."

"I know."

"Then why the fuck didn't you get back to me?"

James sat down on the bottom step which was still smeared with Laura's blood. He didn't seem to notice. The image was surreal. James sitting by his dead wife, looking vaguely sad, yet with an almost imperceptible gleam of relief flickering in his eyes. Alexandre couldn't read him. Had James killed Laura?

"I was in The Priory," James answered solemnly.

The Priory – the British equivalent to the Betty Ford Clinic. Rehab for celebrities who take too many drugs, stuff their faces with too many cakes. Deals were made there – it was a pretty 'hip' place to end up. Some people exaggerated their problems just so they could say they'd been to The Priory. Sounded cool to some.

"I didn't know you had a problem."

James looked down at the corpse and buried his face in his hands. "Nor did I. Well, I did, but I was in total denial."

"What was your drug of choice?"

James swallowed nervously. "How d'you know it was drugs?"

"I figured. You've never been an excessive drinker."

"Smack."

"Heroin? Really? You could have fooled me. How did you get to work every day? How did you make all that money?"

James didn't flinch when he answered, "Well, most of my money went up my arm."

That made sense. He'd only ever seen James wear long sleeved shirts, hand-made in Jermyn Street. He wasn't a T-shirt kind of guy.

James went on, eager to share. Alexandre noticed that people fresh out of treatment were always keen to tell their story. "I was a very controlled junkie. I had the budget for the high grade shit, you know. But things started spiraling out of control – I lost some money on the stock exchange; the tax men were after me. I needed to clean up my act so I went AWOL. My suitcase is still in the hall. I, literally, just got back five minutes ago. And I found *you* here. And Laura dead."

"So, had you spoken to Laura?" A loaded question. What Alexandre really wanted to know was, *how much do you know?*

"Of course. She told me she wanted to get back with you and that you were still in love with her."

Oh fuck! "And you believed her?"

"Well, yes. Why would she lie about that? It's one of the things that drove me into treatment. She was disgusted by me, and rightly so. I was a fuck-up, a disaster. A junkie. How could I have expected her to live with a man like me? There you were, all sorted out. Making a mint. Good looking. Together. And there was I like a fucking loser, jacking up every day."

Alexandre laid a hand gently on James's shoulder. After all, they'd been friends before. Sort of. "What she said wasn't true. I'm in love with Pearl, my fiancée. I have never wanted Laura back. Ever. You have to believe me, James."

James flinched his shoulder and Alexandre took his hand away. "I don't know what to fucking believe. Here we are, the pair of us, sitting next to a dead woman. My wife. The woman I was in love with. The woman I got clean for. I have a feeling you killed her but, obviously I can't prove it."

"James, you don't seem to be that distraught about Laura lying there dead. I could just as easily suppose *you* killed her."

He looked up at Alexandre, his brows furrowed. "And why the hell would I do that?"

"Jealousy. Rage. Revenge. Or simply to stop her taking you to the cleaners. I don't know – you could have a million reasons."

Alexandre thought of the evidence. Was it possible that it was right here, in the house? He was desperate to check it out before the police arrived. He knew how most women's minds worked; they always kept things of value hidden in their bedrooms. "I'm going upstairs to the bathroom."

"There's a bathroom down here, use that."

"I'd prefer to use the one upstairs."

"Why? So you can do a quick robbery while you're at it? Steal Laura's jewelry?"

"Don't be absurd, James."

"Do what you like, the police will be here any second and you can tell them your bullshit excuses about why you broke into our house." He sat like a stone, not budging from the bottom step.

Alexandre skirted around him and mounted the stairs. At the top, he made a right and followed the corridor all the way to the end. The master bedroom door was open. He entered, and scanned his eyes about the room. He'd been to this house on several occasions over the years, and knew his way around. He could hear sirens from two or three vehicles, outside. He looked out of the window, down onto the street. Two police cars and an ambulance had arrived. There was a frantic knock at the front door and he heard James opening it and talking in muffled tones to the police. The living room was filling up rapidly with more voices and commotion. Alexandre didn't have much time. He looked under the bed – nothing. Laura used to like keeping important things in her closet – letters and personal stuff. He opened the closet door, rummaged through hanging dresses, pants and shirts and he glimpsed something shiny at the back – was it the titanium hip? No, just was a silver sequin jacket.

"What the fuck are you *doing?*" It was James standing behind him. Alexandre spun around. James edged closer, a scowl set on his sharp face as if he was about to lash out.

"Nothing. Sorry," Alexandre replied. But James leapt at him, launching his slim body at Alexandre like a missile, his right fist flailing in the air aiming for his face. Alexandre ducked and clamped James's wrists tightly behind his back. Fighting was the last thing he wanted to do.

A policewoman quickly entered the bedroom, and a policeman rushed from behind, barging her out of the way and diving at the two men locked together; Alexandre was still immobilizing James who was thrashing about like a fish on a hook.

The policeman and another colleague, also pushing his way through the room, shouted out, "I want you two to come with us down to the police station."

James shouted out, "This bastard killed my wife! He broke into my house, uninvited. He must have shoved her down the stairs. They were lovers."

Alexandre shook his head and mumbled, "It's not true." What a fuck-up. He knew, though, that the best course of action was to remain calm and wait for his attorney. He'd call Sophie and get their legal team onto it. He had never needed a criminal lawyer before, but they had a good one on HookedUp's payroll, just in case.

Alexandre was silent. He released James's wrists and put his hands up peacefully. Oh shit. He needed his attorney, and fast.

"He basically broke into my house," offered James, nursing the burns on his wrists and glowering at Alexandre.

The policeman, a pale-faced man in his fifties, eyed both men up and down and said, "Look, there is a dead woman below and I don't have time to play Sherlock Holmes. I want you both down at the station, now, to make a statement and give interviews. I'll want to take DNA swabs – meanwhile, the forensic team will tell us if there's been any foul play."

"I know my rights!" James yelled. "Either arrest me now, or leave me be. You have no right to force me to come down to the station, let alone take any bloody DNA samples! I'll give my statement, right here, in my own house, thank you very much."

Alexandre noticed the policeman's thin lips quiver with rage. James answering back in his pompous Etonian accent, had really got his goat.

The officer, a small and 'important' man, told him, "Alright, so be it. I'm arresting you *both* on suspicion of manslaughter." He puffed up his chest and said in a monotone, "You have the right to remain silent, if you give up this right, anything you say can, and will be used as evidence against you in the court of law. You have the right to…"

The man's voice was a swirl of words spinning about in Alexandre's dazed head. He felt as if someone was smothering him with cotton wool. He tented his fingers in front of his face and mumbled, "This is crazy." But he noticed a sneer on the policeman's lily-white face. Damn. He shouldn't have spoken.

The other officer said, in a broad Cockney accent, "What *are* you? Bloody *foreign* or something?"

Alexandre was aware that he shouldn't have opened his mouth. His French accent would not go down well. At all. The English hated the French, it was common knowledge. *Frogs,* they called them. The French, in return, nicknamed the Brits 'Roast Beef', not because of their national dish, but because of the color their bodies turned in summer as they slumped about Mediterranean beaches sporting agonizing sunburns.

James piped up, "It's him you should be questioning, not me! He broke into my house, I tell you."

Alexandre wanted to defend himself, explain he'd been invited, that the back door was open and he had a key to the garage but he bit his lip. He needed to stay calm, wait for his attorney to be present. He simply shook his head.

"So you don't know this man?" asked the policewoman looking at James.

"Yes, I *do* know him, I told you that, downstairs. He's my wife's ex-boyfriend."

"Is this true, sir?" the Napoleon complex officer asked Alexandre.

"I'd rather wait to give my statement down at the station with my lawyer present, if you don't mind," Alexandre answered quietly. He knew his rights. He couldn't be kept at a police station for more than twenty-four hours without being charged, although this could be extended to thirty-six hours with the authority of a police superintendent, and for up to ninety-six hours with the authority of a magistrate, which is exactly what could happen if they got wind of the whole IVF nonsense. He could hear them downstairs now, probably the forensics team – shit, now he thought about it, traipsing upstairs wasn't such a great idea. His footprints would be all over the staircase, proof that he could have pushed Laura. After all, it wasn't his house. James could have his footprints or fingerprints anywhere, and so what? But Alexandre was another story, altogether. That, plus coming in from the back when nobody was home, did not look good at all.

James cried out, pointing his skinny finger like a weapon at Alexandre, "It's him you should be worried about. He was having a bloody affair with my wife!"

The policeman smirked as if he's made a great discovery, and said to James, "So, sir, that would give you a good motive, wouldn't it?"

"Should I handcuff them, sir?" the female officer asked.

"Look, that really won't be necessary," James blurted out. "This is absurd. This is my bloody house! You think I'm going to kill my own wife? I'm the one who called *you*, for Christ's sake? You think I would have made that phone call if I'd been guilty of murder?"

"Actually, a neighbor called 999 before your call came in," the woman said. "She heard a woman scream."

The officer in charge shot her a poisonous look. She'd obviously said too much. She covered her mouth with her hand in embarrassment.

Laura screamed, did she? Alexandre mused. He didn't think that James was capable of murder, but who knew? His mother had killed - and he hadn't imagined Laura would be capable of blackmail. People did strange things under pressure. Maybe Laura was threatening James in some way, and he needed her out of the picture. It seemed strange that she would fall down the stairs in her own house, even with heeled slippers. It wasn't even dark.

"Look sir, we can either do this peacefully and you come with us nice and quietly down to the station for questioning, or we'll have to cuff you."

It was still very civilized in Britain, Alexandre thought. In the USA, he and James would be on the floor by now, wrists cuffed behind their backs and a gun held to their heads. Yet here, they were politely asking them to come along to the station for questioning. He knew a little about the law in Britain and the way the system worked. His new partner, the one he was starting the video game company with, had once been arrested for dealing marijuana. The police in the UK were able to arrest people much more easily than in the States. American police needed probable cause to make an arrest, but in the United Kingdom, officers could arrest just on suspicion.

Alexandre pushed out his wrists in front of him to show good will.

The police officer said, "That won't be necessary, sir. If you men can both come along with us quietly and do not resist, we won't be needing restraints."

"Sure," Alexandre told him, offering a limp smile. His mind raced back to the possibility of the evidence being in the closet. Damn, he'd like to have one more look but it would cause mayhem. James was already suspicious; Alexandre couldn't draw attention to the closet – not even look at it. He'd have no choice but to be led like a lamb to slaughter to the police station, and call Sophie to get his lawyer there ASAP. Meanwhile, he wouldn't incriminate himself, wouldn't give evidence – he had 'the right to remain silent' and he'd damn well use that right.

"Come along please," the small policeman ordered, ushering James and Alexandre out of the bedroom. Alexandre ambled along peacefully but James, disgusted by the Cockney policeman's hand clamped on his wrist shouted, "Get your hands off me!"

Alexandre knew that things would now get worse.

The Napoleon complex officer stood 'tall' and commanded, "On second thoughts, cuff them both. I really don't want any trouble." He pointed a fat finger at James and hissed, "You, sir, need to calm right down."

"He's upset, sir; his wife's just died," the policewoman suggested to her boss.

"Yes, well. I don't want any monkey business when I'm in charge, thank you very much."

It felt humiliating to be arrested and cuffed. Alexandre's mind traced back to the time when he 'cuffed' Pearl with the string of Art Deco pearls, and wondered if she had felt the same; humiliated. Christ, he hoped not, he hadn't meant it that way. Jesus, how embarrassing, his cock started throbbing just thinking about her naked, her hands above her head, her legs splayed open and bound to his brass bed with his blue silk ties – her pussy soaking wet as he licked and sucked her to her first, ever, oral orgasm. Pearl was all his. No other man had given her such pleasure sexually. He loved going down on her – she tasted so sweet. Shit! He felt himself expanding; it was as if his heartbeat was right between his legs. He knew that Pearl nicknamed it his Weapon of Mass Destruction and she was right – it could bring him to ruin if he wasn't more careful. Thank God he was still wearing his overcoat. Jesus, he had a full hard-on now. How he could possibly have an erection in the middle of being arrested was an enigma to him. Pretty fucked-up to be thinking about sex at a moment like this. He'd heard that when men got hung, they found it erotic. It was known as a 'death erection' and 'angel lust.' He'd read, somewhere, that Christ was depicted by several Renaissance artists with a post-mortem erection after the crucifixion. Maybe, that was what was happening now – he knew he was about to be hung, drawn and slaughtered, figuratively speaking.

As they exited, the housekeeper, Mrs. Blake, was bustling towards the front door with a bunch of grocery bags. She looked horrified.

"What on earth is going on?" She gazed at James. "Mr. Heimann, what's happening? I wasn't expecting you back until tomorrow."

"I'm afraid you can't go in there for the now," the policeman in charge said. "Not until the coroner has finished and forensics have done their bit."

James told her in a grave tone, "I'm sorry, Mrs. Blake, Mrs. Heimann took a fall. She's dead."

Mrs. Bake looked at the handcuffs and began to quiver uncontrollably. "But it was an accident, surely?"

"We don't know that yet, madam. Please move aside. I'm sure Mr. Heimann will get in touch with you when you're needed."

"But Mr. Heimann is innocent!" she screeched. "And this gentleman here, Mr. Chevalier. I know him. They would never have hurt Mrs. Heimann. Never! Handcuffs! You are *arresting* them? This is madness!"

"Please move aside, madam. This is being treated as a crime scene until further notice."

James stood erect and said, "Don't worry, Mrs. Blake, it's just a little misunderstanding, that's all. I'll ring you very shortly. Meanwhile, consider it paid leave."

As Alexandre was bundled into the police car and driven away, he thought of Pearl at the George V. He'd had his cell switched off all this time – he thought Pearl calling while he was dealing with Laura would add fuel to the already raging fire. Pearl had probably been trying to call. But now they'd only allow him one phone call and that would have to be to Sophie. In any case, he didn't want to worry Pearl in her delicate, pregnant state. Sophie could deal with everything. He hoped she'd pull out all the guns. Get him out of this mess.

Jesus. What a fucking nightmare.

17

Daisy is now sprawled out on the living room sofa, sozzled from all the pink champagne. I feel responsible, although she doesn't seem to care at all. I left her lying there with a grin spread across her face like the Cheshire Cat.

Amy was rushing about with excitement earlier. I ordered room service for us all, although Daisy was beyond repair and didn't seem interested in eating. I left her with a couple of large bottles of Perrier water on the coffee table and a ceramic bowl next to her to vomit in, just in case. The place is far too fancy to have a bucket and I didn't want to call down. I then gave Amy a sumptuous bubble bath in the grand marbled bathroom and put her to bed.

I return to the living room to check on Daisy and cover her with a blanket. She has miraculously perked up and is in the mood for a chat.

"You're not feeling sick?" I ask.

"No! I'm feeling simply marvelous. Bloody delicious champers – got anymore?"

"No, we've run out," I lie. "But there's lots of delicious mineral water."

"Bore Ring."

"I put Amy to bed."

"Good girl. You, not Amy. You're a good girl for doing that."

Yes, she's tipsy alright. "Okay, I think you're ready now for the delicious soup I ordered for you. Wait there and I'll heat it up. Organic chicken noodle soup with Shiitake mushrooms and ginger."

"Sounds delicious."

"Doesn't it? Give me five minutes and I'll be back."

I hear Daisy glugging down some water as I go to the kitchen. It really is like an apartment here. I could get used to this easy luxury; gourmet food on tap, flower arrangements changing daily.

Still no word from Alexandre. A frisson of fear runs up my spine as I think of all the possibilities. Why hasn't he called? It can only mean one thing: bad news. Laura has persuaded him to do the IVF and he's stalling. He doesn't want to hear me scream and cry about it. I swore to myself I wouldn't; that I'd remain cool, calm and collected, and accept whatever decision he made, but the more I think about Laura pregnant, the sicker I feel.

I return with Daisy's soup on a tray. It smells incredible and I'm tempted to order more, although I had a delicious Club Sandwich, earlier.

As I lay the tray on Daisy's lap, I feel as if I'm feeding an invalid. Chicken noodle soup can heal anything, even an impending hangover. "Are you sure you're not going to take a spoonful and vomit everywhere," I check.

"Ha! You think I'm a wimp, don't you? I used to drink quite a bit, in my day. You should have seen me down the pub; I could drink any man under the table." I spread a napkin like a bib about her neck and she slurps down some of the broth. "Oh my God, this soup is out of this world." She looks as if she's died and gone to Heaven. "Oh, by the way, I forgot to say. Remember when I slipped out of the restaurant this afternoon to go to the chemist to get some Advil?"

"The chemist?"

"Sorry, I mean 'pharmacy' – chemist is English. Anyway, I didn't have a headache at all. I went to buy us some naughty toys."

I widen my eyes with mock disapproval. "From that sex shop we passed earlier?"

Daisy giggles. "Yes. I slipped in and got something for each of us."

"You saucy wench, Daisy."

"I've never used anything like that before in my life, but now that I'm single I thought it was time to experiment."

"Well, I'll have to wait to use mine. I still have to be careful."

"Ah, but I thought of that, Pearl. Yours isn't," she lowers her voice to a tiny whisper, "a *dildo*…it doesn't penetrate, it *vibrates*. It's called the something deux, for the two of you. It splits in half – you'll see how it works." She giggles again. "The 'hers' part is convex and the 'his' part is concave, apparently. Or is it the other way round? Anyway, the saleswoman told me it was very popular with couples, and a best seller."

"So when Amy and I were innocently eating our chocolate mousse you were out buying *sex* toys?"

"I know, isn't it outrageous?"

"Where are they?"

"I left the bags in the closet by the entrance. I hope Amy doesn't find them." She slurps another mouthful of soup. "God this is good, you wanna try some?"

"No, it's okay, thanks."

Daisy studies me for a minute and suddenly comes out with, "Pearl, can I ask you a personal question?"

"Sure."

"Do you have multiple orgasms?"

I don't need long to recollect my memories. "Once or twice it has happened. Only with Alexandre, though. But the truth is, I feel so satisfied…so *satiated* after one, I really don't feel I need another. Why?"

"Oh, just because you're always reading about them and you feel like a kind of freak, you know, just having one, like all other women are having such fun and you, well, you're just…I don't know."

"What's your favorite dish?"

"What's that got to do with it?"

"Just hear me out. What's your favorite thing to eat?"

"Well, I do love a good Sunday roast with Yorkshire pudding and roast potatoes"

"Okay, imagine you've just eaten a full Sunday roast. And it was absolutely delicious. You are full. Best meal you've had for ages. Maybe years. And then you're offered another plate piled high with more of the same. Would you be able to wolf all that down, too?"

"I see your point."

"Believe me, you should be happy with one, good orgasm.

Very happy. A lot of women - and it was how I was for so many years - are starved and don't even get the one, so count yourself blessed. Lots of women don't climax at all during intercourse. Don't believe all you read about multiple orgasms, anyway."

She considers what I've said. I can see the invisible cogs of her mind turning. I know what she's wondering – she's wondering if it's because Alexandre is a god in bed and that's why I've had multiple orgasms, or if I was born that way.

"So no word from Alexandre?" she asks.

"No." Uh, oh, the food is sobering her up; I need to change the subject. "So, tell me more about Zac; we hardly discussed it the other day because of Amy being around."

"Oh my God, Pearl. I mean, when Zac kissed me it made me realize what I'd been missing all these years, you know? He's so *sexy*...so...buffed up." She laughs too loudly and covers her mouth. Maybe she isn't sobering up, after all.

"Funny. You, Natalie and I have all ended up with younger men. Well, that's if you take Zac up on his offer."

"You're right! I hadn't thought of that!"

"We're getting our revenge on the world." I wink at her.

"What do you mean?"

"Well, it's always been guys who get the young girls. Now the tables are turning. There's so much more Girl Power about, have you noticed?"

She sips another large spoonful of soup and sighs at its deliciousness. "Like so many amazing women singers now, and stuff?"

"Exactly. Men need to watch out. Gone are the days when they can sit around getting beer bellies and think their women will be happily waiting for them if they behave like assholes. Women are beginning to call the shots now. I mean, look at *you*. You're not crying your heart out, feeling sorry for yourself. You've moved on. Moved on to a hot, sexy younger model!"

"Don't ya love it?"

I wrinkle my nose. "I hate that word, 'cougar' though, don't you? I find it offensive"

Daisy nods her head as if weighing up the options. "I don't know. I quite *like* the idea of being a cougar. It's a compliment. Cougars are beautiful creatures."

"That's exactly what Alexandre says."

Our girlie chit-chat is interrupted by the phone ringing. Thank God, it'll finally be him. "Oui, hallo?" I say, giving it my French touch.

"Pearl?"

"*Sophie*, is that you?"

"I'm in ze lobby, I'm coming up."

"Great-" The line clicks dead before I get a chance to say anything more.

Daisy arches an eyebrow. "*Sophie's* here? At this hour?"

"I know. A bit odd. Oh, well. We're friends now so…"

"Maybe she wants to come and hang out."

"You think?"

"I can't imagine why. She's so sophisticated. We're such…children compared to her."

"I'm glad you feel that way, too. She's five years younger than I am but I always feel so… so girly next to her."

Daisy laughs. "That's because you *are* girly, Pearl – you'll never be a real grown-up, not even when you're eighty. You're young at heart. You'll always be that way, no matter what happens." She starts singing *Young at Heart* in Frank Sinatra's croon. Actually, she does a pretty good imitation.

"I can hear a knock, that'll be her. I hope nothing's wrong."

When I open the door I can see from the dour expression on Sophie's face that something *is* wrong. Very wrong. My first fear is that Alexandre has died in a car crash or something.

"Is he okay?" My eyes are already pooling with tears. "He's not dead?"

Sophie's lips twitch into a limp smile. "No, he's fine. I mean not fine, but he's not dead, not injured, don't worry."

My heart starts beating normally again. Well, almost. At least he's still alive. "Come in."

She walks in, casts off her sumptuous, cashmere overcoat and slumps herself onto the nearest armchair. "I need a drink."

"Sure, what would you like?"

"A whiskey. Make it a double."

"No problem. Is Alexandre okay?"

"Give me a drink and I'll tell you everything."

"Sure." *Crap, the news must be really bad.* "On the rocks?" I ask her.

"Excuse me?"

"Would you like ice with your Scotch?"

"Yes, lots."

I fix her the drink and gauge her movements from the corner of my eye. I don't know if she has a cold or if she's crying. I slip quietly next door to see Daisy. She has her iPod playing *Young at Heart* and she's spinning about in circles doing a strange sort of ballet. I whisper, "Daisy, I think you'd better stay in here; I have a feeling Sophie's not in the mood to socialize. Do you mind?"

"Actually, I think I'm off to bed now, anyway." She stretches her arms in the air and does a gazelle-like leap. "See you in the morning."

"Don't fall over."

I get extra ice from the kitchen, put some in a bowl and finish fixing Sophie's Scotch. I have no idea how strong a double should be.

I come back into the room and she's still sniffling, biting her lip as if to suppress full-blown sobs. I'm getting frightened now. "Here we go," I say, handing her the drink, my hands trembling. "It might be a little strong." She has been crying. Her dark eyes are like black coal, smudged by mascara. She still looks beautiful and put together, despite it all. "Tell me what happened," I ask, dreading the answer.

"Alexandre has been arrested."

Laura immediately comes to mind. "Oh my God. Why?"

"Don't worry, he's got a hotshot team of lawyers wiz him. Zey have nuzzing on him. I'm sure he'll be released soon."

"But what is he being accused of?"

"In England zey are very quick to arrest, you know? It means nuzzing. They'll let him go soon."

"But what—?

"Laura is dead."

My heart feels as if it's about to leap out of my chest. My first reaction is relief – how wicked is that? But then panic engulfs me as I wonder if Alexandre killed her. Sophie wipes her eyes and relays the story; tells me how Laura either fell down the stairs, or was pushed. How Alexandre slipped in from the back door. And that he and James practically collided into one another, seemingly spotting Laura at the same time, dead at the foot of the stairs; each accusing the other of murder or 'manslaughter.' That James called the police, and because of his finger pointing at Alexandre, they both ended up being suspects.

Sophie begins to weep out loud and I feel awkward. I hardly know her and her tears come as a shock because I have always had her in my mind's eye as a tough-nut. But she looks so tiny and vulnerable, like a fragile bird; and my heart is heavy with sympathy and surprisingly (given our history together), a sort of sisterly love.

"I love Alexandre so much, you know? He is everyzing to me. My bruzzer, my best friend. He is everyzing, Pearl."

I walk over and sit on the arm of the chair and rest my hand on her shoulder. I stroke her soft, dark hair, pulling a few salty strands from her tear-stained face. "It will be alright, I'm sure, Sophie. At least the attorneys are there." I say this calmly but I also have tears in my eyes. I picture the evidence in the safe deposit box, the note to Laura's lawyer if anything should befall her - a life sentence for their mother, even if Alexandre gets let off. *Should I tell Sophie?* No, I've been sworn to secrecy. "What can I do to help?" I ask in a quiet voice. "Should we go to London now? Get on a plane?"

She takes a gulp of Scotch. "Let's wait until tomorrow morning. If zey haven't let him free, zen we'll be in trouble. Ze lawyers will tell me more. We're waiting for ze forensic report."

I think of *CSI* and *Dexter* and am aware that we are now dealing with real life, not genius, fictional super-sleuths with state-of-the-art equipment that can solve cases within minutes and hours. This could drag on forever.

"What do you think happened?" I ask her.

"I don't care what happened. I don't care if he killed ze beach. I just want him home." She scrapes her slim fingers through her hair agitatedly.

I nod. She wouldn't care, either, if their mother went to jail, by the sound of it. She was her step-mother, anyway, not her own flesh and blood, and had betrayed them both when they were minors. From what Alexandre has said, Sophie has never quite forgiven her. I'm itching to tell Sophie about the IVF saga but worry that if I do, I could put my big wooden spoon in a broth with far too many cooks. I bite my tongue. I can do nothing more than comfort her. I wish I knew what Alexandre had told his attorney. Or rather, attorneys, plural. Let's hope his money and power will work miracles. How much, I wonder, do they know? How much of this crazy story has Alexandre revealed to them?

"So Laura's husband James suddenly reappeared, then?" I think of how, in my mind, I'd accused Laura of poisoning him. "Where's he been all this time?"

"Apparently, he went to rehab. He was a heroin addict."

"Heroin? But I thought he was an upper-crust banker!"

"You'd be surprised how people wiz lots of money and connections are ze biggest junkies of all."

What she says makes me remember what her old job was. She used to be a high class call girl, once upon a time, who mixed with the rich, famous and powerful. I guess she would know. "Do you think *James* pushed Laura down the stairs?"

"I wouldn't blame him if he did."

I don't know what else to say, so I offer, "Are you hungry, Sophie? The food's delicious here."

She gets up. "No. I'm leaving now, zank you. I just wanted to come by to see you in person. I'll call you when I have news. Meanwhile, here are ze numbers and emails of ze lawyers." She hands me a business card with extra, hand-written numbers scrawled on them in pen. "My driver's waiting outside. You know, Pearl, you could stay at my house next time. No need to get a hotel."

"I'd love that." *Next time.* Will there *be* a next time? Or is Alexandre going to spend the rest of his life locked up in British jail?

18

I can't sleep. The purple sex toy is lying next to me on my pillow. I thought it would be a good distraction but I wasn't able to bring myself to play with it. I need Alexandre, himself – nothing else can even come close. I need his flesh on mine, the scent of his skin, the taste of his sweet breath. The idea of spending my life without him is horrifying. It has taken me forty years to find true love and now it's being snatched away from me.

Did he kill Laura? Did he push her down the stairs in a rage? It's not his style but he does have a dark side to him; traits about his personality that I will never really know. He kept secrets from me. His Taekwondo, the fact he was in the Foreign Legion. He likes to keep the dark side in the shadows. Yes, he's capable of killing, but if he did kill Laura, I feel like Sophie. I don't care; I just want him safely home.

I mull over James. Not that I have ever met him, but he

sounded like a stalwart citizen. Maybe he's the killer; the nervous junkie who just couldn't take anymore of Laura's antics. He must have gotten wind of the IVF stuff. Maybe that's what drove him to use drugs in the first place. Yes, James could have been her killer. Or was it a simple accident? What are the odds, though, of falling down stairs twice in your life?

Finally, I drift off into a delirious sleep. I know I'm dreaming when I smell Alexandre on me, when I feel him part my thighs and run his hands along my breasts. I know I'm dreaming when I feel his lips on mine, pressing sweet kisses along my neck and my jaw-line, and when I hear his deep, sexy voice whisper in my ear, "I love you, Pearl. You are my life, my love, my rare, precious pearl."

I open my eyes but wonder if I am still in my dream. He's there, leaning over me, his dark hair flopping in front of his face, his five o'clock shadow framing the beauty of his even features, his peridot-green eyes twinkling with humor. "You look so serious, baby," he tells me and smiles; his dimple on one cheek furrowed with amusement. *Serioose.*

"I'm dreaming," I reply to the sexy phantom who has tricked me before. Who has given me orgasms in my sleep and even fooled me into believing he spanks me. This ghost is not the real Alexandre. He looks a little thinner in the face, a touch less hungry for sex.

"You're not dreaming, chérie. I swear."

"I know your tricks," I murmur. "Because I'm feeling it between my legs and my heart's racing. You're just a sexy spirit in my dream," I drift back to my other dream, the one about Rex. Rex is swimming in the sea, his doggie-paddle legs, wild with excitement. I have to spin him around and swim behind him so I don't get scratched.

The phantom crawls into bed beside me and trails kisses along my bare arms. His lips press my hand like a knight in shining armor. He is a knight; his name is Chevalier. Alexandre Chevalier. "Alexandre?"

"Yes, baby. I'm here. I'm back from London."

"But you were in jail," I mutter.

"Not jail, chérie, just at the police station giving a statement. They let me go."

I stir from my hazy slumber and sit up. "You're real? This is true?"

He laughs. "Yes, I'm real. This isn't one of your crazy dreams." He lays the back of his hand on my cheek. "Every-thing's been sorted out."

"But what about Laura?"

He exhales as if all that pent up fear of spending time behind bars is expelled in one long breath. "Someone made a confession."

"James? James killed her?"

"No, not James. He was telling the truth; he'd just got back from rehab, from The Priory."

"Who then? Who killed Laura?"

"The stairs killed Laura. Aided by lots of very slippery furniture polish."

I jolt up and lean back against a pile of soft pillows. I'm well awake now.

Alexandre goes on, "Mrs. Blake, the housekeeper, came to the station to make her statement. She'd polished the stairs that day. Laura was tottering about in kitten-heeled slippers. She fell down the stairs; slid down on her back, ending by crashing her head on the bottom, stone step. It was confirmed by forensics that there was polish all over the soles of her shoes."

"Who polishes stairs? Wasn't that a bit stupid?"

"Stupid or clever, depending which way you look at it."

"Mrs. Blake did it on *purpose?*"

"She told the police that Laura had asked her to polish the staircase but as you say, who polishes stairs?"

"But hadn't she been working for James and Laura for years?"

"Exactly. She hated Laura's guts. Secretly. But stayed because of her loyalty to James. She'd been working for his mother before. Years ago, when I was over there once, I heard Mrs. Blake complaining to the cook. After she made her statement, she asked the police if I could stop by the house. They'd given the case the all clear by that point and somebody had been sent over to clear up the blood. When I stopped by, she told me she had something that belonged to me. At first, I thought she must mean something to do with the Aston Martin. But no, it was the titanium hip parts and teeth."

"But Laura said it was in the safe deposit box."

"She was bluffing."

"But how did Mrs. Blake know that they were yours? How did she *know* that?"

"She said to me, 'Mr. Chevalier, I don't know why this stuff is important to you, or what it all means, but what I *do* know is that Mrs. Heimann was blackmailing you.' Household staff usually know what's going on where they work. She would have heard Laura make phone calls, probably eavesdropped here and there. The ironic thing is that it was stored in the garage, all along. I even had the key."

"The last place anyone would suspect? Especially you."

"Exactly."

"Mrs. Blake told me that she had been planning on calling me and letting me know. When she saw that James and I had been arrested, she was horrified and came down to the police station, straight away, to set the record straight."

"So in the end, you didn't need all those swanky attorneys?"

"The second they realized I was the owner of HookedUp they were putty in my hands. One moment, I was a 'frog', and the next their best mate. Two of them had met their girlfriends through HookedUp. Even if I *had* killed Laura, they were so impressed with me, I think they might have let me go," he jokes.

"What have you done with the evidence?"

"Oh, don't worry, I got rid of it."

My heart's palpitations have steadied now to a more even rhythm. My poor baby, with all the adrenaline swirling about my body, has sure been on a rollercoaster ride tonight. "Does James know about the IVF malarkey?"

"No, luckily Laura hadn't spoken to him about that, although she had told him that I was still in love with her and wanted to get back together."

"So he hates you?"

Alexandre's lips tilt up on one side into his signature crooked smile. "I showed him all the photos of you on my iPhone and shared with him the fact that you were pregnant. He calmed down."

"So you threw the teeth and hip parts away?"

"Too bloody right I did."

"Where?" I ask, fearing they could come back and haunt us like in one of those psychological thrillers. My stomach churns again…oops my baby's getting another ride on the Big Dipper.

"Hopefully, it's all sitting at the bottom of the deepest part of the English Channel. I came back by helicopter."

"Ah, so that's how you got back so quickly. What about Sophie? Did you let her in on the details?"

"Not yet. I'm playing that one by ear."

My questions are like a machine gun. "Does she know you're free?"

"Yes."

"Why didn't she call me, then?"

"I told her not to. I wanted to surprise you, myself."

"So you chucked it all out of the helicopter into the sea?" He nods. "RIP Monsieur Chevalier."

"My father wasn't called Chevalier."

"Really."

"Sophie and I changed our names when we were in hiding."

Another little secret. "Chevalier - Knight. Whose idea was that?"

"Mine, of course. At eight years old, I fancied the idea of being a knight in shining armor galloping on my steed. I was into Sir Lancelot."

"Well your wish came true. Because you *are* my knight in shining armor."

He holds my head in his hands and kisses me gently. "I'm glad you see me that way." Then he leans back on the pillow, stretching out his long legs but his head lands on my new toy. I burst out laughing. "Oops, what's this hard purple thing?" he asks, inspecting the oval-shaped vibrator, the two halves meeting together like a cracked dinosaur egg.

I giggle. "That's a gift from Daisy. She bought it today at the sex shop. It's a 'his and her' design. The man gets his half and the woman hers. It splits in two."

He breaks it open, switches it on and it rumbles in his large hands.

"It's called the Zini Deux. We both get to use it together, apparently, at the same time. You do me and I do you."

"Well, this will be a first."

"I know, me too. I always associated vibrators with lonely, sad women whose husbands can't get it up but, apparently they're big news these days, and very popular with couples."

Alexandre puts his arms around me and draws me close. "Oh, Pearl. You have no idea what's been going through my mind in the last twenty-four hours. It's been hell. First, wondering what the fuck I was going to do about Laura, then finding her dead, the police, James, all that time thinking the evidence was going to come to light, and even if I got off scot free, I thought that it was over for my mother. Jesus, what a rollercoaster of emotions it's been."

"I can imagine. I was going through the same. Thank God Mrs. Blake was so honest. She could have easily kept her mouth shut."

"They would have realized, sooner or later, that it was an accident."

"Yes, but you could have spent weeks, even months, worrying and waiting for that phone call from Laura's attorney – waiting for them to arrest your mother. And how do you feel about Laura being dead? That couldn't have been pleasant, seeing a corpse with her head split open."

"I've seen a lot worse, believe me. But still, I did feel a sort of sadness. Sad that Laura ended up being that way. But I also felt a great sense of liberation, obviously, that she was out of our lives for good. I know that's a cruel thing to say but it's how I felt; how I still feel. It also brought home to me how much I treasure you."

He rests his head on my shoulder, breathes me in as if I were some deliciously scented flower, and we hold hands. This is a quiet moment for us both. Peace at last. We both slip our bodies further down the bed and, entwined in each other's arms, fall into a deep sleep.

Am I asleep? Awake? Alexandre's licking my nipples softly, making me moan. My eyelids flutter open and I remember that he really is here beside me. I lazily stretch out my hand and feel, not the Weapon of Mass Destruction but the Tool of Creation, hard as a rock. Ready. With my eyes half closed, I inch my way down the bed and take him in my mouth, licking, sucking, wrapping my lips about him – I feel a desperate hunger for something and someone who so nearly got taken away from me.

He's groaning, "Oh, yeah baby. Oh yeah, that feels so fucking good. I was thinking about you when I was arrested."

I drag my nails lightly over the delicate skin of his balls and he moans, his hands threading through my hair. I'm still half asleep and realize that we haven't even kissed hello properly, we were so busy talking in the early hours, and then fell asleep. I walk my way up the bed with my hands until our faces touch. I can feel his hardness against my mound and I'm lying on top of him now. He smells so good.

"It was like an eternity," I tell him in a whisper.

"I know."

The tip of my tongue flickers on his lips. He gives me that half-cocked smile, the dimple in his cheek making me remember why I was so smitten the second I laid eyes on him in the coffee shop. Light is pouring through the open parts of the drapes; it must be almost midday. A beam of sun is lighting up his head and I notice shimmers of auburn highlighting his dark hair, which usually looks almost black. He drapes his arms about me, squeezing me against his muscular chest. He gives me an 'Eskimo kiss' rubbing noses gently but what is going on down south is far less innocent.

"I'm trying to control myself, Pearl," he breathes into my mouth. He parts my lips with his tongue and moans. I feel his cock flex against me. His kiss is passionate but brimming over with need and love. I return it with equal fervor, my tongue sliding along his, stroking, flipping under and over and out until our tongues tangle almost into a sexual feast.

"Where's that egg thing?" I whisper.

He cups my ass and I feel his erection tight against me. "Really, you want to have a go?"

"Why not? We'll have to try it at least once, or Daisy will be disappointed. Speaking of Daisy, she and Amy must be up and about."

"I heard them leave a while ago," he tells me in a low voice. "We're quite alone and I put a Do Not Disturb sign on the door."

He leans over and takes the big purple oval from the bedside table and holds it up. He smirks.

"Pull it apart. Let's see how it works." I take one half from him and switch on the lowest setting. Even on 'low' it's still very buzzy. "This fits you right here," I say, cupping his balls with it. But it seems as if it's too ticklish for him because he jiggles about.

"Let's see what happens when we light you up," he says. He switches on the 'hers' half and pushes it underneath me so it cups around my form perfectly. The sensation is different from anything I've ever tried, not so unlike the shower head; intense, unrelenting. I slide further down his chest, back to my last position with my face resting on his erection and I begin to sweep the base of his cock with my tongue as vibrations massage my clit. I press another setting for me and it pulsates in waves. I look up at Alexandre and see him observing me, biting his lip as I run my tongue along his length. He simultaneously, from his half, must feel the vibrations on his balls.

"I need to see more of you, baby," he says sitting up, taking his half from me and switching it off. "We can do me another time. Right now, I want to concentrate on you. On your back."

"What?"

"Do as I say. Roll on your back."

He gets off the bed, pulls me by the legs so my butt is on the edge of the mattress. He grabs my ankles and hoists me up so they are resting on his shoulders. "Hook your pretty feet around my neck."

I do as he says. He's standing before me, a veritable vision of beauty; the Greek god again. That delightful V so prominent with the marble statues, but unlike their little fig leaf offerings I observe Alexandre's massive centerpiece, smooth and proud. His pecs flex as he maneuvers me into position. He wants to see all of me. I curl my toes about his neck and lift my arms above my head. The last time I did this he impregnated me, but now he brings the vibrator and presses it into its rightful position. It feels amazing – almost too intense. I buck back a touch and he gets the hint; he switches it down a notch and I'm writhing about – this feels great.

"Open your eyes, baby," he commands, and I do. I observe him, as with one hand he holds the gadget against me, and with the other he grips his cock. "In a minute, I'm going to come all over you." His index finger is massaging between my butt crack as he holds the Zini in place with his large hand. It's zapping my clit and vibrating at my entrance relentlessly. Meanwhile, I focus on his erection, tight in his fisted hand as he pleasures himself. I'm thrashing about, thrusting my hips at him, controlling the waves of pleasure by either pulling back a touch or grinding my hips forward.

"Lick your fingers and play with your nipples, Pearl." I do, and his hand works faster, jacking his cock with racing speed. I tug at my nipples and feel a rush of electricity shoot between my legs. Mixed with the intense vibrations, it feels amazing.

"I love watching you, so wet, so hot, so beautiful – when I fuck you, your pussy's so tight around my cock, your tits so sexy…" He presses another button and the rhythm changes to a pulse. I watch him grow even bigger, the crown swollen and full as his hand races up and down his thick length.

I push my hips forward and feel a spasm rip through the core of me. My legs are quivering like an out of control sewing machine. "I'm coming Alexandre."

"Me too," he shouts out. "Me too, chérie." Hot cum spurts out all over my stomach. Alexandre is still holding the Zini against me – it's too much, I want him to stop…but then…"Oh my God…" Another wave rolls over me and I realize that I'm climaxing again. My body jerks as if I've been electrocuted; my clit feels numb from the buzzing and he turns off the contraption. I slowly come down from my man-made orgasm and wonder if this little gadget could get addictive.

As if reading my thoughts, Alexandre says, "I can see I might have competition. We'll have to keep this little minx of a machine under control." He kneels down below me and seals his mouth around my clit, pressing his tongue against me, hard and flat. I still feel the buzzing between my legs even though it's no longer there, like when you get off a boat and still feel yourself swaying. He flickers his tongue around my sensitive clit without touching it, and starts sucking hard. I can hardly believe it. Yet another spasm tingles through me and I climax again. This is insane.

"Alexandre, oh my….oh my God." He's growling into me like an animal eating its prey with his strong hands clinching my thighs apart, spreading my legs wide open. I'm shuddering as he lashes his tongue at my opening and I feel more contractions rolling through my core. All my energy has been stolen from my center as I slowly come down, moaning and whimpering like a dying person. There is nothing left of me. I am totally spent.

A wry smile spreads across my lips and I think about what I said to Daisy about multiple orgasms.

Sometimes God plays ironic tricks on you, and you have to laugh.

19

Even I have to admit, I looked beautiful today. It is St. Valentine's Day, the day of my wedding to Monsieur Alexandre Chevalier, also known as the knight in shining armor to a Pearl Robinson, now Pearl Chevalier.

Pearl Chevalier. Those two words roll off my tongue and take flight like tiny sparkles of snow-dust into the cool, Lapland atmosphere.

Pearl Chevalier.

All my wishes have come true and, as I look up at the sky above me and at the face of the man who is now my husband, I see that my wishes are *still* coming true every second.

Every millisecond is a moment to celebrate and cherish.

We are both transfixed by the swirls of color in the sky. I lean back in the open-air sled drawn by reindeer and nuzzle against Alexandre's shoulders. My feet are entwined with his as we gaze at the northern lights; nature's firework display. The sky looks like a pastel drawing that a giant has come along and smudged with his thumb. Blues and greens are dancing through the heavens in great twirls and whirls; ribbons of paler light ripple through the colors, creating surreal shapes and forms.

"Tell me why the colors are the way they are again, baby?" I ask my husband (how I love that word HUSBAND).

"Well as you know, the real name is Aurora Borealis. The northern lights are basically particles that are hurled into space after storms on the sun's surface. They're attracted by the magnetic North Pole, and the South Pole, and enter the atmosphere in a ring-like zone around the poles. We're incredibly lucky to see this spectacle; it's never guaranteed, you know."

"It's breathtakingly beautiful."

"*You* are breathtakingly beautiful," he tells me, his green eyes not so different in color from the northern lights. "You looked ravishing in your wedding gown earlier. Simply stunning. I have never seen a more beautiful bride."

A grin spreads across my happy face, proud that the day pattered along so flawlessly. We didn't need confetti because light snowflakes fluttered from the sky as everybody cheered. My white gown sparkled and shimmered. *I* sparkled and shimmered. Pearl, shimmering like my namesake.

Little Amy was clutching her basket of baby ivy and pink roses, and Elodie was holding my train, dressed in her Zang Toi gown, draped low at the back, also pink.

The ceremony was in a chapel made of ice and just our close friends and family were there to celebrate. They are still here enjoying the three-day party.

Alexandre's mother is not the dragon I imagined, at all. She is charming. Tall and elegant and very quiet and unassuming.

Alexandre's new video partner has come; he couldn't tear his gaze away from beautiful Elodie as she walked slowly behind me, making sure my gown was perfect. Amy's eyes were shining like an eager puppy, and Daisy looked on, mopping her tears. Even Sophie cried. Alexandre was right – she's not as tough as she pretends to be; she and I have a lot in common, after all.

My father looked so proud of me, and Zang Toi was also pleased with his creation, making sure that not a hair was out of place and that my gown was fit for a princess. I *was* a princess today. An ice princess. And Alexandre my prince. He was dressed in tails – he looked so chic, so elegant.

Alexandre's deep voice stirs me from my reverie. "How are those babies doing? Do you think they feel the colors of the northern lights?"

"I think they're swirling about in their own magical colors in there," I say patting my stomach.

"Well, I'm betting that our little boy and girl are feeling the vibe of happiness, no matter what."

"Monsieur Chevalier, the doctor said they couldn't be a *hundred* percent sure of their sex at this stage; that we needed to wait an extra week, or so."

"She said ninety percent, that's good enough for me. Anyway, my instinct tells me it's one of each. I'm never wrong. We have a girl and a boy cooking in that little oven of yours, I just know it."

"Is Louis still your number one boy's name?"

"I think Louis Chevalier sounds perfect, as long as Americans don't pronounce the S."

"Yes, I like Louis. It sounds quite regal, actually. Louis Chevalier…I love it. I can't decide between Angelique and Madeleine. I think Madeleine because it works in both countries."

"In America and France, you mean?"

"Yes, of course; they *will* both grow up bilingual, I'll make sure of that. Madeleine. One of my favorite books as a child was *Madeline's Rescue* about the little girl and the dog Genevieve and their adventures in Paris. My mother used to read it to me over and over again."

"That was written by the artist Ludwig Bemelmans – there's a painted mural of his at The Carlyle Hotel."

"How funny. The Carlyle. I won't forget that in a hurry, when you stormed out on me during breakfast."

He throws his head back and laughs. "We've had our fair share of dramas, haven't we?"

"That's for sure. We've really put each other through the wringer."

He rests his hand on my thigh. "But here we are. Together. Married, till death do us part."

"And two little ones on the way." I breathe in the cool, crisp air. "Madeleine it is, then. I'll never forget how my heart broke in two that day. When you left me there, weeping into my linen napkin - everyone staring at me. That's when I realized how insanely in love with you I was. My whole world fell apart that day."

He grins. "Little did you know there was worse to come."

I raise an eyebrow. "And then I met Rex and I couldn't choose between you both. I have to say, you had real competition there."

"Yes, Rex became quite the traitor."

"Because I had him on my side, in my heart of hearts, I knew that I'd win you back."

"You never lost me, chérie. I was yours from word Go. All

yours. I always have been and I always will be." His words are sweet as music to my ears.

"It was like a fairytale today, wasn't it?" I say.

"It still *is* a fairytale. Look at that sky."

"Which reindeer is your favorite?"

"The pale one. The one with the soulful eyes," he says.

"I like the frisky one that tried to nip my bottom earlier. They look so cute with their white ribbons on their massive antlers. Wow, that was some ride sailing through the snow. We went so fast."

"And now we're doing it again." Alexandre tilts his head up to the sky. "What do you think they're all doing now?"

"The stars? The space people? The *Starman* waiting in the sky who'd like to come and meet us but he thinks he'd blow our minds?" I say quoting the David Bowie song.

He laughs. "No, our guests."

"Well, Daisy and Anthony were weeping. And drinking. I last saw them standing by the ice sculptures. Earlier, though, I did catch Daisy out of the corner of my eye flirting outrageously with my dad, so who knows what's going on. Or, they're probably telling embarrassing stories about us. Sophie and Alessandra had a midnight walk planned. Natalie and Miles will probably still be dancing." I laugh, conjuring up a picture of Anthony in his outlandish outfit. "How adorable did Ant look, squeezed into his pink suit? Oh my God, Alexandre! I forgot to tell you. Bruce proposed to him. While we were having the cake."

Alexandre licks his lips. *Those beautiful lips that I'm going to kiss later.* "Both of those cakes were out of this world."

"Weren't they?" I sigh with happiness. "This has been the most perfect wedding possible. The most beautiful day, ever."

"I have to admit, I'm glad we didn't get married in Vegas."

"What? Even though I escaped from you, clambered out of a toilet window and caused mayhem and heartbreak?"

"I caused you a fair share of heartbreak, as well, chérie. I think we're about even on that score."

"We made it, though."

"Yes, we did. We made it."

We are ensconced in our cozy, log cabin. There is a fire burning in the hearth. Outside, it is snowing lightly; a blanket of powdery white covers the ground and tops the pine trees.

I'm lying on the king size bed; nude, expectant and literally, feeling like a virgin on my wedding night. It *is* my wedding night. Alexandre hasn't been inside me for three months. My heart is in my stomach as it whips around in an eddy of emotions, twirling and swirling like the northern lights. I observe Alexandre, my husband, walking around the room naked, unwittingly parading his beautiful body. He is stoking the fire enjoying, perhaps, the latent fear that is mounting inside me. He must know how nervous I feel. The orange blaze of the fire glows on his golden torso; he bends down, his muscles rippling in his forearms and thighs.

I gaze at him, already moist between my legs, just imagining what he's going to do to me. He turns around, narrows his eyes and says, "You are so exquisite, Pearl." His legs are astride and I watch his erection flex into a hard rod. He's biting his lower lip without being aware that he's looking so predatory. A tingle of fearful adrenaline spikes me in my solar plexus.

"Do you have any idea how much I've been longing for this, Pearl?"

"I have a pretty good idea," I reply, blood pumping through me in a hot rush.

"Do you know what I want to do to you?"

The Big Bad Wolf, I think.

He saunters towards me slowly, standing above me as I lie there. His eyes trail up and down my body – just the thought of him has my nipples erect, but when he touches me, tingles shoot through me. He holds my chin in his hands, leans down and kisses me, parting my lips with his tongue; his glittering green eyes locking with mine, not leaving me for a second. "I want to kiss every inch of you. Your mine, Pearl, all mine." He straddles me, his strong thighs either side of my hips, his solid erection resting against my stomach. I grip onto his sinewy biceps, raise myself up a little to meet his lips once more, and I moan hungrily into his mouth.

"Please, Alexandre."

He inches his way down the mattress and I feel the tip of him resting on my clit, which is throbbing in anticipation. I begin to buck my hips at him in desperation. I need him inside me. He shifts his weight a touch and his soft crown rests at my entrance.

"You're so wet, baby. How I've missed this." He enters me just a millimeter and I cry out.

"Alexandre!"

"How does that feel?" he murmurs into my mouth.

"Incredible." I wriggle beneath him. "I want more."

"I know you do, and you bet I'm going to give it to you, baby." He pushes himself an inch inside me, his mouth still on mine. "So juicy, so hot and ready for me."

"Ahh…" I groan, writhing under him.

He eases himself in further. "Are you okay? Is that too much?"

Are you kidding? "Please," I beg.

He groans and thrusts himself all the way in. "Oh, Pearl. Oh Pearl." He's stretching me, filling me slowly and I scream out. He circles his hips and pulls out a touch, waits a beat and then comes back down into me. I respond by grabbing his butt and thrusting myself at him.

"Alexandre."

He can't help it and nor can I. He's fucking me rhythmically now, and I rise up to meet each delicious plunge. I hook my feet around his ankles so he's in deep, and claw onto his butt tighter to control the pace. Each time he comes down on me I drive my hips forward, my clit rubbing hard against his pubic bone. I grasp his ass so tightly so our groins are united as one, and I freeze the movement so each time our centers meld, my clit slaps hard against him; tremors pulsating and ringing through me. He is thick and hard inside me, filling me on all sides, molded to my form.

"We were designed for each other, Pearl," he murmurs. "Made to fuck together. Forever and ever."

"Oh, baby, this feels so good."

His focus is just *me*. His forehead is on mine; his thrusts are making me delirious. His hands cup my ass possessively. We are locked together. He says, almost in a growl, "You. Are. All. Mine. This. All. Belongs. To. Me." Each thrust is punctuated by a word. "Love. Honor. And. Obey."

I want to laugh but maybe what he says isn't so silly, after all.

Because on a hard plunge on 'obey' my inner fireworks explode – the northern lights of my core swirl and dance inside me like never before. I cry out in ecstasy and feel his hot release pounding through me, as his lips meld with mine.

"Yes, yes, *yes*," I scream into his mouth.

"What are you saying yes to, Pearl Chevalier?" he says on one last thrust.

"I swear to love, honor and obey you for the rest of my life."

"That's what I wanted to hear," and he kisses me again.

Epilogue

Eight months later.

The leaves have turned golden and the sun is lighting up a crisp, cobalt blue sky. Louis and Madeleine are dozing like two cherubic angels, their cheeks rosy and round, their eyelids fluttering into deep slumber, as I roll the twin stroller through the Ramble in Central Park. Rex is guarding the babies as if they were his very own, his ears pricked up expectantly, making sure no curious squirrels might leap upon them. I tilt my face up to the sky; the autumnal sun is shimmering in dappled shadows through the trees.

I love Central Park in fall - never more than now with my life being the way it is. Complete. Fulfilled. I am not here to stalk Rex, nor to run away from Alexandre. I am here as a mother to two beautiful, healthy babies, as a wife, and as a woman who has finally gained confidence in herself. I am enjoying my family, bathing in the caress of their unconditional love and a heartening sense of finality.

This is it. I have arrived. I am here.

Out of the corner of my eye I sense Alexandre watching me. I'm lapping up the sun's gentle, warm rays but I can feel the intensity of his peridot-green eyes upon me, his gaze focused - he probably wants to know what thoughts are flitting through my mind.

"What are you staring at?" I murmur softly without looking at him.

I can hear the smile in his voice when he answers, "How do you know what I'm doing?"

"Because that's what happens with husbands and wives; they get to read each other, even with their eyes half closed."

"What are you thinking about, Pearl, with that serene look on your face and that satisfied smile?"

I laugh.

"No really, what's going on in that pretty head of yours?"

A bird swoops above me and some leaves drop to the ground like golden confetti. "I was wondering when you'd ask me what I was thinking," I reply.

"Come on!"

"I'm not kidding."

I hear him sigh with contentment and he links his arm with mine. "You want to know what *I* was thinking?" he asks.

"Maybe about what we're going to have for dinner, even though we've just had lunch," I tease, knowing how he and his family are forever discussing *haute cuisine* recipes. He's been cooking up a storm lately, impressing me with his gourmet meals. I cock my head to see his reaction. His eyes glitter with amuse-ment – a man who knows how to laugh at himself; one of the many reasons I fell in love with him.

He squeezes my arm. "Actually, no. Although I have to admit that did pass through my mind ten minutes ago. I was just going over the events in my head…you know, everything that led us here; all the trials we put each other through. I still wouldn't have had it any other way, though." He pauses, then adds. "Okay, perhaps a few less hours of labor pains for you would have been a bonus. But still, we've been rewarded nicely."

"We really are lucky." I stop walking for a minute and look at him. A little lurch causes my stomach to flip as if I've just set eyes on him for the first time. "Funny. I'd forgotten all about that, the labor pains. I think women are programmed to have a sort of amnesia after birth because I was just remembering how smoothly it all went, how effortless." I lean down to check the babies and tuck the soft blankets about their tiny, alabaster necks. "Madeleine's developing your dimple, Alexandre."

My husband's lips curve up and the dimple in his cheek confirms my observation. "I was just thinking how much like *you* she is, chérie."

"Like me? But her hair's dark. She even has your French pout. No, she's you in a nutshell."

"In character, I mean. She's a little indecisive."

"Give her a chance, she's only a month old." I frown. "Am I indecisive?"

He winks at me. "Hard to catch. You weren't easy to convince."

I love the fact that he sees me as having been hard to catch when I was so obviously *his* right from the second I set eyes on him in the coffee shop. I say nothing, although a tiny smirk sneaks its way onto my lips. I am unashamedly happy – the cat with all the cream. Double-cream, no less.

Alexandre turns to face me and folds me in his arms. I lean my head on his shoulder and feel the slow steady beat of his heart.

Madeleine makes a little murmur but then falls back into a deep sleep. I observe Rex who looks at her and then at Louis. Finally, his wide, black head checks up with us for approval. This is my family, dog and all. We are a team.

Team Pearl.

As if reading my mind, Alexandre says, "We're in this for the long haul. Are you ready for the ride, chérie?"

I hesitate for a minute and ask myself, am I really equipped for this, to be a good mother to my children, keep my autonomy as an independent career woman who can hold her own and also be a loving wife to a man as headstrong as Alexandre? Yes, I think. I *am* ready and more than capable. I have come a long way in the last nine months. Life is not about me anymore. It's about us.

I reply, "Am I ready for the ride, chéri? You bet I am."

Shimmers of Pearl Playlist

Sweet Dreams - Patsy Cline

I Will Survive - Gloria Gaynor

Ben - Michael Jackson

Little Things - One Direction

Nobody Does It Better - Carly Simon

Mon Ami - Kim

Here Comes The Sun - The Beatles

Non, Je ne Regrette Rien - Edith Piaf

Young At Heart - Frank Sinatra

Starman - David Bowie

To listen to the Shimmers of Pearl soundtrack

http://ariannerichmonde.com/music/shimmers-of-pearl-sound-track/

Thank you so much for reading my book which I hope you enjoyed. For more information about me please visit my website: www.ariannerichmonde.com

Available at Amazon

Part 1 of *The Pearl Trilogy*, **Shades of Pearl**
Part 2 of *The Pearl Trilogy*, **Shadows of Pearl**
You can also get the entire collection of
The Pearl Trilogy

I have also written **Glass, a short story**.

Join me on Facebook:
http://facebook.com/AuthorArianneRichmonde

Twitter: @A_Richmonde

If you would like to be the first to know about my next book release please go to: http://ariannerichmonde.com/email-signup/
Your details are private and will not be shared with anyone else. You can unsubscribe at any time.

I love hearing from readers. Feel free to send me an email at ariannerichmonde@gmail.com.

Teaser for *Pearl*

It was raining in New York City. The sort of rain that felt vaguely tropical because it was summertime and the muggy heat was broken by a glorious downfall. Very welcome, because my sister and I had just given a talk at an I.T. conference and she was feeling hot and bothered—really getting on my case.

The rain eased the tension.

Sophie was driving me nuts that day. It wasn't easy going into business with a sibling, but if it hadn't been for her shrewd business savvy, I wouldn't have had the same luck. Sophie inhaled HookedUp. Exhaled HookedUp. Being as obsessed with money as she was, she wouldn't rest until we'd practically taken over the world. And, as everyone now knows, social media really *has* taken over the world so she was onto something big. Clever woman.

Sophie had moved our conference talk forward by an hour because she was in a foul mood—wanted to get it over and done with—get the hell out of there. I, on the other hand, felt bound by some odd sense of duty to share our success story; inspire people to jump into the deep end as we had done. To go for it.

At the conference, someone in the audience asked me how I would describe myself and I replied: "I'm just a nerd who found programming fascinating. With a keen eye for patterns and codes, I pushed it to the limit and got rich. I'm a lucky geek, that's all." People laughed as if what I said was a silly joke. But I meant it.

I'm still not used to being a billionaire. Even now, if I ever see an article written about the power of social media and HookedUp, it's as if I'm taking a glimpse into someone else's life; a driven, ambitious, 'ruthless businessman' (as I've often been described), when I'm still just a guy who likes surfing, rock climbing and hanging out with his family and dogs. Just an ordinary man. Others don't perceive me that way—at all. I suppose I should be flattered by their attention, although I'm a private man and hate the limelight.

I took a chance, worked hard, and got lucky. A Frenchman living the American Dream.

That's what I love about American culture. Everybody gets a shot if you get off your ass and have the will to succeed. Not so in France. It's hard to break away from the mold; people don't like to see others rise above their station. Maybe I'm being hard on my country, judgmental, but all I know is if I'd stayed there, HookedUp wouldn't be the mega-power it is today. Not even close. The USA has given us all we have and I'm grateful, even though having this much money still feels sinful at my age. Or any age, for that matter.

Funny how Fate pans out; you never know what life has in store for you.

I nearly didn't go into the coffee shop that day. Sophie needed a shot of caffeine and I really wasn't in the mood to argue, so we dashed in from the rain and stood in line.

Our conversation had been heated, to say the least. We'd been discussing the HookedUp meeting we had scheduled in Mumbai in a couple of weeks time. It was a mega-deal that she'd been feverishly working on all year. I didn't think HookedUp could get any more global and powerful than it already was, but I was wrong. That deal was going to make us silly money. Really silly money. I knew I was going to be able to buy that Austin Healey I had my eye on. Hell, I could have bought a fleet of them. Aircrafts too. Whatever I wanted.

Sophie took out her Smartphone from her Chanel purse and said in French—her voice low so that nobody would overhear, "Look, Alexandre, this is the guy we're meeting in Mumbai." She scrolled down to a photo of a portly man with a handlebar mustache. "This is the son of a bitch who's squeezing us for every dime. He's our enemy. He's the one we need to watch."

"But I thought you said he's the one we're signing with—"

"He is," she interrupted. "Keep your enemies close." She brushed her dark hair away from her face and narrowed her eyes with suspicion—a habit I had myself. I remember thinking how elegant and beautiful she looked; yet in 'predator mood,' she was also formidable. I was glad to have her on my side.

Half listening to my sister gabble on about the Mumbai deal, I noticed a woman rush through the door—a whirlwind of an entrance. She was flustered, her blonde hair damp from the summer rain, her white T-shirt also damp, clinging to her body, revealing a glimpse of perfectly shaped breasts through a thin bra. I shouldn't have noticed these sorts of things, but being your average guy, I did. She was battling with an enormous handbag— what was it with women and those giant handbags? What did they carry in those things—bricks?

"Arrête!" Sophie snapped and proceeded for the next couple of minutes to berate me for not paying attention. She was rolling her eyes and puffing out air disapprovingly. Ignoring her, I wondered, again, why I had gone into business with her because she was really bugging me. She added, "If you want to fuck that girl you're staring at, you can you know—American women put out on the first date."

I hated it when my sister talked like that to me—it made me cringe—especially her sweeping generalizations about other countries and civilizations.

"She doesn't strike me as that type," I mumbled back in French. The pretty lady was now closer and I couldn't take my eyes off her. She had her head cocked sideways and was staring at the coffee menu, chewing her lower lip in concentration. She was beautiful, like a modern version of Grace Kelly—she looked about thirty or so.

My eyes raked down her perfectly formed body. She was dressed in a tight, gray skirt which accentuated her peachy butt. The slit on the pleat revealed a pair of elegant calves, but her chic outfit was marred by sneakers. Somehow, it made her all the more attractive as if she didn't give a damn. As my gaze trailed back up to her breasts, I saw that she was wearing an *InterWorld* button. *Good,* I thought, *we have something in common—I can chat her up.*

I cleared my throat and moved a step closer. "So how did you enjoy the conference?"

She jumped back in surprise; her eyes fixed on my chest. I felt as if I was towering above her, although she was a good five foot six. I looked a mess—T-shirt and old jeans with holes in the knee. So far, she was not responding. I knew that New Yorkers could be just as rude as Parisians so I wasn't fazed.

She flicked her gaze at me but said nothing. I was right—she hadn't answered my question, just continued to look at me; stunned, as if she really didn't want to have a conversation at all.

I smiled at her. I felt like a jerk, but dug myself in deeper. "Your name tag," I said. "Were you at that conference around the corner?" I decided that she obviously thought I was a total jackass as her response was clipped, terse.

"Yes I was," is all she said and then cast a glance at Sophie.

I realized that this woman—her nametag said **Pearl Robin-son**—must have assumed that Sophie was my girlfriend—the perils of hanging out with my beautiful sister. Or maybe Pearl Robinson wasn't smiling simply because she wanted me to shut the hell up and leave her alone.

But I didn't back off. "I'll pay for whatever the lady's having, too," I told the girl serving our coffee. I wanted to say, 'Whatever Pearl's having' but thought that Pearl would peg me for some kind of stalker. Why I continued to pursue her I wasn't sure, since she was clearly not interested. But I couldn't help myself. "For Pearl," I added, wondering why I was not getting the response I was after. Not to be arrogant, but women did normally smile at me, if not give me the eye. They still do. Daily. But Pearl was not buying it. I wanted her to flirt, brighten up my dull day.

I went on, undeterred—for some reason I didn't feel like giving up; she had really piqued my interest. "Pearl. What a beautiful name." *Jesus what did I sound like? A typical French gigolo type, no doubt.* "I've never heard that before. As a name, I mean."

In my peripheral vision, I caught Sophie rolling her eyes, again, and she whispered in French, "Bet you anything you'll have that woman on her back in no time." *Shut up!*

Pearl Robinson finally reciprocated with a beautiful big smile. *Nice.* Pretty teeth. Sexy, curvy lips. She told me about her parents being hippies or something—explaining her name. I wasn't listening. I'd got her attention, that's all I cared about. I could tell she liked me. *Took long enough for her to warm up, though—all of forty seconds.* I felt triumphant. Why? I met pretty women all the time. But there was something about this one that really captured my attention. She was poised and elegant, yet unsure of herself.

There was a childish, vulnerable quality about her which I found disarming, even beguiling. She was rifling through her enormous handbag, trying to find her wallet. Why are American women so keen on paying for themselves? Was she embarrassed because I was buying her a coffee?

"What's your name?" she asked, while simultaneously staring at my nametag.

Good...ironic sense of humor, I thought. I laughed and introduced myself. Introduced Sophie, too.

Pearl went to shake Sophie's hand and her wristwatch caught on my T-shirt. I looked down at her other hand. No wedding ring. *Good.* I felt my heart quicken with the physical contact of her delicate wrist brushing against my chest—the intimacy—and I knew....in that nanosecond, I knew; I was going to have to fuck this girl.

The way she was looking at me was giving me the green light. Yet her big blue eyes were unsure of me. She looked down at the floor, and then up again at me. She may not have even known it herself at that point—women rarely do—but she wanted me to claim her. I could almost hear her screaming my name. I pictured myself pinning her up against a wall, all of me inside her.

I wanted her. And I was going to have her. You bet. Every last inch of her.

"Remember to use protection," Sophie whispered in French, "she may look like an nice Upper East side WASP, but you never know."

I retorted, also in French. "Get your coffee, or whatever you're drinking, and *leave* because I've had enough of your snippy conversation for one day."

Sophie cocked her eyebrow at me and smirked. I turned my

attention back to Pearl Robinson and prayed that her French was limited or non-existent. I gazed at her, right into her clear blue eyes. *Yes,* I decided, *I want this woman.*

And she wanted me. I was pretty damn sure. She was jittery, nervous, tongue-tied—couldn't get her sentences out straight. Why? Because I was running my eyes up and down her body, mentally undressing her, and she could sense the electricity. The heat. She was all flustered. She could read my mind. She was fumbling for something in her monster-bag again. Her apartment keys, she told me. Was she planning on inviting me over?

"Nice to meet you, Pearl," Sophie said, giving her the once-over. "Maybe see you around some time?" The innuendo was so thick you could have cut it with a machete.

Sophie sashayed out of the coffee shop and I exhaled with relief. *Thank God, now I can get down to business. Real business.*

"I got the drinks to go, but do you want to sit down?" I suggested to Pearl. She nodded.

Why I was so taken with this New Yorker, apart from her obvious good looks, I wasn't quite sure—she had a quirky kind of charm. I liked her. And I decided right there and then—I didn't just want to fuck Pearl, I wanted to get to know her, too.

She eased her way into an armchair but was unsure whether to cross or uncross her legs. Like a schoolboy, I found my eyes wandering to her crotch and imagining what lay beneath, but she was too demure for that. Her legs crossed closed, and she smoothed that sexy pencil skirt over her thighs. I thought about fucking her again—I couldn't stop myself. I wondered if what Sophie said was true: that Pearl would put out on a first date. I'd have to find out....

We were interrupted by a phone call from my assistant, Jim,

telling me to snap up the Austin Healy I'd had my eye on—they'd accepted my offer. So the conversation with Pearl swung around to cars. I felt like a jerk. I knew what women were like; feigning interest about bits of machinery when they really couldn't give a damn. Pearl was no different. Still, she did a good job of pretending. She nodded and smiled and widened her pretty eyes. Meanwhile, I had one thing on my mind: to get her into the sack ASAP.

But then she took me off guard. She started talking about reruns of old sitcoms, classic novels, and old songs and I began to think we had something in common besides physical attraction. Then, when I mentioned my black Labrador, Rex, that was it. I began to mentally tuck my tackle back into my pants, so to speak, because she admitted that she was crazy for dogs, too. She loved the fact that I could take Rex to restaurants in Paris and a flash of our future ran before my eyes. I swear. I had a vision of us together eating something delicious, Rex at our side, and something told me that Pearl and I would make the grade. It does sound crazy, that. Call it a premonition—I think it was.

She was telling me about her childhood Husky.

"My dog was called Zelda," she said, her liquid eyes flashing with happy memories.

"Like Zelda Fitzgerald?" I asked. "Scott Fitzgerald's wife?"

She looked up at me, surprised. "Yeah, you know about her?"

"Of course I do. She was a little bit crazy, wasn't she? *The Great Gatsby* was partly inspired by her."

"Well, like Zelda Fitzgerald, our Zelda was a little out to lunch. I mean, literally. She loved chickens. Went on several murderous escapades."

"The way you say that with a little smile on your face makes me believe you didn't have much sympathy for the innocent, victimized chickens," I teased.

"They were going to be slaughtered anyway, poor things." She put her hand on her mouth as if she'd put her foot in it. "Sorry, Alexandre, are you a vegetarian?"

I loved the way she said *Alexandre* with her cute American accent, trying to accentuate the *re*. "No, you?"

"No red meat. Only organic chicken. I know…kind of ironic considering what Zelda did. I do have a conscience—I'm against intensive farming, you know, animals spending their lives in tiny cages, so small they can't even turn around. Cows being forced to eat grain, not grass—being pumped full of antibiotics. People don't like inviting me to dinner. I'm a tricky customer."

"Not for me, you're not," I found myself saying. "I'd be delighted if you came for dinner. I'll cook you something wonderful." I narrowed my eyes at her. Fuck she was sexy.

Her eyes, in return, widened and her lips clamped around her straw, as she sipped her iced cappuccino, seductively. Jesus, I felt my cock harden watching her mouth. I shifted in my seat and leaned forward to hide my bulge. As I leaned down, I let my hand brush against her golden calf. Smooth, soft legs. *Nice*. This unexpected coffee date was getting too hot to handle so I tried to turn the conversation around to stop myself from mentally undressing her. She got there first, asking me why I chose to live in New York.

"France is a great country," I began. "Beautiful. Just beautiful. Fine wine, great cuisine, incredible landscape—we really do have a rich culture. But when it comes to opportunity, especially for small businesses, it's not so easy there."

"You own a small company? What do you do?"

Interesting. This woman has no idea who I am. Refreshing. She won't be after my money—she doesn't have an agenda. Good.

"That's why I was at that conference," I explained.

I expanded a bit, gave her the usual blab about 'giving back,' and how I liked to share a few tricks of the trade with others.

"And you?" I asked, wondering what the hell this unlikely sexpot was doing at an I.T. conference. She so didn't look the type. "What were *you* doing there?"

She flushed a little, slid down into her chair as if she wanted to disappear and shifted her gaze to her feet. She looked acutely embarrassed. Maybe she had a very boring job, I reasoned, and didn't want to spoil the mood. I dropped the subject. So we brought the conversation back to me again, and she *had* heard of HookedUp, after all. Of course she had. Who hadn't? Everyone and his cousin hooked up with HookedUp, even married couples. But Pearl didn't seem particularly impressed by me, even when I let it slip that I was the CEO.

"So when you're not working or zipping about in your beautiful classic cars, or hanging out with Rex, what do you do to relax?"

"I rock-climb," I replied, already having planned in my head that rock climbing would be the perfect first date for us. Not too 'date-like,' not typical—she'd go for it.

"Oh yeah? I swim. Nearly every day. It's what keeps me sane."

Ah, so that accounts for her tight peachy ass and sculpted legs. We discussed the benefit of sports—how it was good for one's mental state of mind as well as keeping your body fit. This woman had me intrigued. I was getting more than a hard-on talking to her. She made me laugh. She was bright, opinionated. Had read the classics, loved dogs and sure, I couldn't deny it, she had a body like a pin-up and the face of an angel. Besides, with all her straw-sucking, I knew what was going through her mind. She wanted to see me with my shirt off. Yes, damn it, I could tell. She couldn't take her eyes off my chest. She even licked her luscious lips while she was ogling me, and then said—her eyes all baby-doll...all come-and-fuck-me-now:

"I tried rock climbing once. I was terrified but I could really understand the attraction to the sport."

On the word, *attraction*, I swear to God, she looked at my chest, then my groin, and back again to my chest before she finally fastened her gaze on my face. Oh yeah, believe me, I knew what was going on in Pearl's mind. Her smart attire, educated voice and expensive handbag didn't fool me. Still, her come-on would have been imperceptible to an un-trained eye—not slutty, not over-flirtatious...just a split second of wanton lust on her part, which I bet she thought I hadn't clocked onto.

But...Miss Pearl Robinson, daughter of hippies, lover of dogs, quasi-vegetarian temptress....I had your number.

I knew everything there was to know—instinctively.

I wanted her quirky ass and I was going to have it. And everything that went with it, too. All of it. I was going to put my mark on that peachy butt.

I presumed I had her all worked out. Clever me.

Little did I know that I was dead wrong.

Things weren't going to be quite so simple.

Made in the USA
San Bernardino, CA
21 February 2014